TEACHERS FOR TOMORROW'S SCHOOLS

ANALYSIS OF THE WORLD EDUCATION INDICATORS

2001 Edition

ORGANISATION FOR ECONOMIC CO-OPERATION AND DEVELOPMENT
UNESCO INSTITUTE FOR STATISTICS
WORLD EDUCATION INDICATORS PROGRAMME

ORGANISATION FOR ECONOMIC CO-OPERATION AND DEVELOPMENT

Pursuant to Article 1 of the Convention signed in Paris on 14th December 1960, and which came into force on 30th September 1961, the Organisation for Economic Co-operation and Development (OECD) shall promote policies designed:

– to achieve the highest sustainable economic growth and employment and a rising standard of living in Member countries, while maintaining financial stability, and thus to contribute to the development of the world economy;

– to contribute to sound economic expansion in Member as well as non-member countries in the process of economic development; and

– to contribute to the expansion of world trade on a multilateral, non-discriminatory basis in accordance with international obligations.

The original Member countries of the OECD are Austria, Belgium, Canada, Denmark, France, Germany, Greece, Iceland, Ireland, Italy, Luxembourg, the Netherlands, Norway, Portugal, Spain, Sweden, Switzerland, Turkey, the United Kingdom and the United States. The following countries became Members subsequently through accession at the dates indicated hereafter: Japan (28th April 1964), Finland (28th January 1969), Australia (7th June 1971), New Zealand (29th May 1973), Mexico (18th May 1994), the Czech Republic (21st December 1995), Hungary (7th May 1996), Poland (22nd November 1996), Korea (12th December 1996) and the Slovak Republic (14th December 2000). The Commission of the European Communities takes part in the work of the OECD (Article 13 of the OECD Convention).

UNESCO

The constitution of the United Nations Educational, Scientific and Cultural Organization (UNESCO) was adopted by 20 countries at the London Conference, in November 1945, and entered into effect on 4 November 1946. The Organization has currently 188 Member States.

The main objective of UNESCO is to contribute to peace and security in the world by promoting collaboration among nations through education, science, culture and communication in order to foster universal respect for justice, for the rule of law, for the human rights and fundamental freedoms which are affirmed for the peoples of the world, without distinction of race, sex, language or religion, by the Charter of the United Nations.

To fulfil its mandate, UNESCO performs five principal functions: 1)prospective studies on education, science, culture and communication for tomorrow's world; 2) the advancement, transfer and sharing of knowledge through research, training and teaching activities; 3) standard-setting actions for the preparation and adoption of internal instruments and statutory recommendations; 4) expertise through technical co-operation to Member States, for their development policies and projects; 5) exchange of specialized information.

The UNESCO Institute for Statistics (UIS)

The UNESCO Institute for Statistics (UIS) is the statistical office of UNESCO and is the UN depository for global statistics in the fields of education, science and technology, culture and communication.

The Institute for Statistics was established in 1999. It was created to improve UNESCO's statistical programme and to develop and deliver the timely, accurate and policy-relevant statistics needed in today's increasingly complex and rapidly changing environment.

Currently based in UNESCO Headquarters in Paris (France), the UIS will be permanently located in Montreal (Canada) from September 2001.

TABLE OF CONTENTS

FOREWORD

The 1990s have witnessed growing demand for learning throughout the world. Compelling incentives for individuals, economies and societies to raise the level of education have been the driving force behind increased participation in a widening range of learning activities by people of all ages, from earliest childhood to advanced adulthood. The challenge, in this era of spreading and diversifying demand for learning over the lifetime, is how best to meet rising demand while ensuring that the nature and types of learning respond to needs in a cost effective manner. There is an increasing recognition that teachers play the central role in efforts aimed at improving the functioning of education systems and raising learning outcomes. But do government policies consistently reflect this awareness? How do they help teachers promote excellence and thus influence levels of learning achievement? Teachers are expected to respond to an increasing range of societal demands, but how are they enabled to do so?

In searching for effective education policies, governments are paying increasing attention to international comparative policy analysis. Through co-operation at the international level, governments are seeking to learn from each other about how to secure the benefits of education for all and how to manage teaching and learning in order to promote learning throughout life.

In many countries, this attention has resulted in a major effort to strengthen the collection and reporting of comparative statistics and indicators in the field of education. In keeping with these national efforts, the OECD and UNESCO have adjusted their statistical programmes in an attempt to meet the growing demand for information on education systems.

As part of such efforts, the OECD has, over the past 13 years, developed and published a broad range of comparative indicators that provide insights into the functioning of education systems, reflecting both on the resources invested in education and their returns to individuals and societies. These indicators have become a unique knowledge base, underpinning public policies which attempt to improve access to education in order to make lifelong learning a reality for all, to raise the quality of educational opportunities, and to ensure effective use of resources and fair distribution of learning opportunities.

Building on the OECD indicators programme, eleven countries, together with UNESCO and the OECD and with financial support from the World Bank, launched the World Education Indicators programme in 1997. These countries were Argentina, Brazil, Chile, China, India, Indonesia, Jordan, Malaysia, the Philippines, the Russian Federation and Thailand. They first met on 10-12 September 1997 in order to:

- explore the OECD education indicator methodology;

- establish mechanism whereby participating countries could agree on how to make common policy concerns amenable to comparative quantitative assessment;

- seek agreement on a small but critical mass of indicators that genuinely indicate educational performance of relevance to policy objectives and measure the current state of education in an internationally valid, efficient and timely manner;

- review methods and data collection instruments in order to develop these indicators; and

- determine the directions for further developmental work and analysis beyond the initial set of indicators and establish an operational plan and schedule for the implementation of the pilot programme.

Since then, participating countries have contributed in many ways to conceptual and developmental work, have applied the WEI data collection instruments and methodology at national levels in collaboration with the OECD and UNESCO, have co-operated in national, regional and international meetings of experts, and have worked jointly on the development of the indicators. Further countries, including Egypt, Paraguay, Peru, Sri Lanka, Tunisia, Uruguay and Zimbabwe joined the project subsequently. In 1999, the growing demand for policy-relevant, timely, reliable and comparable statistics at the international level led to the creation of the UNESCO Institute for Statistics. The UNESCO Institute for Statistics has become not only an important contributor to the further conceptual and methodological development of the World Education Indicators programme, but is also progressively incorporating many WEI activities in its own programme of work. It is extending the WEI objectives and processes to a much wider range of countries, through both regional and national development programmes.

This report is the second in a series of publications that seek to analyse the indicators developed through the WEI programme in areas of key importance to governments, bringing together data from countries participating in the WEI programme with comparable data from OECD countries. Its main objective is to shed light on the demand and supply of qualified teachers in WEI countries, in the face of increasing recognition of the role of teachers in improving the functioning of education systems and ensuring positive learning outcomes. Chapter 1 sets out the broader macro-economic context of education systems in WEI countries, and its influence on public policy; examines trends in educational finance and governance, with particular attention to how they relate to teachers and teaching conditions; and reviews patterns of access and participation in education system to signal changes in the demand for teachers. Chapter 2 examines expected changes in the demand for teachers over the next decade under different enrolment scenarios and explores their financial implications; compares what is demanded of existing and prospective teachers in terms of general expectations, required qualifications and expected workload with what is offered to them in terms of financial incentives and career prospects; and finally reviews the policy choices and trade-offs that countries make when balancing expanded access to education against the need to attract and retain good teachers. Finally, Chapter 3 provides a statistical profile of important determinants of the demand and supply of qualified teachers in each country participating in the WEI programme, highlighting relative strengths and weaknesses of education systems in the light of the characteristics of other education systems in both WEI and OECD countries.

Despite the significant progress that has been accomplished during the first three years of the WEI programme in delivering policy relevant and internationally comparable education indicators, the indicators presented should not be considered final but have been, and continue to be, subject to a process of constant development, consolidation and refinement. Furthermore, while it has been possible to provide for comparisons in educational enrolment and spending patterns, comparative information on the quality of education in WEI countries is only beginning to emerge. New comparative indicators will be needed in a wider range of educational domains in order to reflect the continuing shift in governmental and public concern, away from control over inputs and content towards a focus on educational outcomes.

The countries participating in the World Education Indicators programme, together with UNESCO and the OECD, are therefore continuing with the development of indicators and analyses that can help governments to bring about improvements in schooling and better preparation for young people as they enter an adult life of rapid change and increasing global interdependence.

John Martin
Director for Education, Employment,
Labour and Social Affairs,
OECD

Denise Lievesley
Director
UNESCO Institute for Statistics

Ruth Kagia
Director, Education Sector
Human Development Network
World Bank

INTRODUCTION

Education and training play a crucial role in helping individuals and societies to adapt to profound social, economic and cultural change, and foster the development of the human capital needed for economic growth. The ability of education and training systems to fulfil these roles depends on whether educational institutions themselves respond to change, and on whether teachers develop and deliver educational content in ways that meet the needs of today's and tomorrow's citizens.

Policy-makers and society at large have high expectations of teachers as professionals, role models and community leaders. Teachers are asked to manage the far-reaching changes that are taking place in and outside schools and to implement the complex reforms of education systems that are under way in WEI countries.

Educational policy-makers face a difficult balancing act in managing teacher deployment effectively and efficiently. They need to ensure that the investment made in teachers is sufficient and proportionate to the demands placed upon them. This means both that the qualifications of the teaching force must be adequate and that the salaries and working conditions of teachers must be sufficiently competitive to attract and retain people with the desired qualifications into the teaching profession.

■ RISING DEMAND FOR EDUCATION AND TEACHERS

Rising enrolment rates, in some cases combined with an expanding school-age population, are increasing the demand for new teachers in many WEI countries, notably in those with the lowest levels of economic development.

In the majority of WEI countries, the population of primary-school age has stopped growing or even started to decline. On the other hand, unlike the situation in most OECD countries, where the population at the age of secondary and tertiary education has tended to decline, the number of individuals beyond primary-school age is still growing in most WEI countries. The slowdown in population growth, which began in the 1970s in most countries, will still take many years to translate into fewer children at secondary and tertiary levels. Moreover, while most WEI countries have achieved or are close to achieving universal enrolment in primary education, enrolment rates for the population of secondary-school age vary widely, ranging from 87 per cent in Chile to 48 per cent in Indonesia.

These changes in student numbers will have significant implications not only for teacher training and recruitment but also for the financial resources which countries need to invest in education if they are to achieve universal education for all children of primary-school age and to increase, or merely to maintain, current enrolment rates in secondary education.

And yet, despite an increasing population of secondary-school age, the next few decades will provide a unique window of opportunity for many WEI countries to improve the quality of educational services. Because of the relative decline in the size of the cohorts of primary-school age, the proportion of people of working age will grow faster over the next few decades than that of children in many WEI countries. As a result, countries will be in a better position to mobilise resources for public services, including education, and should find it easier to fund their education systems. Policy-makers can use this opportunity to shift the focus from expanding the coverage of the education system to improving the quality of educational provision and outcomes, including reducing the high proportion of over-age students, repeaters and late entrants enrolled in primary education which is still found in certain WEI countries.

The ability to meet demand at secondary and tertiary levels has been constrained in some countries by the capacity of the teaching force. Teachers and non-teaching staff account for a sizable percentage of national labour resources. In most WEI countries, at least one in twenty-five of all employed persons works in the education system. In Tunisia, this ratio is even higher - one in ten. Moreover, teachers are often among the most educated workers: in Indonesia, more than half of those members of the labour force who have a tertiary qualification are in the education sector.

The proportion of the teaching force meeting national qualification standards differs markedly between WEI countries. Six WEI countries have more or less reached the standard of requiring tertiary qualifications for teaching in primary, lower and upper secondary education. The lowest proportions of teachers with tertiary qualifications are found in Brazil, China and Tunisia. The first two of these countries also have the lowest percentages at the lower secondary level. The situation in Tunisia, where only 14 per cent of teachers at the primary level have a tertiary qualification, contrasts sharply with that in Jordan, where almost all primary teachers have such a qualification. Data from a recent international assessment show nonetheless that there is still sizable demand for qualified mathematics and science teachers in secondary education in both countries.

A better-trained teaching force is an important factor in educational quality and efficiency, but there are also organisational considerations. Policies that give children more access to educational opportunities, such as larger classes and multiple-shift schooling, are common in many WEI countries but may place additional burdens on teachers. These practices are closely connected to the issue of repetition: in Brazil, Paraguay, the Philippines and Zimbabwe, between 30 and 50 per cent of pupils of secondary-school age are enrolled in primary school as repeaters or late entrants. In such situations, teachers face greater difficulties in managing classrooms and delivering curricula.

■ RESOURCE LEVELS FOR EDUCATION AND HOW MONEY IS SPENT

In order to meet the goals of expanding educational opportunities and improving quality, additional resources will be needed. Furthermore, this report recognises that sustainable strategies for the deployment of teachers require a stable flow of resources, since unexpected declines in the level of financial support will make it difficult, if not impossible, to adhere to the strategies adopted. Rapid macro-economic changes in the global and national economies mean that strategies must also have the flexibility to respond quickly, yet in a considered manner.

However, WEI countries are limited in what they can spend on education by shrinking public budgets, except in those few instances where the economy, and hence public budgets, have expanded. Governments are therefore asked to take decisions on which aims can realistically be achieved in the light of the resources available.

Countries that faced an economic crisis in the 1990s must meet the double challenge of building sustainable educational reform in an unstable macro-economic environment. Some WEI countries have had to respond to diminished public resources by redistributing public funding between levels of education and categories of expenditure. In the Russian Federation and Southeast Asia, the proportion of spending on teachers has remained relatively stable, while the amount available for spending on other types of educational needs has fallen. Experience in these countries also suggests that in economic downturns, greater pressure is placed on households to make private contributions to the costs of education.

This raises the more general question of who should pay for the expansion of educational opportunities. The funding of a national education system should be equitably distributed across the population. Nevertheless, private expenditure plays an important role in financing secondary and tertiary education in most WEI countries. In a number of countries, parents and communities help to cover costs by directly or indirectly subsidising teachers' salaries in state-run schools, or by directly employing and paying teachers. The extent of private funding of education reaches high levels in some countries, accounting for more than 40 per cent of total educational expenditure in Chile, Peru, the Philippines and Thailand. These figures are well above the OECD mean of 19 per cent.

In the quest for solutions to the issue of funding, it should be borne in mind that one of the main goals of a national education system is to make the benefits of education accessible to all. Several WEI countries have made special efforts to this end, most notably Brazil, where indicators show that progress was made in the second half of the 1990s in widening educational access in the impoverished Northeastern region. However, while access to education has improved, enormous gaps between Brazilian regions remain in educational quality, as measured by the availability of qualified teachers, adequate infrastructure and other indicators of teaching conditions.

Investing in the educational process also means providing enabling environments for teachers and students. Well-qualified and motivated teachers are a necessary but not a sufficient condition for good learning outcomes, and adequate investment in teaching materials and school infrastructure is also required. According to data from an 1999 international student assessment, a large proportion of 8th-grade students were affected by shortages of teaching materials and poorly equipped or poorly maintained schools. For example, over 80 per cent of students in the Russian Federation, Thailand and Tunisia were in schools that reported 'a lot' of problems with the availability of teaching materials. An essential part of ensuring good learning outcomes is providing teachers with the tools needed to deliver the curriculum.

■ WHAT TEACHERS ARE ASKED AND WHAT THEY ARE OFFERED

Expectations of teachers are high. They need to be experts in one or more specific subjects, and this demands an increasing level of academic qualifications. They must continually update their expertise and knowledge since, in order to provide tomorrow's world with the knowledge and skills on which economic and social progress so critically depends, educational institutions and teachers need to respond by developing and delivering appropriate educational content. Moreover, teachers' subject-matter expertise must be complemented by pedagogical competence, with a focus on the transmission of a range of high-level skills, including the motivation to learn, creativity and co-operation. In some WEI countries, technology is becoming a new feature of professionalism in teaching, requiring an understanding of the pedagogical potential of technology and the ability to integrate it into the teaching-learning process. Finally, professionalism in teaching can no longer be seen as an individual competence, but must include the ability to function as part of a "learning organisation" and the capacity and willingness to move in and out of other careers and experiences that can enrich teaching ability.

The global trend towards moving decision-making in education to lower levels of government also affects teachers in the WEI countries in several ways: first, by bringing decisions about teachers (aside from statutory salary scales) closer to the locality and the school and, second, by asking teachers to play a greater role in managing the system. Some countries have adopted a model in which schools operate within a centrally determined framework of curricula and standards, but are given a considerable amount of autonomy and responsibility for decisions.

The demands placed on teachers are therefore considerable. The balance between what is required of teachers and what is offered to them has a significant impact on the composition of the teaching force and the quality of teaching. Attracting skilled individuals and retaining them in the teaching profession is an essential prerequisite for ensuring high-quality education in the future.

This report considers the challenges posed by the need to secure a skilled and motivated teaching force, and examines some of the policy choices and trade-offs that countries make when balancing expanded access to education with the need to attract and retain good teachers.

The relative level of teachers' salaries and the availability of salary increases during the course of teachers' careers can affect the decision by qualified individuals to enter or to remain in the teaching profession. At the same time, the pressure to improve the quality of education is often subject to tight fiscal constraints, and teachers' salaries and allowances are the largest single factor in the cost of providing education, accounting for two-thirds or more of public expenditure on education in most countries. The impact of various elements of the total compensation package varies from country to country, and within a given country, over time. If the compensation package is too generous there will be a surplus of qualified applicants for the profession. In addition, teaching is sometimes one of the few occupations available to individuals with a high level of education in developing countries. In such cases, there is no effective market alternative, and even low levels of compensation will attract qualified applicants. As other areas of the economy begin to develop, however, there is likely to be a sudden exodus of the best-qualified teachers from teaching into more attractive new positions.

While uniform salary scales are transparent and simple to administer, they do not help to motivate teachers to perform at their best, nor do they help to solve problems of shortages of teachers in certain subjects or in rural areas. Among the policy options that many WEI countries have not yet fully exploited are bonuses as a means of adjusting the remuneration of teachers without altering the basic government scales. Such adjustments may serve different aims, such as rewarding teachers who take on responsibilities or duties beyond statutory norms, attracting better candidates to the teaching profession, encouraging teachers to improve their performance, or attracting teachers into subject areas where demand is greater than supply, for example science and mathematics, or to rural locations where there is a scarcity of applicants.

The payment of bonuses has to be weighed carefully, however, and their impact evaluated from case to case since there is evidence that they may elicit responses from teachers that have an effect opposite to that which is intended, impairing school effectiveness and hence student achievement. The examples of pay schemes discussed in this report show nonetheless that bonus schemes can be effective.

Material incentives for teachers are not the only factors of significance in attempts to improve the quality of education. This report examines other important indicators of the working conditions of teachers, including hours of teaching and instruction, class size and student-teacher ratios. If the working conditions for the teaching force and their associated costs are to be judged accurately, all of these indicators need to be considered in combination rather than in isolation. Together, they can help to show whether teachers are being asked to do too much or too little, and whether trade-offs are well balanced. An unbalanced system may lead to poor morale among teachers, difficulties in recruiting qualified staff, and an exodus from the profession. It may also reflect a less efficient teaching process, leading to higher costs of teaching. A balanced system contributes to more effective teaching and hence to better learning outcomes.

When governments decide on their education budgets, they need to make trade-offs between factors such as the level of teachers' salaries, the size of classes, the number of teaching hours required of teachers and the intended instruction time for students.

Some countries seek to increase the competitiveness of teachers' salaries and/or to raise enrolment levels by increasing student-teacher ratios, sometimes in combination with the introduction of new teaching technologies. However, while this may be a viable option for improving the effectiveness of education systems in some WEI countries, student-teacher ratios already exceed 40 students per full-time equivalent teacher in others, where it will be difficult to respond to the increased demand for teachers by raising the ratio further without risking a deterioration in the quality of educational provision.

This report shows that countries make different policy choices about these trade-offs. In some countries, a lower than average teaching load is compensated by larger class sizes, while in other countries, smaller than average class sizes add to a light teaching load, increasing the salary costs per student. In Chile, the Philippines and Thailand, comparatively high statutory salaries for primary teachers are compensated by a high number of teaching hours or larger than average classes, while in Indonesia, low salaries and a high number of teaching hours are partially offset by smaller classes. Uruguay, on the other hand, combines small primary-level classes with a low number of hours of instruction and low salaries.

These examples illustrate that there are a various approaches for managing teacher deployment. The question of which approach is better may be a natural one, but not entirely appropriate. Each education system is a working system, which to a greater or lesser degree has satisfied the requirements of its society. The different policy choices discussed in this report represent a long history of decisions taken nationally and are subject to a certain inertia that makes it difficult to introduce substantial changes overnight, if for no other reason than that some features of the system are subject to negotiation in the framework of collective bargaining agreements. The success of an approach may also depend on less quantifiable characteristics of the education system, such as the teaching methods used or the extent of remedial help available. The interplay between, for example, class size and teaching methods is far from clear. Small classes may mean that more attention to individual students is possible, but in the absence of curriculum reform or of a change in teaching practices, for example, the expected benefits may not be forthcoming.

While it is difficult to assess the effectiveness of the different policy options conclusively, the analysis in this report shows that there is room for choice and that international comparative analysis can be a useful instrument for informing the debate. Future research is needed to elaborate the potential impacts of the different strategies adopted by countries. It needs to identify countries that ask too much or too little of teachers, or give too much or too little to teachers in return. More information is needed about teachers and the effectiveness of instructional strategies, particularly at the classroom level. Proposed changes in the levels of resources invested, in the management of teachers, or in teaching and learning conditions, need to be seen in the context of overall public policy, which governs the complex relationship between teacher deployment, the internal efficiency of the education system, and learning outcomes. More extensive micro-level data, especially more comprehensive and reliable measures of student achievement, are required in order to understand this relationship. The provision of such data remains one of the most important future objectives for the WEI programme.

READER'S GUIDE

Definitions and methods

The World Education Indicators programme (WEI) places great importance on the cross-country validity and comparability of the indicators. To accomplish this, participating countries have endeavoured to base the collection of data on a common set of definitions, instructions and methods that were derived from the OECD indicators programme. Annex A2 to this report provides definitions and methods that are most important for the interpretation of the data in this publication as well as notes pertaining to reference periods and data sources.

Five annexes are presented at the end of the report:

• **Annex A1** provides general notes pertaining to the coverage of the data, the reference periods and the main sources for the data;

• **Annex A2** provides definitions and notes that are important for the understanding of the indicators presented in this publication (the notes are organised alphabetically);

• **Annex A3** provides a cross-reference between tables and notes;

• **Annex A4** provides the full set of data used in this publication;

• **Annex A5** documents the classification of 18 WEI countries educational programmes according to the International Standard Classification of Education (ISCED).

The full documentation of national data sources and calculation methods is provided in the OECD's 2001 edition of *Education at a Glance* and is also available on the Internet (http://www.oecd.org/els/education/ei/index.htm).

In order to enhance the comparability of the indicators, countries participating in the WEI programme have also implemented a new standard for the classification of educational programmes, ISCED97, which was developed by UNESCO to enhance the comparability of education statistics.

While comparability of the data is a prerequisite for the validity of international comparisons, it often poses challenges for the interpretation of the indicators within the national institutional context. This is because the implementation of comparable standards and classifications requires countries to diverge from national institutional structures. For example, education that is classified as ISCED level 1 in this report (primary level of education) does not correspond strictly in all countries to the grades in which primary education is provided, because the number of grades associated with primary education varies greatly between countries. The detailed allocation of individual national educational programmes according to ISCED97 is provided in Annex A5b of this report.

Coverage of the data

Although a lack of data still limits the scope of the indicators in many WEI countries, the coverage extends, in principle, to the entire national education system regardless of the ownership or sponsorship of the institutions concerned and regardless of education delivery mechanisms. Generally, all types of students and all age groups are meant to be included: children (including those classified as exceptional), adults, nationals, foreigners, as well as students in open distance learning, in special education programmes or in educational programmes organised by ministries other than the Ministry of Education, provided that the main aim of the programme is the educational development of the individual. However, vocational and technical training in the workplace, with the exception of combined school and work-based programmes that are explicitly deemed to be parts of the education system, is not included in the basic education expenditure and enrolment data. Educational activities classified as "adult" or "non-regular" are covered, provided that the activities involve studies or have a subject-matter content similar to "regular" education studies, or that the underlying programmes lead to potential qualifications similar to those gained through corresponding regular educational programmes. Courses for adults that are primarily for general interest, personal enrichment, leisure or recreation are excluded.

Calculation of international averages

The OECD country average, which is often provided as a benchmark, is calculated as the unweighted mean of the data values of all OECD countries for which data are available or can be estimated. The country average therefore refers to an average of data values at the level of national systems and can be used to illustrate how an indicator value for a given country compares with the value for a typical or average country. It does not take into account the absolute size of the education system in each country.

Chapter 1

TEACHERS TODAY

Prepared by Albert Motivans, Mathieu Brossard and Douglas Lynd
(UNESCO Institute for Statistics)

■ INTRODUCTION

There is an increased recognition of the role of teachers in improving the functioning of education systems and ensuring positive learning outcomes. But do government policies consistently reflect this awareness? How do they help teachers, promote excellence and thus influence levels of learning achievement? Teachers are expected to respond to an increasing range of societal demands, but how are they enabled to do so? Government policies are often contradictory – greater expectations are often accompanied by fewer resources. Because of this, some observers have warned that teachers are at risk of becoming casualties rather than catalysts of change (Hargreaves, 2000). In order for societies to meet the changing demands of the 21st century, policy-makers need to foster a well-qualified, well-equipped and motivated teaching force.

Teachers are expected to respond to an increasing range of societal demands, but greater expectations are often accompanied by fewer resources.

From the perspective of sheer numbers, teachers represent a considerable force that can be mobilized to meet changing demands. The number of teachers in the 18 WEI countries exceeded 23 million in 1998 according to head-count data, which by comparison, is greater than the combined population of Australia and New Zealand. This figure represents an increase of 10 per cent over the 1990 total, with the biggest gains at the secondary and tertiary levels.

The number of teachers in WEI countries is 23 million and growing. The number has increased faster in secondary and tertiary education.

While not all WEI countries have fully met the goal of universal primary education, they are coming close, so that there is growing pressure on governments to provide additional places and teachers in subsequent levels of education. Most national policy-makers see the main challenges facing the education system lying at the secondary and tertiary levels, reflecting the growing need to enhance human capital by raising levels of skills among the population in order to compete economically in an increasingly global market. However, the goal of greater participation at secondary and tertiary levels of education presents difficult choices and trade-offs, especially for countries that also seek to improve the quality of primary education. Trade-offs are an inherent part of the allocation of limited financial and human resources, and investing in adequate training and support for primary-school teachers will contribute to later educational achievement and attitudes that enable the pursuit of lifelong learning.

This also raises the issue of targeting those in greatest need of the benefits of education. For example, a key question in most WEI countries is how to recruit and support teachers in difficult conditions, often in rural or remote areas. This raises policy issues both of ensuring quality throughout the education system and, more specifically, of targeting the deployment of teachers and redistributing resources in an effort to overcome the effects of multiple disadvantages (poverty, poor infrastructure and lack of qualified teachers) in certain regions, cities or school districts.

The size, qualifications and working conditions of the teaching force are linked to a number of different institutional, historical, social and economic factors. This chapter examines how, in particular, economic factors help to establish the parameters in which countries make choices about policy in terms of teachers and conditions for learning. This sets the stage for the next chapter, which focuses on the specific policy trade-offs related to teacher deployment (*e.g.*, class size, instruction hours, salary scales) that are used to achieve desired outcomes.

- *Section 1* sets out the broader macro-economic context, and its influence on public policy. In the 1990s, national income levels sometimes changed dramatically, resulting in either additional government revenue or more severe budget constraints on public spending. Such trends can have an immediate impact on government (and private) support for education. Moreover, there is a need to go beyond aggregate measures of national income and to examine how income is distributed among the population. Education systems and teachers in societies with wide social inequality face the difficult challenge of distributing the benefits of education more equitably.

- *Section 2* examines trends in how educational systems are financed and governed, with particular attention to how they relate to teachers and teaching conditions. It surveys the levels of funding and how education spending is allocated. Are governments in WEI countries paying sufficient attention to the level of investment in education, and specifically in the teaching force? On the basis of a 1998 WEI survey and another recent study, this section also looks at trends in decision-making in education. Who makes decisions about teachers, and what is the margin of autonomy granted to schools in this regard? To what extent are teachers given authority to make certain decisions at the school level?

- *Section 3* looks at current trends in participation in education in WEI countries and reviews how students progress through the education system. It also discusses certain characteristics of educational systems (*e.g.*, promotion policies or multiple-shift schools) and the implications for teaching staff. This section also compares results from an international assessment of 8th-grade science and mathematics achievement in eight WEI countries that participated in the study. The same study also provides, among this sub-group of WEI countries, a look at how teachers and students use new information and communication technologies (ICT) in the classroom, and some indicators of education quality: shortages or inadequacies that affect schools' capacity to provide instruction and how well teachers feel they are prepared to teach certain topics.

- The *final section* presents a profile of the current teaching force in WEI countries and looks at differences in patterns of gender, age and qualifications. The profile of teachers helps educational planners anticipate, for example, an aging teaching force or identify the gaps in teacher qualifications, although in other cases it is not always easy or desirable for countries to define specific benchmarks. This section examines the characteristics of today's teaching force that may present challenges and opportunities related to expanding educational opportunities and improving educational quality into the next decade.

■ MACRO-ECONOMIC CONDITIONS AND RESOURCES FOR EDUCATION

Changing macro-economic conditions can have an immediate impact on the public resources available for education by influencing levels of government revenue and expenditure. In some cases, this may lead to budget constraints on public social spending, particularly in the area of education. Macro-economic conditions also affect households and can have a considerable impact on the level of private spending on education. They may even influence individuals' decisions about pursuing or continuing education.

Macro-economic changes can have an immediate impact on levels of public and private spending on education.

In the late 1990s, the macro-economic situation in WEI countries, as reflected by levels of GDP, sometimes changed dramatically. In some countries, rapid economic growth meant higher government revenue and hence a greater pool of potential resources for education. Other countries faced declines in national income, tighter government budget constraints and fewer financial resources for education.

Countries in transition from heavily centralised systems, such as Russia, face particular challenges in rebuilding institutions and educational curricula in the face of severe budget constraints. As shown in Figure 1.1, the Russian Federation was the only country to see a decline in GDP throughout the 1990s. Southeast Asian countries that suffered from the financial crisis in the late 1990s, notably Indonesia, Thailand and Malaysia, showed positive growth rates during that time, but at a far slower pace than at the start of the decade. In 1998, they then suffered sharp declines in GDP, of 13.2, 9.4 and 7.5 per cent respectively (World Bank, 2001). These countries face difficulties in maintaining achievements in education, especially among those segments of the population hardest hit by the economic downturn. On the positive side, China stands out as the country with the most rapidly expanding economy in both the early and the late 1990s, with GDP levels in Argentina, Chile and Jordan also growing at a brisk pace. More recent events signal an economic downturn in Argentina, and quite possibly in the Philippines and Zimbabwe, where there was marginal economic growth in the late 1990s.

Economic instability has limited public funding for education in the Russian Federation and in Southeast Asia, but in growing economies such as Chile and China, more funds have become available.

Measures of national income are perhaps too general for an adequate assessment of the potential impact of macro-economic changes on education.

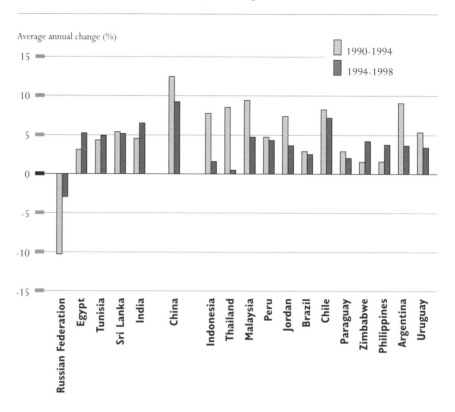

Figure 1.1
Average annual change in GDP growth, 1990-1994 and 1994-1998
(in percentages)

Countries are ranked by direction and magnitude of change between periods.
Source: World Bank (2001).

The level of government revenue more accurately depicts the potential pool of resources for education, although expenditure generally exceeds revenue in the WEI countries. Figure 1.2 shows the wide variation in levels of government revenue among WEI countries in the 1990s, although the focus here is on the change over time.

In the 1990s, government revenue as a percentage of GDP declined in about half the WEI countries, reducing the potential proportion of national income that can be spent on education.

As a proportion of GDP, government revenue in Jordan and Tunisia is twice as high as in China, India and Peru. A comparison of levels in 1990 and 1998 shows that WEI countries fall into two groups. About half of the countries, mostly in Asia (especially Malaysia and Sri Lanka) experienced a decline in revenue as a percentage of GDP while the other half, mostly in Latin America (particularly in Uruguay and Peru) saw increased government revenue.

Changes in revenue and expenditure have obvious implications for education spending. While unexpected and rapid declines in revenue often lead to lower

Figure 1.2
Government revenue as a percentage of GDP, 1990 and late 1980s
(in percentages)

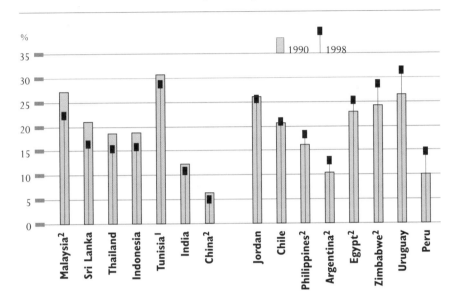

Countries are ranked by percentage point change between years.
1. Year of reference 1996.
2. Year of reference 1997.
Source: World Bank (2001).

educational expenditure, countries may respond by redirecting resources from one level of education or type of expenditure to another. It is also necessary to examine the breakdown of revenue between different levels of government and geographical regions. Particularly in federal states, such as Brazil, China or Russia, education systems are funded through complex arrangements between different levels of government, from the central to the local. As local social expenditure often exceeds local revenue (Klugman, 1997) this imbalance calls for central government transfers in order to equalise regions with less capacity to generate their own revenue.

Another measure, GDP per capita, represents the theoretical division of national income between all members of a population, and is therefore commonly used to compare national income between countries because it adjusts for population size. As shown in Figure 1.3, WEI countries vary widely in national wealth. The 1999 level of GDP per capita in Chile, 8 612 dollars, converted using purchasing power parities (PPP), was nearly four times that in India (2 217 PPP dollars) but still less than half that of the OECD mean. Between 1995 and 1999, the largest gains were recorded in China (31 per cent), Tunisia (18 per cent), India (16 per cent) and Chile (14 per cent).

GDP per capita varies widely between WEI countries: the level in Chile is nearly four times that in India. In the late 1990s, GDP per capita fell in seven WEI countries.

Figure 1.3
GDP per capita, 1995, 1997 and 1999

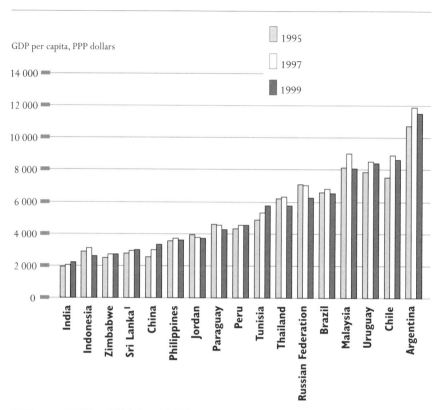

OECD mean (1997) = PPP dollars 18 788.
1. Year of reference 1998.
Sources: World Bank (2001); OECD (2001).

Partly because it has the highest rate of population increase among the WEI countries, GDP per capita in Jordan actually declined, despite considerable growth in national income. In 1999, GDP per capita also fell below the 1995 level in six further countries: Brazil, Indonesia, Malaysia, Paraguay, the Russian Federation and Thailand. The largest decline occurred in the Russian Federation, where GDP per capita fell by 12 per cent.

High rates of inflation mean that fewer goods and services can be bought with the same amount of money, reducing the purchasing power of educational institutions and the real value of teachers' salaries.

In certain countries, changes in national income were accompanied by high rates of inflation. Thus, expressed in constant terms, the real value of these figures after adjusting for inflation are lower. Between 1995 and 1999, the majority of countries showed steady economic growth, with relatively small increases in consumer price indices. However, high rates of inflation were recorded in Indonesia, Russia, Uruguay and Zimbabwe, the first two of which faced financial crises in the second half of the 1990s. Aside from its deleterious effect on general welfare, the reduced real value of wages has an impact on employment, and raises concerns about the ability to retain qualified teachers, let alone to attract new teachers to the profession. How governments respond can have an impact on the skill levels and composition of the teaching force. Governments may, for instance, protect the real value of public sector salary scales by linking them to some type of price index in order to offset their declining real value.

Private contributions to education, as will be discussed in the following section in greater detail, play an important role in financing the provision of education in WEI countries. Thus, it is important to examine also how national income is actually distributed in terms of individual income, rather than as though it were shared equally by each member of the population.

Several WEI countries are among those with the most unequal distribution of income in the world. In Brazil, for example, the richest ten per cent of the population have more than 48 per cent of the wealth (World Bank, 2001). The Gini coefficient, which measures the level of inequality, is plotted against GDP per capita in Figure 1.4. The higher the coefficient, the more unequal the distribution of income (perfect equality is equal to zero and perfect inequality is equal to one). This shows that some of the WEI countries in Latin America, namely Brazil, Chile and Paraguay, have highly unequal distribution of income. Inequality is an issue in other WEI countries, but to a lesser extent

WEI countries in Latin America are among the most unequal in terms of income distribution, with concentrations of the very rich and the very poor.

Figure 1.4
GDP per capita and income disparity in the 1990s

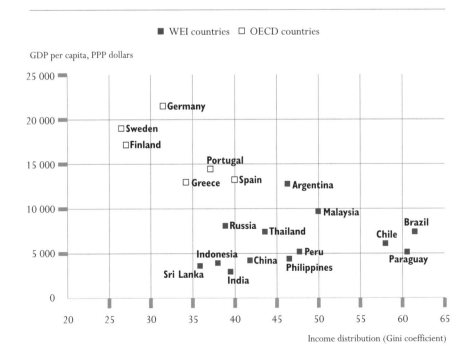

■ WEI countries   □ OECD countries

Source: UNU-WIDER/UNDP World Income Inequality Database.

than in Latin America. While there is general movement towards greater equality as national income increases, the Russian Federation is one example where income inequality has risen.

The links between the distribution of income and educational opportunities have been discussed widely, particularly in the context of Latin American countries. As average educational attainment increases, inequality in income tends to decline. In countries such as India, however, education is even less equally distributed than income, suggesting that yet greater efforts will be necessary to counteract the imbalance there (World Bank, 2001).

This situation places added pressure on governments to distribute educational opportunities, and the benefits associated with them, more equally.

In the light of this debate, pressure is often placed on policy-makers to counteract the negative social and economic effects of inequality, and education is often cited as a key factor since it can help to provide the skills needed to overcome poverty and social exclusion. In most WEI countries, compensatory programmes have been targeted at communities and school districts with high proportions of low-income households. Some countries have also sought to facilitate participation in different types of early childhood education programmes. There is a growing body of evidence suggesting that these programmes can be effective in redressing unequal opportunities.

2 TEACHERS AND THE FUNDING AND GOVERNANCE OF EDUCATION

Teachers are essential factors in the funding of education systems. Expenditure on education can account for up to half of all public social spending. Salaries and wages generally account for the major part of this sum. Teachers and non-teaching staff also account for a sizable percentage of the national labour force. In most WEI countries, at least one in twenty-five of all employed persons work in the education system.

Education is the largest area of public social expenditure, and those employed in the sector can account for up to 10 per cent of the total labour force.

In Tunisia, this ratio is even higher – one in ten. Moreover, they are some of the most educated workers: in Indonesia, more than half of the labour force with tertiary education are teachers. While most administrative functions related to the education sector are dealt with by non-teaching staff, teachers play a major role in implementing decisions at the school level. While government and administrative personnel technically "govern" education systems, teachers "govern" classrooms.

This section looks at the availability of public resources and how they are allocated. It also examines the role of teachers in the decision-making process, and the levels of government at which the decisions that affect teachers are taken.

Availability of public resources

Levels of public spending as a proportion of GDP reflect levels of commitment to educational provision.

Public spending on education as a percentage of GDP is often interpreted as the level of commitment which a state makes towards educational provision. As shown in Figure 1.5, levels of public spending on education in 1998 ranged from 1.4 per cent of GDP in Indonesia to 6.8 per cent in Tunisia. In most WEI countries, the figure falls well below the OECD mean (5.0 per cent in 1998). The level of public spending as a percentage of GDP may also reflect differences in the balance between public and private funding of education. As noted earlier, in Tunisia educational staff account for a considerable percentage of public sector employees and thus of the public wage bill. This goes some way to explaining the higher public spending on education in Tunisia than in other countries with similar levels of GDP.

Levels of public spending as a proportion of GDP reflect levels of commitment to educational provision.

There were notable changes in patterns of public spending in the period between 1996 and 1998. These may reflect unexpected changes in GDP as much as decisions on levels of public spending on education. For example, between 1996 and 1998, public spending on education increased by more than a third in Paraguay, from 3.1 to 4.2 per cent of GDP, and by a fifth in

Between 1996 and 1998, the proportion of GDP devoted to education grew most in Argentina, Chile, Paraguay and Thailand.

Figure 1.5
Public expenditure[1] on educational institutions as a percentage of GDP, 1998

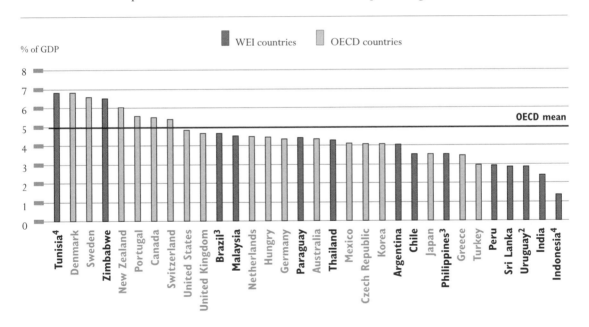

1. Including public subsidies to households attributable for educational institutions. Including direct expenditure on educational institutions from international sources.

2. Direct expenditure on educational institutions from international sources exceed 1.5% of all public expenditure (1998).

3. Year of reference 1997.

4. Year of reference 1999.

Source: OECD/UNESCO WEI, Table 4 in Annex A4.

Argentina, Chile and Thailand. The proportion among other countries remained relatively stable, although it is important to keep in mind that in an expanding economy, real expenditure still increases if the percentage of GDP devoted to education remains the same.

Spending on education as a proportion of total public expenditure is generally higher in WEI than in OECD countries, accounting for more than one quarter of public expenditure in Thailand in 1998.

Another measure of a government's commitment to education is the proportion of total public expenditure devoted to education. WEI countries often allocate a percentage higher than the OECD mean (12.8 per cent in 1998). Thailand, for example, spent 27.2 per cent of public expenditure on education in 1998, more than twice the OECD mean, and a substantial increase from the level of 21.8 per cent recorded in the previous year. The percentage in the Philippines fell from 28.3 to 19.7 during the same period. Thus, countries that spend a proportion of GDP lower than the OECD mean may still be devoting a percentage of total public expenditure to education which is at or above the OECD mean.

Private sources play a more important role in funding education in WEI than in OECD countries.

Private sources of funds play a significant role in financing educational systems. It is common in all countries for public expenditure on education to be supplemented by private contributions. When private spending is taken into account, combined public and private expenditure in Chile, the Philippines and Thailand exceeds the combined mean of the same measure among OECD countries.

The extent of private funding of education is striking, accounting for more than 40 per cent of total educational expenditure in Chile, Peru, the Philippines and Thailand. These figures are well above the OECD mean of 19 per cent (OECD, 2001). In Egypt, Jordan and Tunisia, private expenditure is lower, since there are few private providers. There are, however, a number of countries where parents and communities help to cover costs by directly or indirectly subsidising teachers' salaries in state-run schools, or by directly employing and paying teachers. One example is Indonesia, where parents' organisations make small contributions to staff welfare at the primary and lower secondary levels (OECD, 1998).

National averages can conceal considerable variation in spending within countries. For example, expenditure per student in China can be up to five times greater in some regions than in others.

Substantial government support for private education is found in several WEI countries, especially at the primary and secondary levels of education. Three WEI countries are well above the OECD mean (10 per cent) in this respect, although there is wide variation among OECD members. At the primary and secondary level, about one third of educational spending goes towards government-dependent private institutions in Chile and India, and 13 per cent in Argentina.

The distribution of educational expenditure can also vary widely within a country. Expenditure per student can differ by a factor of as much as 5.1 between regions in China, or 3.8 in Argentina (NCES, 2001). Another study

Figure 1.6
Expenditure per student by educational level, 1998

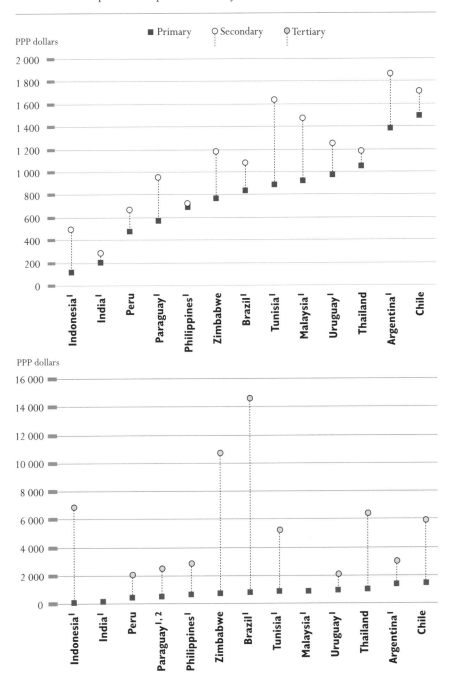

Based on full-time equivalents.

1. Public institutions only.
2. Tertiary refers only to type B programmes.

Source: OECD/UNESCO WEI, Table 8 in Annex A4.

has shown that the variation between regions actually increased in Russia during the 1990s, and that even after intergovernmental transfers, there remained significant differences in the distribution of resources for education (Klugman, 1998). Some countries have sought to address regional disparities in levels of resources. In Brazil, a special fund was set up in 1996 (Fund for Primary Education Development and for Enhancement of the Value of the Teaching Process – FUNDEF) to distribute funds to states and regions where expenditure per student falls below a nationally established level. Money in School is another programme in Brazil that transfers cash directly to schools.

Use of public resources

The cost of educating a child at the primary level can vary from 116 PPP dollars in Indonesia to 1 500 in Chile.

Expenditure per student also differs widely between educational levels in WEI countries, although comparisons should be made with caution, as figures reflect differences in levels of national income. As shown in Figure 1.6, expenditure at the primary level ranges from 116 PPP dollars per student in Indonesia to 1 500 in Chile. As in the OECD countries, the cost per student increases at higher levels of education. The OECD average expenditure per secondary student is 40 per cent higher than that per primary student, while in WEI countries the difference ranges from only 5 per cent in the Philippines to several hundred per cent in Indonesia.

The data show marked changes in several countries between 1997 and 1998, although these may be the result of either changing patterns of expenditure or the number of students enrolled. Moreover, these figures are in current dollars, meaning that in countries with high inflation rates, such as Zimbabwe or the Russian Federation, the real value of the expenditure might be much less if it were measured in constant terms.

When educational spending had to be cut in the late 1990s, Malaysia reallocated funds to maintain primary education at the expense of higher levels of education.

Countries react in various ways to the need to cut expenditure. In the case of Malaysia, GDP fell by 7.5 per cent in 1998 as a result of the economic crisis. Figure 1.7 shows that public resources devoted to primary education were maintained while cuts were made at the secondary and tertiary levels. An initial policy to cut primary spending by 18 per cent in 1997 was reversed in 1998, and additional funding was allocated to support social safety net programmes (Knowless *et al.*, 1999). As a result, net enrolment rates in primary education remained stable during this period. However, negative effects on secondary school enrolments were reported, especially among girls and in rural areas, due to higher fees and higher opportunity costs (*ibid*).

After adjustment is made for differences in national income, wide variation in unit costs in education tends to disappear.

It should be noted that expenditure per student, expressed in PPP dollars, may distort comparisons by not taking into account the level of a country's national income. A measure that addresses this issue compares expenditure per student with a country's resources, *i.e.*, GDP per capita. As shown in Figure 1.8, the large differences between countries tend to disappear at lower

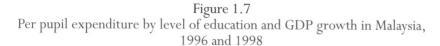

Figure 1.7
Per pupil expenditure by level of education and GDP growth in Malaysia,
1996 and 1998

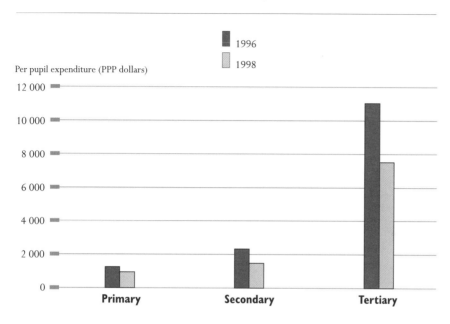

Source: OECD/UNESCO WEI, Table 8 in Annex A4; OECD (2001).

levels of education. For example, after adjusting expenditure per primary student by national income, Chile, the Philippines and Thailand reflect levels similar to the OECD mean. Both Tunisia and Zimbabwe spend a higher proportion per secondary student than the OECD mean and other WEI countries. At the tertiary level, however, differences remain considerable and indicate that some countries, such as Zimbabwe, Indonesia and Brazil may pursue a policy of supporting tertiary education at the expense of other levels of education.

The allocation of resources also differs by type or category. Educational spending is conventionally divided into two categories – current and capital expenditure. The former refers to spending on goods or services that are consumed in the year of expenditure (*e.g.* teachers' salaries), while the latter represents longer-term investment in school buildings or equipment. Capital expenditure may be higher as a percentage of total spending in countries where expansion of the education system involves the construction of new school buildings. The majority of recurrent educational expenditure goes towards the salaries (and pensions where relevant) of teaching and non-teaching staff in the education system.

Figure 1.8
Expenditure per student as a percentage of GDP per capita, 1998

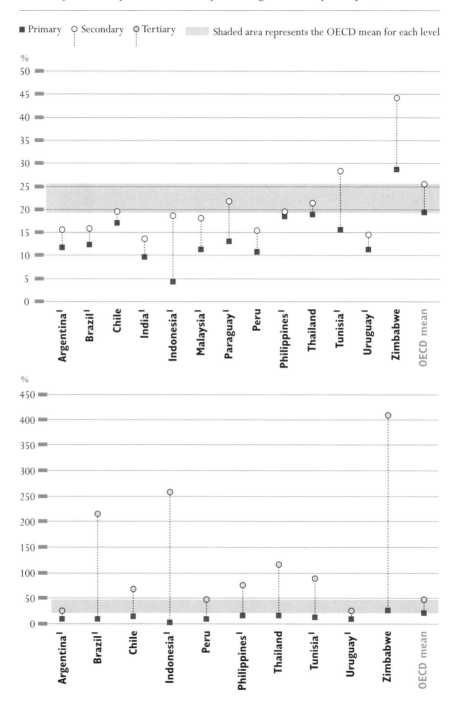

Based on full-time equivalents.

1. Public institutions only.

Source: OECD/UNESCO WEI, Table 9 in Annex A4.

WEI countries tend to spend only a small part of the education budget on capital expenditure. In Indonesia, for example, 4 per cent of total public spending on education at the primary and secondary levels is allocated to capital expenditure. In other countries, the percentage is closer to the OECD mean (8 per cent in 1998). Both OECD and WEI countries tend to allocate a higher percentage to capital expenditure at the tertiary level, as this level requires greater long-term investment. Malaysia, for example, spends 12 per cent of total public spending on education on capital expenditure at the primary and secondary level, and three times that figure (37 per cent) at the tertiary level (see Table 7 in Annex A4). These differences may reflect a temporary effort to expand the capacity of the system quickly.

Capital costs tend to be highest in countries which are expanding educational provision.

It has been widely suggested that high proportions of compensation-related expenditure, which is often more inflexible to change, may be at the expense of other current or capital expenditure. Figure 1.9 shows that among WEI countries, countries with a high levels of compensation-related expenditure

Figure 1.9
Capital and compensation-related expenditure as a proportion
of total expenditure in primary and secondary levels, 1998
(in percentages)

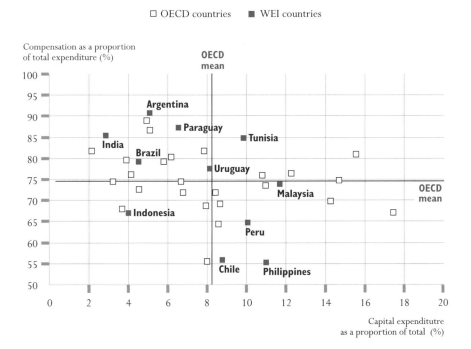

Note: WEI data refer to public institutions only. See notes to Table 7.
Source: OECD/UNESCO WEI, Table 7 in Annex A4.

in primary and secondary education, such as India, Brazil or Argentina, tend to have lower capital spending. And higher levels of capital spending are found in the Philippines, Chile and Peru, where the shares of total expenditure going towards compensation are considerably lower.

Salaries for teaching and non-teaching staff account for the largest share of current spending, but the proportion by type of staff can vary considerably.

Figure 1.10 breaks down salary costs for teachers and for all educational personnel as percentages of current expenditure in selected WEI countries. Indonesia and Peru spend more than two thirds of the money allocated for current expenditure on teachers' salaries at primary and secondary levels. The breakdown of expenditure on salaries by category of personnel reflects wide differences in the use of non-teaching staff. In Peru, the salary costs for teachers represent 70 per cent of current expenditure while other staff account for only 2 per cent. In the case of Argentina, however, the salaries of non-teaching staff account for a considerable proportion of wage costs. This difference can be seen in the ratio of classroom teachers to school administrators, which is almost 30 to 1 in Peru but only 4 to 1 in Argentina.

The next chapter discusses teacher salary scales in greater depth both from a comparative perspective and in terms of overall costs.

Governance of schools

Reforms involving the decentralisation of decision-making in education were introduced in many WEI countries in the 1990s.

Many WEI countries are in the process of decentralising financial and management responsibilities to regional or municipal authorities, or even to individual schools, as part of broader reform policies. These efforts may have a considerable impact on the context of teaching. However, there are also some WEI countries which are at a different stage of the policy cycle and, sometimes as a reaction to over-hasty decentralisation, are seeking to re-centralise certain aspects of decision-making.

While the rationale for decentralising decision-making is well-established, it is difficult to assess its effects, particularly on teachers.

The decentralisation of responsibilities from central to regional and local authorities has been motivated by a wide range of concerns. The aim of these reforms is to improve efficiency and student performance, and to increase community involvement. Decentralisation policies aim to give communities and schools greater power to select and manage their own personnel, to choose certain areas of the curriculum and to control some aspects of financial resources. In principle, the rationale underlying these steps is that local decision-makers know their own needs best. It is also thought that this policy should lead to greater accountability, as parents are encouraged to participate actively in school governance, and ultimately, to improved student performance. In practice, however, it is difficult to assess the actual impact on teachers because of the complexity of the process of decentralisation. Nonetheless, it is possible to draw some general conclusions from experience in a number of countries.

Figure 1.10
Compensation for teachers and other staff as a proportion of total current expenditure by level, 1998

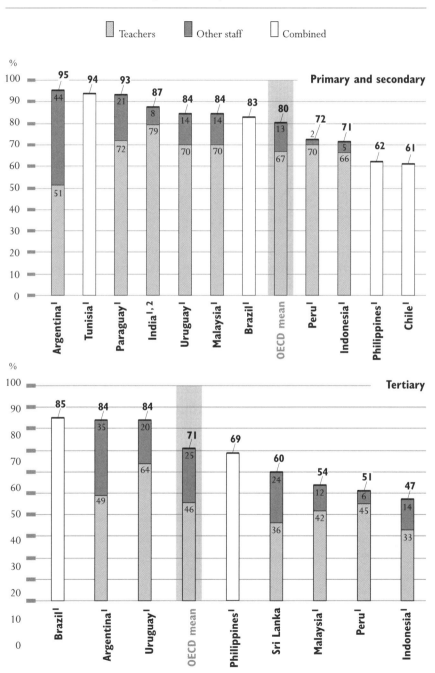

1. Public institutions only.
2. Public and government-dependent private institutions only.

Source: OECD/UNESCO WEI, Table 7 in Annex A4.

The potential impact on teachers is considerable, and teachers themselves may be asked to play a role in the decision-making process.

The decentralisation of responsibilities may affect teachers' working lives in different ways. For example, local municipalities or school principals may be given greater power over certain aspects of personnel management, such as recruitment of teachers and pay awards, or for use of resources. The ability to reallocate expenditure within an overall budget or to raise local resources, for example, may have a substantial impact on the funds available for staffing or in-service training. Teachers themselves may be asked to carry additional responsibilities in the areas of curriculum development or school management.

Box 1.1 looks more closely at the results from a recent comparative study of policy trends related to decentralisation in education.

Box 1.1
The effects on teachers of decentralising education systems

A recent study has examined the role of regional governments in the funding and governance of primary and secondary education in 21 countries (NCES, 2001). The study included six WEI countries, four with federal systems of government (Argentina, Brazil, India and Russia) and two non-federal systems (China and Indonesia).

Overall, the study found that 10 of the 21 countries had moved towards decentralisation in six different areas of decision-making in the 1990s. Five countries remained basically centralised in their decision-making, and others had a mixed profile. Two of these countries had moved towards more centralised decision-making: the United Kingdom in the areas of curriculum, duration of schooling, examinations and inspection, and Australia in the area of finance. In the six WEI countries, the study found the trends summarised in Table 1.1.

Table 1.1
Shifts in levels of authority over educational decision-making, 1990s
(primary and secondary education)

| C-R: Central to regional | C-L: Central to local | R-C: Regional to central | L-C: Local to central |
| C: Central | R: Regional | L: Local | |

	Curriculum	Hour/year	Exams	Credentials	Inspection	Finance	Overall
Argentina	C-R	R	L	R	C-R – C-L	C-R	C-R
Brazil	C-R	C	C/L	~	C-R	C-R – C-L	C-R – C-L
China	C-R	C	R	C	C-R – C-L	C-R – C-L	C-R – C-L
India	R-C	R-C	R-C	R-C	L	L-C	R-C – L-C
Indonesia	C-R	C	C	C	C	C	C
Russian Federation	C-L	C-L	C-R – C-L	C-R – C-L	C-R – C-L	C-R – C-L	C-R – C-L

~ : No information available.
Source: NCES (2001).

In general, decisions in some fields are traditionally made at the regional or local level, such as those relating to curriculum choices and inspection; others, concerning the duration of schooling or examinations and qualifications, are more likely to be the responsibility of central authorities. Decisions about personnel supervision and budgets are made at various levels in the WEI countries. For example, decisions in these areas are the responsibility of central authorities in India and Indonesia, while they made at the regional and local level in the other WEI countries reviewed in the study.

The special survey conducted among WEI countries in 1998 showed that the level at which decisions about teachers are made differs from country to country, but tends to be fairly consistent within each country. The only exception is statutory salary scales, which are set at the central level in nearly all countries. This diversity is shown in Table 1.2: in Indonesia, central government is responsible for hiring and firing teachers, for prescribing teachers' duties and conditions of service, and for determining teachers' career progression, while in India these same decisions are made at regional level and in Chile, largely at local government level. It should also be noted that decentralised decisions are frequently taken within a framework laid down by central government, usually with some degree of consultation with regional and local governments.

Within countries, most decisions that affect teachers are made consistently at the same level of government, whether central or local, but the salary structure is always a matter for central government.

It is widely held that well-trained and motivated teachers are a major factor in a school's performance. In addition to strong teaching skills, teachers need a supportive environment that fosters continuing training and teamwork and makes time available for new responsibilities related to school management.

Table 1.2
Levels of authority over educational decision-making at ISCED 1/2, 1997
(decision taken at central, regional, local or school-level)

C: Central	R: Regional	L: Local	S: School	m: missing
	Hiring/firing teachers	**Setting wages**	**Duties and condition**	**Influence career path**	**Allocation of resources**
Indonesia	C	C	C	S	C
India	R	R	R	R	R
Chile[1]	L	C	L	L	L
Philippines	R	C	C	S	R
Thailand	C	C	S	S	C
Argentina	m	m	m	m	R

1. Data refer to public institutions only in 1996.

Source: OECD (1998).

Some countries have adopted a model in which schools operate within a centrally determined framework of curricula and standards, but are given a considerable amount of autonomy and responsibility for decisions. One example of school-based decision-making is the team-teaching approach adopted in Peru, which identifies and proposes solutions to problems such as professional development and community outreach (ILO, 2000). New educational legislation, such as that in Thailand, may call for the creation of school-based management committees comprising parents, teachers and community leaders (ibid).

3 TEACHERS AND THE ORGANISATION OF LEARNING

Over the last decade, access to schooling has expanded at all levels, and educational attainment among young people has increased several-fold over that of their parents' generation. In most WEI countries, the focus of education policy has moved increasingly from access to primary education to higher levels of education, and to issues of quality throughout the system. This has meant a greater focus on teachers, particularly in the context of growing demand at secondary and tertiary levels.

This section looks at the education systems in which teachers serve in WEI countries. Systems differ widely in the demands they place on teachers, in levels of participation in the education system and in the organisation of educational programmes. The section examines the available evidence on educational quality, such as what student assessments can tell us about the conditions that teachers face in the classroom.

Growing levels of participation in education

"School expectancy", the expected number of years of schooling, is a measure of aggregate enrolment across the school-age population.

One indicator which reflects overall changes in participation in education is the average number of years of schooling which a five-year-old child can expect, conventionally termed "school expectancy". This measure captures aggregate patterns of enrolment by adding together the net enrolment rates for single years from the age of five (and dividing by 100). It represents the number of years for which students are enrolled in the system, but does not indicate any particular level of achievement. Higher school expectancy is usually found in countries with higher enrolment rates and more developed systems of tertiary education, but expectancy may also be increased by high levels of repetition. This indicator should therefore be interpreted with caution.

Higher school expectancy is not always associated with higher levels of GDP.

School expectancy varies widely in WEI countries, more years not always being associated with higher levels of GDP per capita. Figure 1.11 shows that countries have achieved similar results in expected years of schooling with widely differing GDP per capita. For example, Peru has achieved a level comparable to that of Malaysia, but with only half the GDP per capita. Chile has a level similar to that of Argentina, but much lower national income. This

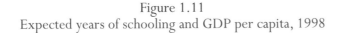

Figure 1.11
Expected years of schooling and GDP per capita, 1998

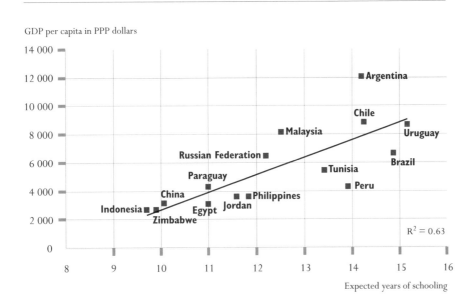

Sources: OECD/UNESCO WEI, Table 12 in Annex A4; World Bank (2001).

is not to say that this measure captures educational quality per se, but rather access to education, and particularly at post-secondary levels. Nonetheless, WEI countries with the lowest GDP per capita, such as China and Indonesia, are found clustered together, having similarly low values for school expectancy.

Figure 1.12 shows estimated school expectancy in WEI countries in 1996 and 1998. The level rose over this short period in five of the nine countries where data are available, especially in Chile, Malaysia, Paraguay and Uruguay. Girls, in particular, benefited from the expansion of educational opportunities in Uruguay. Generally, levels were still far below the OECD mean, where continuation to tertiary education is more widespread. The gender gap remained relatively stable among the 14 countries with data for 1998: girls had more expected years of schooling than boys in seven countries (Latin American and others) and fewer years in the other seven (African and others).

Between 1996 and 1998, school expectancy increased in five of the nine countries for which data are available.

School expectancy figures cannot capture actual learning outcomes, however. Data from comparative student assessments in Latin America show that the type of school matters. Students attending elite private schools score considerably higher in mathematics and science tests than their peers in rural public schools (World Bank, 1999). Although the socio-economic differences underlying these outcomes may play a large role, good teaching and learning conditions also clearly encourage good results. While the increase in school expectancy is a positive achievement in itself, it is not sufficient to ensure either the equitable distribution or the quality of educational opportunities.

The expected number of years of schooling does not reflect the real outcome of education: learning achievement.

Figure 1.12
Expected years of schooling under current conditions, 1996 and 1998

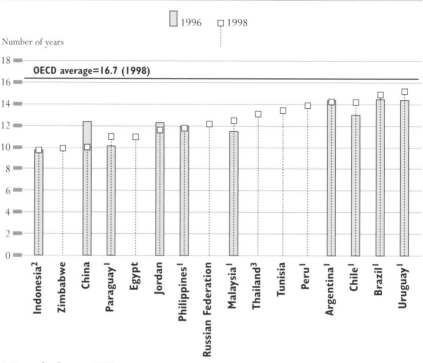

1. Year of reference 1998.
2. Year of reference 2000.
3. Full-time participation only. Participation by adults in part-time education accounts for about five more years of school expectancy.
Sources: OECD/UNESCO WEI, Table 12 in Annex A4; OECD (2000).

Despite progress, there are still challenges to be met in extending education to those who need it most.

An important issue is who benefits from additional education. Not surprisingly, it appears that children from poor households or living in remote areas are the hardest to reach. Evidence from household surveys carried out over a number of years in several WEI countries suggests that the poor are the last to benefit from increased access to education (Vandermoortele, 1999). Governments have therefore made efforts to create incentives for teachers to work in remote areas. In Malaysia, for example, higher remuneration and promotional schemes have been introduced for teachers working in schools in remote areas. In Russia, Sri Lanka and other countries, the state provides subsidised housing and special hardship allowances for this category of teachers. Nevertheless, recruiting and retaining qualified teachers remains a challenge in most WEI countries.

Participation in early childhood programmes exceeds the OECD mean in some countries, such as Peru and the Russian Federation.

Educational opportunities have expanded not only at secondary and tertiary levels, but also through access to early childhood education. These programmes are spreading along with the recognition that early intervention in education is an effective way of providing the basis for lifelong learning and helping to break the cycle of poverty. In the WEI countries, rates of participation in early childhood development programmes often reach levels comparable to those in OECD countries. For example, more than 80 per cent of five-year-olds attend programmes in Peru and the Russian Federation.

The importance of basic education in WEI countries is underscored by the fact that attendance is compulsory at both primary and lower secondary levels (which together last for between seven and 11 years). In the last few decades, most WEI countries have theoretically achieved universal primary enrolment, although net enrolment rates still show large gaps at certain ages in some countries. There are still pockets of out-of-school youth in most WEI countries.

Public provision of primary and secondary education is predominant, as is shown in Figure 1.13, but substantial proportions of students are enrolled in private institutions in Chile (44 per cent), Jordan (24 per cent) and Argentina (22 per cent). Private provision at tertiary level is more common, as elsewhere in the world, and is particularly high in Indonesia (85 per cent of students), the Philippines (74 per cent) and Chile (71 per cent). The comparable OECD mean is 26 per cent. Private tertiary enrolments represent only 5 per cent of the total in the Russian Federation, however.

Enrolments in private education are highest in Argentina, Chile and Jordan at the primary and secondary levels, and in Chile, Indonesia and the Philippines at the tertiary level.

Figure 1.13
Share of students in private educational institutions by level of education, 1998

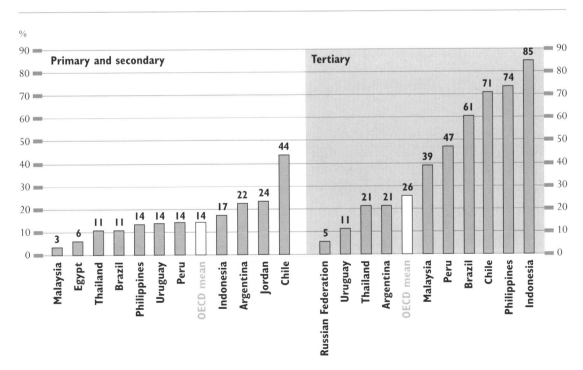

Source: OECD/UNESCO WEI, Table 14 in Annex A4.

Figure 1.14
Proportion of students repeating current grade by educational level, 1998

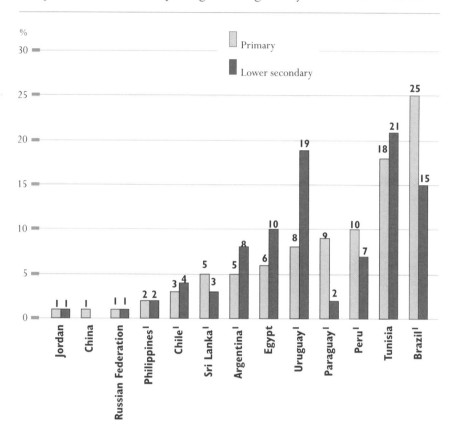

Countries are ranked by primary level.
1. Year of reference 1998.
Source: OECD/UNESCO WEI, Table 15 in Annex A4.

High repetition rates persist in several WEI countries, lowering the efficiency of education systems and creating problems for teachers.

Most WEI countries have been able to promote progression through the primary and secondary grades, but high rates of repetition persist in several countries. Figure 1.14 shows that in Brazil and Tunisia, repetition at the primary and lower secondary levels remains a serious problem. While there is still wide debate on how best to measure the scope of the problem accurately (Klein, 1999), it is clearly a pressing issue. From the perspective of teachers, classes with large numbers of repeaters make it more difficult to deliver the curriculum and to manage the classroom.

Increasing the number of students who complete secondary schooling is vital for enhancing human capital and improving economic performance. Despite the often high rates of non-completion noted in some WEI countries, levels of secondary school completion have risen sharply in many WEI countries, though still at levels below the OECD mean. Figure 1.15 shows the range of

Figure 1.15
Upper secondary graduation rates by type of programme, 1998

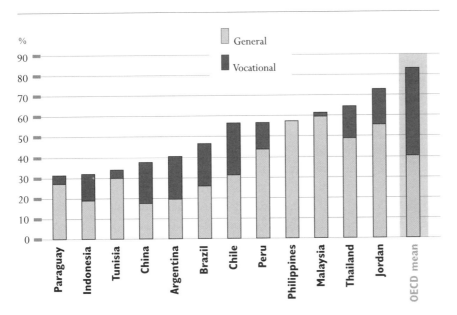

Ratio of upper secondary graduates to total population at typical age of graduation (multiplied by 100), by type of programme.
Source: OECD/UNESCO WEI, Table 18 in Annex A4.

graduation rates in WEI countries. Data over time show that completion rates have been increasing in countries with available data, with the exception of the Philippines.

As reflected by secondary completion rates, education systems vary in the emphasis of their provision. Young people are more likely to follow a predominantly academic programme in Philippines (100 per cent), Malaysia (97 per cent), Tunisia (88 per cent) and Paraguay (87 per cent), and a more vocational programme in China (54 per cent) and Argentina (53 per cent).

Education systems vary in the emphasis of upper secondary education, from predominantly academic to predominantly vocational.

Greater demand for secondary schooling has partly been the result of the increased numbers of children completing primary education. Government-dependent and independent private schools are therefore frequently playing an increasing role in the provision of secondary education, as indicated above (see Figure 1.13).

An extensive tertiary education system is needed to build the scientific and technological infrastructure to respond to the emerging needs of knowledge-based economies. Improving access to upper secondary and tertiary education therefore remains an important goal, as there is still widespread inequality in many countries.

There has been modest growth in tertiary enrolment rates in WEI countries in recent years. Generally, however, tertiary enrolment rates are considerably lower than those in OECD countries. And as shown in Figure 1.16, graduation rates can also vary substantially by country and by type of programme in WEI countries. A greater number of students graduate from professional programmes (Tertiary-type B) in WEI countries compared to the OECD mean, although university-degree programmes are strong in the Russian Federation and the Philippines.

Multi-shift, multi-grade and boarding schools are common in some WEI countries, but little is known as yet about the implications of such arrangements.

Although governments have had some success in expanding educational opportunities, one of the main problems has been an adequate supply of teachers. As a result, some countries, as noted in Table 1.3, make considerable use of multi-shift schooling at both the primary and secondary level. While research in Brazil, Chile, India and Malaysia has shown that the use of multi-shift schools has not led to poorer learning outcomes than single-shift schools, it has raised concerns about difficult working conditions for teachers (Bray, 2000).

Figure 1.16
Tertiary graduation rates by type of programme, 1998

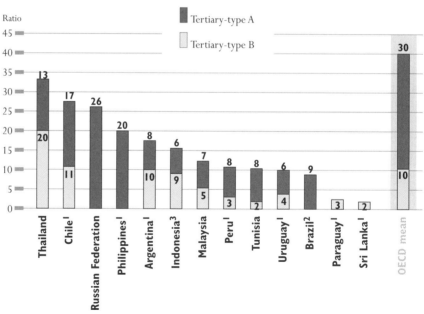

Ratio of graduates to population at typical age of graduation in public and private institutions.

Note: The total of tertiary graduation rates might be overestimated due to double counting across types of programmes.

1. Year of reference 1998.
2. Year of reference 1997.
3. Year of reference 2000.

Source: OECD/UNESCO WEI, Table 19 in Annex A4.

Table 1.3
Prevalence of multiple-shift schooling, late 1990s

● Common	■ Rare	n: none	m: missing

	Primary	Lower secondary	Upper secondary General	Upper secondary Vocational
Brazil	■ / ■	● / ●	● / ●	n/n
Chile	●	●	●	m
Egypt	m	m	m	m
Indonesia	m	●	●	●
Malaysia	● / ■	●	●	m
Peru	n	●	n	n
Philippines	■ / ■	■	■	m
Russian Federation	■ / ■	■ / ■	■	m
Sri Lanka	n	n	n	n
Thailand	n	n	m	■
Tunisia	n	n	n	n
Uruguay	● / ●	● / ●	● / ●	● / ●
Zimbabwe	n	n	n	n

Note: First or only symbol refers to double shift classes/schools; second symbol refers to triple shift classes/schools.
Source: OECD/UNESCO WEI.

While national indicators supply valuable information at a general level about teachers' working conditions, they say less about what happens at the classroom level. Additional evidence from an international study conducted in 1999 is therefore included (see Box 1.2). This timely study helps to provide a better understanding of some aspects of the challenges faced in teachers' day-to-day situation. Moreover, it raises the vital issue of maintaining adequate levels and distribution of resources at the school level. An essential part of enabling teachers is ensuring that they are well-prepared and well-equipped to meet the needs at the school level.

Box 1.2
What happens in the classroom? Evidence from international assessments

Growing concern about the quality of education has focused on the outcomes of learning, but this is an area that is very difficult to measure or monitor. For the most part, efforts have concentrated on testing knowledge of the prescribed curriculum in certain areas such as mathematics and sciences.

The Third International Mathematics and Science Study (TIMSS), for example, was conducted in 1999 in 38 countries, including eight WEI countries. It tested the curriculum-based achievement of students in grade 8 (generally aged 13-14 years). In terms of national average achievement scores, WEI countries tended to cluster at the lower end of the scale, as shown in Figure 1.17. Countries with levels of GDP per capita similar to those of WEI countries, mostly in Central and Eastern Europe, achieved considerably higher average achievement scores.

Figure 1.17
National achievement scores in mathematics and sciences, 1999

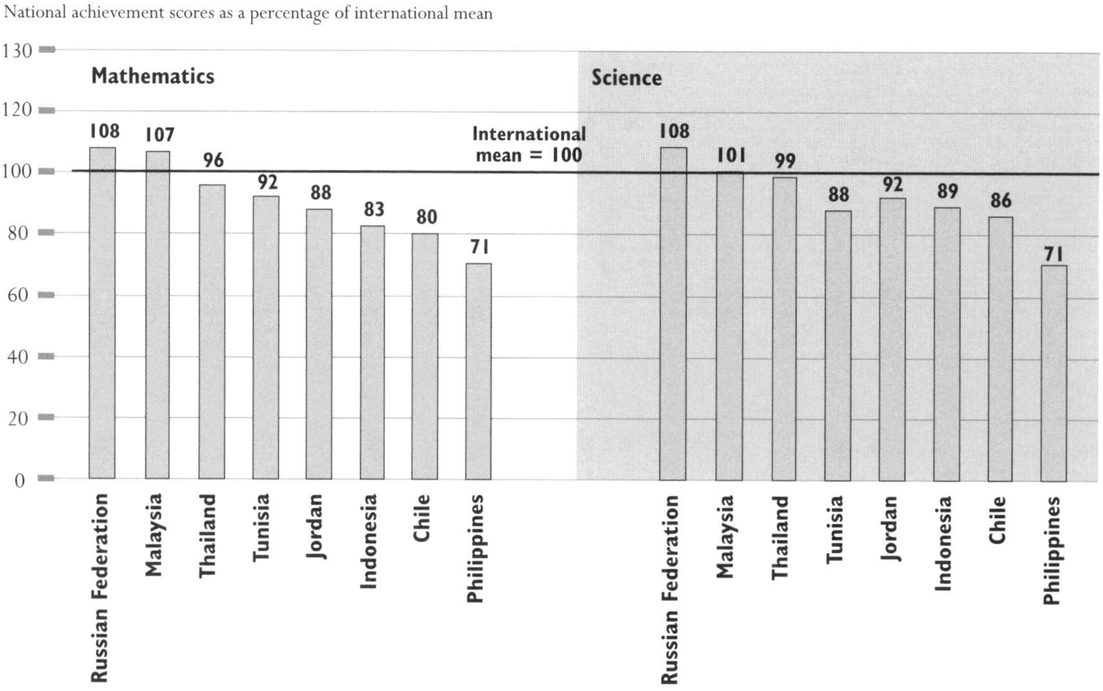

National achievement scores as a percentage of international mean

Sources: Martin *et al.* (2000); Mullis *et al.* (2000).

In terms of science achievement, Malaysia and the Russian Federation were the only WEI countries scoring above the international average. Girls did as well as or better than boys in science in 22 of the 38 countries, and in five of the eight WEI countries. Boys achieved higher scores than girls in Chile, the Russian Federation and Tunisia. In mathematics, Malaysia and the Russian Federation again exceeded the international average.

Besides assessing students' knowledge of mathematics and science, however, the study also collected detailed information about the characteristics of schools and teachers. Several issues that it examined were the use of information and communication technologies (ICT) in the classroom, the "preparedness" of teachers to teach mathematics and science and shortages or inadequacies that affect schools' capacity to provide instruction.

There is much public discussion of the need for ICT in the classroom, but because of the speed of changes, much less knowledge about how ICT actually improves teaching and learning. The benefits of greater access to information are clear, but how new technologies are incorporated into curricula and how teachers are trained to use these new tools are important issues for the immediate future.

According to the TIMSS study, the percentage of students whose schools have access to the Internet ranges from 98 per cent in Finland to near zero in Indonesia, Iran and Morocco. The highest access rates in WEI countries are found in Chile, where 23 per cent of 8th-grade students have access to the

Internet in their school. Thailand and Malaysia show the next highest figures, 17 and 16 per cent respectively. The level of access in the Russian Federation is lower than might have been expected, only 5 per cent.

There is some indication of the extent to which teachers and students are using computers to demonstrate ideas in science classes. According to TIMSS data, the use of computers in science teaching is still relatively limited in Indonesia, Malaysia and Tunisia, and is more frequent among teachers than students in the Philippines and Thailand. The highest proportion of students using computers in science is in Jordan, although at a level still below the international mean.

The study also measured access to the Internet and found that even in countries with low levels of access at home or at school, much larger percentages of students reported having access elsewhere. While it is possible that students have access through libraries, cafés and other places, it is also likely that some students do not have a clear idea of what is meant by Internet access (Martin *et al.*, 2000).

Figure 1.18
Shortages or inadequacies that affect schools' capacity
to provide science instruction (in percentages)

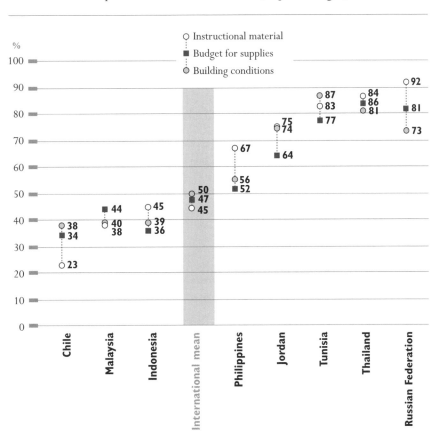

As part of background questionnaires completed by headmasters of participating schools in the TIMSS assessment, these figures refer to the proportion of 8th-grade students affected by a shortage or inadequacy as reflected by the answer categories "some" and "a lot".

Source: Martin *et al.* (2000).

While the use of new technologies in the classroom is frequently looked to as a valuable tool for teachers and efforts to widen access in schools have increased in WEI countries, the associated costs are often large and compete with expenditure on other educational goods, such as instructional materials. The shortages in learning materials or the inadequate availability of supplies or poor building conditions that affect a schools' capacity to provide instruction were reported by head-teachers in the eight WEI countries and give an interesting perspective of school conditions (Figure 1.18). Countries that have faced shrinking educational budgets, such as Thailand and the Russian Federation showed the greatest problems, with the shortage of instructional materials affecting 80-90 per cent of the 8th grade students. Fewer problems were reported in Chile, Malaysia and Indonesia, although the share of students affected still ranged between 20 and 40 per cent. While these results should be interpreted with caution, they may imply that in terms of enabling teachers, governments need to look more closely at improving access to traditional tools of teaching and learning and not only in terms of access to the latest technology.

Figure 1.19 provides an indication of how confident teachers are in their ability to teach 8th grade mathematics and science classes. The index was calculated based on self-reported responses by teachers and uses the level of "preparedness" to teach different sub-topics in science or mathematics (*e.g*, life science, biology, chemistry, algebra, geometry).

Figure 1.19

Teachers' confidence in their preparation to teach science and mathematics topics
(in percentages)

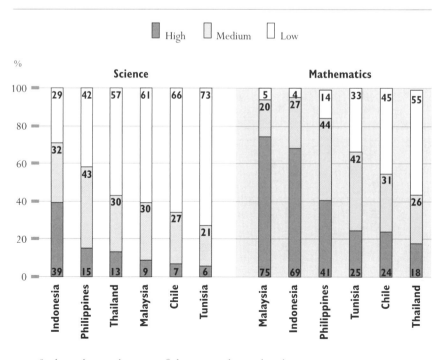

Students whose teachers report feeling prepared to teach each topic.
Sources: Martin *et al*. (2000); Mullis *et al*. (2000).

Generally, teachers were more confident about their preparedness to teach in the area of mathematics than in science. For example, in Malaysia, the proportion of mathematics teachers who reported their level of preparedness as *low* was only 5 per cent cent compared to 61 per cent in science. More than half of the mathematics teachers in Thailand felt poorly prepared while more than half of science teachers felt the same way in Thailand, Malaysia, Chile and Tunisia. While further research is needed to see how these variables are associated with students' actual learning achievement, they do give a general indication of teachers' views about their training and therefore provide useful background information for looking at teachers' qualifications in the next section. However, as they represent teachers views, they may not reflect actual differences between countries in terms of qualification standards and required training.

4 PROFILES OF THE TEACHING FORCE

This section identifies some of the key characteristics of the existing teaching force in WEI countries: age and gender distribution, and qualifications. These are significant variables and need to be monitored in order to respond to changing patterns of enrolment and availability of financial resources.

The composition of the teaching force in terms of age and gender helps to provide insights into the state and status of the teaching profession. The age profile of the teaching force not only reflects the supply of teachers and the rate of renewal of the teaching force (which has implications for the forward planning of teaching staff requirements) but also provides a proxy for the overall level of teaching experience. The gender composition of the teaching force to some degree reflects national social norms and traditions, but also gives an indication of the labour market situation of teachers. However, it is difficult to define a right balance between young and old or female and male teachers. Generally, these indicators can inform policy merely by identifying serious imbalances.

While a reasonable balance between age groups and genders in the teaching force is a justified policy goal, it is difficult to relate these characteristics to student achievement.

The age distribution of the teaching force is of particular concern. Policies on the recruitment, deployment and retention of teachers will obviously influence, and be influenced by, the balance between younger, less experienced, and older, more experienced teachers. Countries with predominantly older teachers, such as Chile, clearly have more accumulated experience in the teaching force. Countries with significant proportions of younger teachers, such as Indonesia, may have less accumulated experience, but the introduction of new curricula may prove to be easier among younger teachers who have been trained more recently. Perhaps more importantly, they incur a smaller wage bill, with the result that education systems can reach more pupils at a lower cost.

Figure 1.20
Distribution of teaching staff by age and level of education, 1998

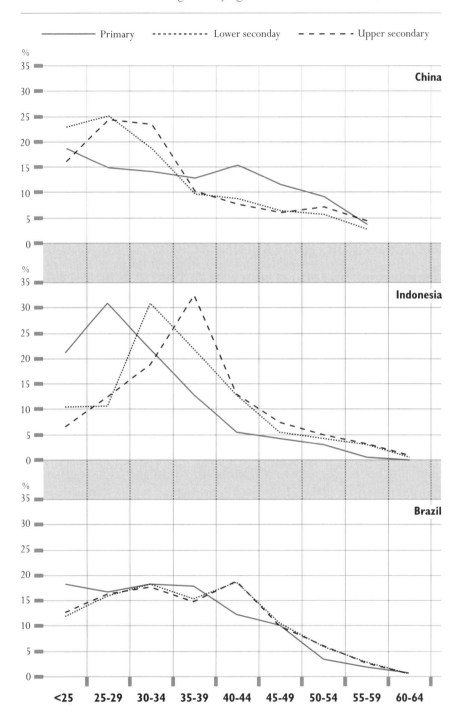

Age group

Source: OECD/UNESCO WEI, Table 22 in Annex A4.

Figure 1.20 and Table 22 show the age distribution of teaching staff by level of education. In primary education, younger teachers are most prevalent in Brazil and Indonesia. In Indonesia, teachers under 30 years of age make up more than half of the primary-level teaching force. The age profile of primary teachers is considerably higher in Chile and China. In Chile, the data clearly indicate that a renewal of the teaching force is rapidly becoming a necessity, even taking into account the falling number of students due to decreasing fertility rates. Over half of the teachers employed at the primary level are older than 45 years of age.

In primary education, young teachers are in the majority in Brazil and Indonesia.

In secondary education, there are fewer teachers under 25 years of age, partly because many may still be in training to meet the higher qualifications necessary to teach at the secondary level. Age profiles are very similar in both lower and upper secondary education, except in Indonesia, where there are more older teachers at the upper secondary level. The youngest secondary-level teaching force in the WEI countries is in China, where the majority of teachers are under 35 years of age. In Chile, over 50 per cent of the teachers in lower secondary, and 40 per cent in upper secondary education are older than 45 years of age.

The age profiles of secondary teaching staff vary widely, from China, where over half are under 35 years old, to Chile, where nearly half are over 45 years of age.

Figure 1.21
Proportion of women among teaching personnel and GDP per capita, 1998
(in percentages)

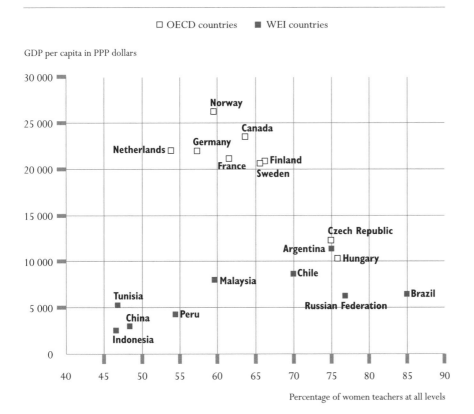

Sources: OECD/UNESCO WEI; World Bank (2001); Table 23 in Annex A4.

The gender distribution of the teaching force relates more closely to social norms and labour market issues than to level of national income.

The policy implications of the gender composition of the teaching force are sometimes contradictory. On the one hand, development literature points to the positive impact of female input and of the involvement of women in education, especially in encouraging greater participation among girls. On the other hand, a very high proportion of women in teaching, as in the Russian Federation, may reflect unsatisfactory labour market conditions and/or an imbalance between the genders in the completion of tertiary education.

As shown in Figure 1.21, the proportion of women among teachers at all levels of education is not clearly associated with national levels of GDP per capita. Two countries with roughly similar levels of GDP per capita, Brazil (6 625 PPP dollars) and Tunisia (5 404 PPP dollars), have very different proportions of women employed as teachers, 85 per cent in Brazil but only 46 per cent in Tunisia. The proportion of women tends to be influenced rather more by other criteria, such as cultural traditions, social norms, and labour market conditions. For example, Central and Eastern European, and European OECD countries, tend to cluster together in the scatter-plot.

The majority of primary school teachers are women in WEI countries, except in China, India and Tunisia. Women account for an even higher proportion in private education, except in Zimbabwe.

In WEI countries, primary teachers are predominantly women, with the notable exceptions of China, India and Tunisia, where women represent 50 per cent or less of the total number of teachers. In all countries, the percentage of women among teachers in upper secondary education falls below the percentage at the primary level, as shown in Figure 1.22, although women still form the majority of the teaching staff in upper secondary education in three of the six countries with available data. The lower proportion of women in upper secondary education may be explained in some countries where upper secondary education is largely vocational by the fact that the occupations for which students are prepared have a similar gender imbalance themselves (*e.g.* agriculture and some industries).

In the provinces of China, women tend to work as teachers rather than administrators, but where there is a high proportion of women among teachers, so there is among non-teaching staff.

Some gender differences may be associated with the type of school (public vs. private). The proportion of women in public education tends to be higher than that of men at all levels in almost every country (except Tunisia). In private education, the proportion of women is also higher in Malaysia (61 per cent in public and 84 per cent in private) and Thailand (58 per cent in public and 79 per cent in private education). The opposite is the case in Zimbabwe, where the proportion of women in private education is only 40 per cent.

Although data on gender distribution are not broken down type of staff (teaching, non-teaching and administrative) as part of the WEI project, data from China for the year 1998 show that despite the high proportion of women in the teaching profession, the percentage of administrative positions occupied by women (between 8 and 58 per cent) was substantially lower in every province than the similar percentage of full-time teaching positions (between

Figure 1.22
Share of women among teaching personnel by level of education, 1998
(in percentages)

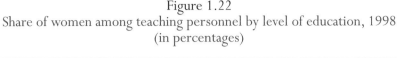

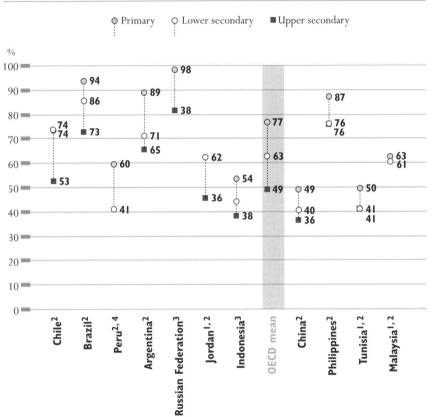

Includes teaching staff in public and private institutions based on head counts.

1. Public institutions only.
2. Year of reference 1998.
3. Year of reference 2000.
4. Refers to lower and upper secondary.

Source: OECD/UNESCO WEI, Table 23 in Annex A4.

30 and 72 per cent) (Ministry of Education – China, 1999). The data also show that the higher the percentage of women teachers, the higher also the proportion of women in administrative positions.

The qualifications profile of the teaching force reflects its age distribution to some extent, in that the minimum qualifications required to teach at a given level of education have changed considerably over time. For example, a teacher at the upper secondary level in Chile would today need to have at least a tertiary qualification, *i.e.*, a degree from a university or teacher-training college, whereas 20 or even ten years ago the minimum qualification for entering the field was non-tertiary.

The qualifications required for teaching have risen over the years, but the current teaching force may not reflect these new standards yet.

Six WEI countries now require tertiary qualifications from all primary and secondary teachers. The lowest proportions of teachers with tertiary qualifications are found in Brazil, China and Tunisia.

Qualifications also differ according to the level of education taught, and there are significant differences between WEI countries. As shown in Figure 1.23, six countries have more or less reached the standard of requiring tertiary qualifications for teaching in primary, lower and upper secondary education. The lowest proportions of teachers with tertiary qualifications are found in Brazil, China and Tunisia. The first two of these also have the lowest percentages at the lower secondary level. There may be large differences between countries within the same world region, as between Tunisia, where only 14 per cent of teachers at the primary level have a tertiary qualification, and Jordan, where almost all teachers at the same level have such a qualification. In general, the proportion of teachers with a tertiary qualification increases at the secondary level, where more advanced types of training are expected.

Information collected from the eight WEI countries participating in the TIMSS assessment reflects a seemingly contradictory situation with regard to the qualifications of mathematics and science teachers. In most, the percentage of students whose science or mathematics teachers had primarily studied the subject that they were teaching was close to the international average. The two exceptions were the Philippines and Thailand, although this result may be affected by pre-service training policies in those countries. At the same time, headteachers

Figure 1.23
Share of teachers with tertiary-level qualifications, 1998
(in percentages)

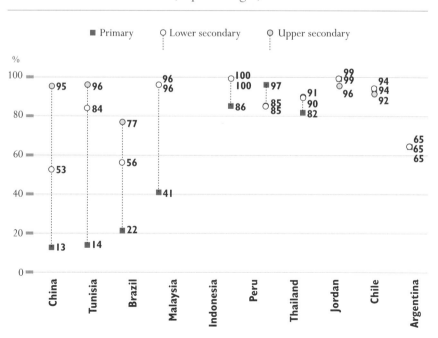

Countries are ranked by the difference between primary and upper secondary values.
Source: OECD/UNESCO WEI.

reported shortages in qualified teachers. The percentage of students in schools reporting such shortages was highest in Jordan and Tunisia.

As shown in Figure 1.24, the distribution of qualified teachers may vary more within one country than between countries. This is illustrated by the case of Brazil, where teachers in less developed regions are much less likely to have tertiary qualifications than those in better-off regions. The variation between Bahia, which ranks twentieth out of the 27 regions in Brazil in terms of the human development index, and Sao Paolo, which ranks third, is striking. Pro rata, Sao Paolo has 14 times as many primary teachers with tertiary qualifications as Bahia, and at the lower secondary level, where qualifications may matter even more, the proportion is two and a half times greater in Sao Paolo. The challenge of improving standards in less developed regions must be met if educational quality is to be enhanced and students' life-chances improved.

The distribution of qualified teachers can favour some regions over others, as illustrated by the case of Brazil.

Having examined the contexts in which teachers work — the impact of macro-economic indicators on the funding of education systems, the organization of education systems and some of the challenges that teachers face in the classroom — we turn in the next chapter to some of the policy trade-offs which both influence and are influenced by these contexts.

Figure 1.24
Share of teachers with tertiary-level training
by level in selected states of Brazil, 1998
(in percentages)

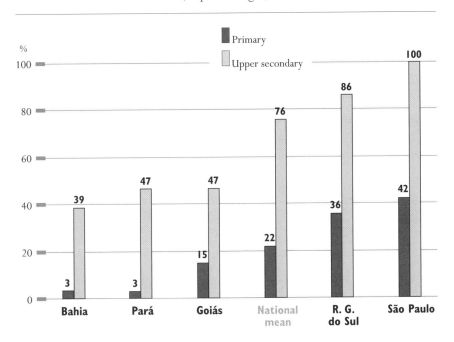

Source: Ministerio da Educação (2000).

REFERENCES

Bray, M. (2000), *Double-Shift Schooling: Design and Operation for Cost-Effectiveness*, Commonwealth Secretariat and International Institute for Educational Planning, London.

Hargreaves, A. (2000), "The paradoxical profession: teaching at the turn of the century", *Prospects*, Vol. XXX, No. 2 (June), International Bureau of Education, Geneva.

ILO (2000), "Lifelong learning in the twenty-first century: The changing roles of educational personnel", Report for discussion at the Joint Meeting, ILO, Geneva.

Klein, R. (1999), "Repetition and dropout in Brazil: changes and prospects: measurement issues", in Randall, L. and Joan Anderson (Eds.), *Schooling for Success: Preventing Repetition and Dropout in Latin American Primary Schools*, M.E. Sharpe, Inc., Places.

Klugman, J. (1997), "Decentralization: a survey from a child welfare perspective", Innocenti Occasional Papers, Economic Policy Series, No. 61, UNICEF International Child Development Centre, Florence.

Klugman, J. (1998), "Education and equity in the former Soviet republics: disruption and opportunities in financing and governance", UNICEF International Child Development Centre, Florence, Mimeo.

Knowles, J., Pernia, E. and **Racelis, M.** (1999), "Social consequences of the financial crisis in Asia", Economic Staff Paper, No. 60, Asian Development Bank, Manila. Paper is available at the URL address: http://www.adb.org/Documents/EDRC/Staff_Papers/ESP060.pdf.

Martin, M., Mullis, I. *et al.* (2000), *TIMSS 1999 International Science Report: Findings from IEA's Repeat of the Third International Science and Science Study at the Eighth Grade*, College, International Study Center, Boston.

Ministerio da Educação (2000), *Geografia da Educação Brasileira*, Ministerio da Educação, Brasília.

Ministry of Education (1999), *Educational Statistics Yearbook of China – 1998*, People's Education Press, Beijing.

Mullis, I., Martin, M. *et al.* (2000), *TIMSS 1999 International Mathematics Report: Findings from IEA's Repeat of the Third International Mathematics and Science Study at the Eighth Grade*, Boston College, International Study Center, Boston.

National Center for Education Statistics (2001), *The Role of Regions in Education Governance and Finance*, National Centre for Education Statistics, Washington, DC.

OECD (1998), *Education at a Glance – OECD Indicators 1998*, Paris.

OECD (2000), *Investing in Education – Analysis of the 1999 World Education Indicators*, Paris.

OECD (2001), *Education at a Glance – OECD Indicators 2001*, Paris.

Schiefelbein, E. and **Wolff, L.** (1995), "Repetición y rendimiento inadecuado en escuelas primarias de América Latina: magnitudes, causas, relaciones y estratégias", The Major Project of Education in Latin America and the Caribbean, UNESCO-OREALC, Santiago.

UNESCO (1995), *World Education Report*, UNESCO Publishing and Bernan Press, Paris.

UNU/WIDER-UNDP World Income Inequality Database, Version 1.0, September 2000, Helsinki: UNU-WIDER. Database is available at the URL address : http://www.wider.unu.edu/wiid/wiid.htm.

Vandermoortele, J. (2000), "Absorbing social shocks, protecting children and reducing poverty: the role of basic social services", EPP Staff Working paper 00-001, UNICEF, New York.

World Bank (1999), *Educational Change in Latin America and the Caribbean*, World Bank, Washington, DC.

World Bank (2001), *World Development Indicators*, CD-ROM, World Bank, Washington, DC.

Chapter 2

TEACHERS TOMORROW

Prepared by Andreas Schleicher, Michael Bruneforth,
Maria Teresa Siniscalco and Karine Tremblay
(OECD)

■ INTRODUCTION

There is robust evidence that knowledge and skills are a significant factor in economic growth and social development. Education and training play a crucial role in fostering the development of the human capital needed by the economy, and in helping individuals and societies to adapt to profound social, economic and cultural change. The ability of education and training systems to fulfil this role depends on whether educational institutions themselves respond to change, and on whether teachers develop and deliver educational content in ways that meet the needs of today's and tomorrow's citizens.

Educational policy-makers need to ensure that the investment made in teachers is sufficient and proportionate to the demands placed upon them. This means both that the qualifications of the teaching force must be adequate and that the salaries and working conditions of teachers must be sufficiently competitive to attract people with the desired qualifications into the teaching profession.

This chapter considers the challenges posed by the need to secure a skilled and motivated teaching force, and examines some of the policy choices and trade-offs that countries make when balancing expanded access to education against the need to attract and retain good teachers:

• *Section 1* examines changes in the demand for teachers during the first decade of the 21st century under different enrolment scenarios. It also explores the financial implications of changes in the size of the teaching force.

• *Section 2* looks at what is demanded of existing and prospective teachers: it considers the general expectations that policy-makers in WEI countries place upon teachers, and the required qualifications and expected workloads of teachers. These aspects are examined in the context of national income per capita.

• *Section 3* then examines what is offered to teachers for fulfilling their tasks. The section includes a comparative analysis of financial incentives and career prospects.

• The *concluding section* brings the factors examined in the preceding sections together, with the aim of quantifying the cost of changing the structural characteristics that determine the interplay between what is demanded of teachers and what is offered to them.

While the analysis in this chapter encompasses both OECD countries and the countries participating in the OECD/UNESCO World Education Indicators (WEI) programme, the focus is on teacher supply and demand in WEI countries.

1 DEMAND FOR TEACHERS IN THE NEXT DECADE

Rising enrolment rates, in some cases combined with an expanding population of school age, are increasing the demand for new teachers in many WEI countries, most significantly often in those with the lowest levels of economic development. This has significant implications not only for teacher training and recruitment but also for the financial resources which countries need to invest in education if they are to achieve universal education for all children of primary-school age and to increase, or merely to maintain, current enrolment rates in secondary education.

The demand for teachers in the context of population and enrolment trends

The number of teachers has steadily increased in the developing world; but the increase has not always been sufficient to outweigh the growth in the school-age population.

Teachers represent some 1.6 per cent of the world's 15-64 year-olds and comprise the largest single group of white-collar highly skilled professionals. The total number of teachers in formal education systems (in all countries and at all levels) has increased by more than seven million in just seven years, rising from 52 million in 1990 to 59 million in 1997. In 1997, more than two thirds of these teachers were employed in the developing world, up from 63 per cent in 1990 (ILO, 2000).

However, the steady increase in the supply of teachers in the developing world has, on average, been counterbalanced by a comparable growth in the number of school-age children. Therefore, despite significant efforts made during the 1990s to train new teachers and to improve education, many developing countries still experience severe shortages of teaching personnel and must seek to go on training large numbers of new teachers at low cost and to retain them with limited scope for monetary incentives.

In most WEI countries, demographic pressure has somewhat eased at the primary level but is increasing at the secondary and tertiary levels.

In the majority of WEI countries, the population of primary-school age has stopped growing or even started to decline. On the other hand, unlike the situation in most OECD countries, where the population at the age of secondary and tertiary education is also tending to decline, the number of individuals beyond primary-school age is still growing in most WEI countries. The slowdown in the average number of children per woman, which began in the 1970s in most countries, will still take many years to translate into fewer children at secondary and tertiary levels.

Moreover, while most WEI countries either have achieved or are close to achieving universal enrolment in primary education, enrolment rates for the population of secondary-school age range from 87 per cent in Chile to only 48 per cent in Indonesia (see Table 20 in Annex A4). Furthermore, in Brazil, Paraguay and the Philippines, between 20 and 45 per cent of pupils of secondary-school age are enrolled in primary school as repeaters or late entrants (see Table 20 in Annex A4), so that the proportion of the relevant school-age population actually enrolled in secondary education is significantly lower than suggested by total enrolment rates. This is very different from the situation in most OECD countries, where virtually all individuals enter the secondary level of education and where, on average, 79 per cent of an age cohort gain a qualification at the upper secondary level of education (see Table 18 in Annex A4).

Comparing current enrolment rates and student-teacher ratios with the projected school-age population provides a rough approximation of the changes required in the supply of teachers. In what follows, four benchmarks are used to quantify the demand for teachers over the period 1998-2010, on the assumption that student-teacher ratios remain constant.

Comparing current enrolment rates with the projected school-age population provides a rough approximation of changes in the demand for teachers.

• A "current enrolment scenario for the population of primary-school age" depicts the changes in the supply of teachers that would be required to maintain current enrolment rates while compensating for population growth at primary-school age;

• A "universal primary enrolment scenario" depicts the changes in the supply of teachers that would be needed to enrol all children of primary-school age by 2010;

• A "current enrolment scenario for the population of secondary-school age" depicts the changes in the supply of teachers that would be required to maintain current secondary enrolment rates;

• A "best practice scenario for the population of secondary-school age" depicts the increase in the supply of teachers needed to enrol 87 per cent of children of secondary-school age, which is the average of the three best-performing WEI countries, by 2010.

These scenarios represent an attempt to quantify the efforts required of WEI countries in order to meet the demand for teachers at the end of the decade. When the figures are interpreted, it should be borne in mind that the challenge is often not solely to increase the number of teachers but also to raise their qualifications through appropriate pre-service and in-service training arrangements.

Obviously, these projections oversimplify the real situation in a number of ways:

• First, they do not take into account the demand for new teachers due to the turnover of existing teaching staff, which is significant in some WEI countries.

• Second, the assumption of constant student-teacher ratios is not always realistic since the remaining percentage of students may be geographically or socially harder to reach and hence require a lower ratio. On the other hand, raising the student-teacher ratio may be a useful expedient in the short term in order to address temporary shortages of qualified teachers and, in some of the WEI countries where there are signs of over-staffing, perhaps even in the medium and long term.

• Third, demand for teachers based simply on the populations of primary and secondary-school age cannot be taken as an indication of the true demand for primary and secondary teachers, given that the figures do not distinguish, within the student population of secondary-school age, between students enrolled above the normal age in primary education and students actually enrolled in secondary education.

Figure 2.1 shows the demand for teachers in 2010 under the "current enrolment scenario" and the "universal primary enrolment scenario".

In three out of 13 WEI countries, the projected growth in the population of primary-school age over the period 1998-2010 will increase the demand for teachers by more than ten per cent.

For each country, the bottom part of the bar illustrates the "current enrolment scenario", that is, what percentage change (1998=100) is needed in the teaching force in order to maintain current enrolment rates in the population of primary-school age until 2010. The top part of the bar illustrates the "universal primary enrolment scenario", that is, the percentage change in the teaching force required to enrol all children of primary school age by 2010.

Figure 2.1
Estimated change in the demand for teachers due to changes in the population
of *primary-school age* under different enrolment scenarios,
1998-2010

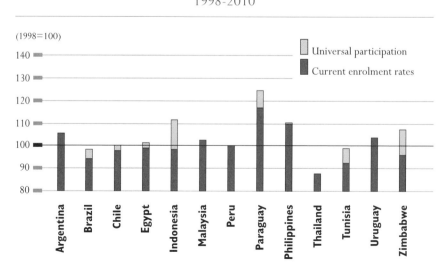

Source: OECD/UNESCO WEI, Table 37 in Annex A4.

The figure shows that as a result of the growth in the population of primary-school age, nine out of 13 WEI countries will have to expand their teaching force by between 1 and 24 per cent over the period 1998-2010 in order to achieve or maintain universal primary education with current student-teacher ratios (see Table 37 in Annex A4). Again, this is unlike the situation in most OECD countries, which have all achieved full enrolment and where the size of the teaching force is likely to decline because of demographic factors, except in Ireland, Japan, Luxembourg and Turkey (see Table 3 in Annex A4). In Argentina, Malaysia, the Philippines and Uruguay, the WEI countries where universal primary education has already been achieved, the increase in the demand for teachers is therefore entirely driven by changes in the population of primary-school age.

In Indonesia and Zimbabwe, on the other hand, where the population of primary-school age is expected to level off or decrease during the first decade of the 21st century, the teaching force will still have to expand in order to achieve universal primary enrolment by 2010 (see Table 37 in Annex A4). In Paraguay and the Philippines, both population growth and rising enrolment will lead to an increased demand for teachers. In Paraguay, the Philippines and Indonesia, this extra demand is expected to exceed 10 per cent at the primary level. The scale of the need for teacher training becomes even more striking when the percentages are translated into actual numbers. Indonesia will have to employ some 125,000 additional teachers, Paraguay 12 000 and the Philippines an additional 38 000 teachers. Conversely, in Chile there will be no significant change in the demand for teachers between 1998 and 2010, and in Brazil and Tunisia, the demographic projections suggest that in 2010 the demand for teachers will be slightly below 1998 levels. Finally, in Thailand, the demand for teachers is expected to be about 12 per cent lower in 2010 than it was in 1998.

Countries that still have growing school-age populations, such as Paraguay and the Philippines (see Table 3 in Annex A4), will have to invest significant additional resources in order merely to maintain enrolment rates at the 1998 level. In countries where the pressure of the school-age population has levelled off or started to decline, such as Brazil, Chile, Egypt, Indonesia, Thailand and Zimbabwe, every additional sum invested in the teaching force will be a step towards universal primary education, where this has not yet been achieved, and/or will allow access to higher levels of education to be expanded, and quality to be enhanced (e.g. by reducing class sizes, increasing teachers' qualifications and salaries, or addressing problems of disparity in educational opportunities).

Figure 2.2 shows the expected change in the number of teachers for the population of secondary-school age, under the "current enrolment scenario" and under the "best practice scenario".

Figure 2.2
Estimated change in the demand for teachers due to changes in the population of *secondary-school age* under different enrolment scenarios, 1998-2010

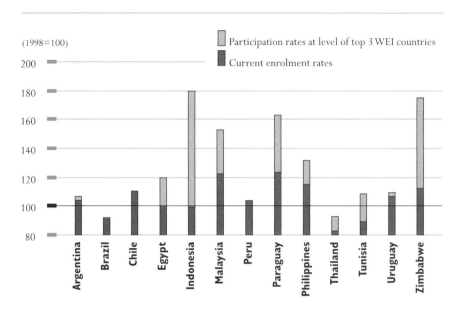

Source: OECD/UNESCO WEI, Table 37 in Annex A4.

In five out of 13 countries, the projected growth in the population of secondary-school age is expected to increase the demand for new teachers by between 10 and 23 per cent, in order merely to maintain current enrolment rates.

For each country, the bottom part of the bar illustrates the "current enrolment scenario", that is, what percentage change (1998=100) will be needed in the teaching force in order to maintain current enrolment rates in the population of secondary-school age by the year 2010. The top part of the bar illustrates "best practice", that is, the percentage change in the teaching force that will be required to enrol 87 per cent of the population of secondary-school age by 2010, the figure reached today by the three WEI countries with the highest enrolment rates.

In nine out of 13 countries, the demand for teachers is expected to increase between 1998 and 2010 in response to the growth in the population of secondary-school age (whether enrolled in primary or secondary education) in order merely to maintain current enrolment rates (see Table 37 in Annex A4). Among these countries, in Chile, the Philippines and Zimbabwe the increase in the demand for teachers is expected to exceed 10 per cent, while in Malaysia and Paraguay, it is expected to exceed 20 per cent.

Raising enrolment rates in secondary education, which is a policy target in many WEI countries, would further expand the demand for new teachers. If the current average enrolment rate of the three best-performing WEI countries (Brazil, Chile and Peru) is taken as a benchmark (87 per cent), then Indonesia and Zimbabwe would need to recruit 79 and 76 per cent more teachers respectively by 2010 (*i.e.*, more than 500 000 and 23 000 teachers, respectively) than they have today (see Table 37 in Annex A4), followed by Paraguay, Malaysia, the Philippines and Egypt, where the required expansion in the teaching force would range from 20 to 63 per cent. On the other hand, in Argentina, Chile, Peru, Tunisia and Uruguay, there would be limited demand for new teachers because of demographic changes in the population of secondary-school age. In some of these countries, as in most of the OECD countries, the ageing of the existing teaching force (see Table 22 in Annex A4) is likely to be a more important factor in the demand for new teachers than the demography of students.

These figures show that, despite the significant progress made by many WEI countries in containing population growth, it will still be very difficult for them to enrol, say, three quarters of the population in secondary education.

Student-teacher ratios

Student-teacher ratios need to be taken into account in evaluating the demand for and supply of teachers.

The ratio of students to teaching staff, which needs to be distinguished from class size (see Box 2.1) is an important indicator of the resources which countries devote to education. Figure 2.3 shows current student-teacher ratios in WEI and OECD countries by level of education.

Box 2.1
Class sizes and student-teacher ratio

It is important to distinguish student-teacher ratios from class sizes. The relationship between these two measures is complicated by many factors. These include differences between countries in the length of the school year, the number of hours for which students attend class each day, the length of the teacher's working day, the number of classes or students for which a teacher is responsible (*e.g.* in systems of multi-grade teaching or where there are multiple shifts of students with the same teacher), the division of the teacher's working time between teaching and other duties, the grouping of students within classes and the practice of team-teaching (OECD, 2000*a*).

Figure 2.3
Student-teacher ratio by level of education, 1999
Calculations based on full-time equivalents

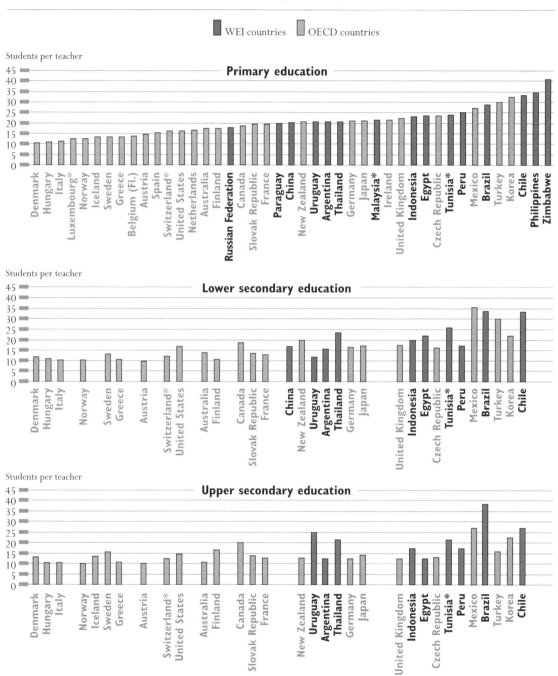

Countries are ranked by the student-teacher ratio at the primary level of education.

* Public institutions only.
Source: OECD/UNESCO WEI, Table 21 in Annex A4.

Student-teacher ratios vary greatly among the WEI countries. At the primary level, the number of students per teacher ranges from a low of 18 in the Russian Federation to a high of around 40 in Zimbabwe (see Table 21 in Annex A4). It should be noted that the lowest student-teacher ratio among the WEI countries is still only at the level of the OECD average (18 students per teacher at the primary level). Ratios for the remaining 16 countries with comparable data are between 20 and 41 students per teacher, well above the OECD average.

The student-teacher ratio ranges from 18 to 40 students per teacher at the primary level and from 12 to 36 at the secondary level.

At the secondary level, Argentina, Paraguay and Russia have the lowest ratios, below 15 students per teacher, while at the opposite end of the scale the Philippines and Brazil have more than 30 students per teacher at the lower and upper secondary level, respectively (see Table 21 in Annex A4). Student-teacher ratios at the secondary level tend to be considerably lower in OECD countries than in WEI countries, ranging from nine students per full-time equivalent teacher in Belgium to 32 in Mexico.

In both WEI and OECD countries, the student-teacher ratio declines as the level of education rises. In a few WEI countries, however, the number of students per teacher is higher at the secondary level than at the primary level. These include Brazil and Thailand and Uruguay (at the upper secondary level only). Differences in student-teacher ratios between the various levels of education may indicate the priority given to particular levels of education, but they may also reflect delays in matching the teaching force to changing population and enrolment patterns.

Differences in student-teacher ratios between levels of education may reflect either policy choices or delays in matching the supply of teachers to changing demographic patterns.

As countries face increasing constraints on education budgets, the decision to decrease student-teacher ratios needs to be weighed against the goals of increased access to education, competitive salaries for teachers, and investment in school infrastructure, equipment and supplies. Student-teacher ratios are, however, at critically high levels in three countries, where the demand for new teachers is expected to increase significantly over the next decade, that is, in the Philippines at both the primary and secondary levels and Chile and Zimbabwe at the secondary level. In these countries, it will be difficult to respond to the increased demand for teachers by raising student-teacher ratios further without risking a deterioration in the quality of educational provision.

Financial implications

Expanding the teaching force implies funding the education of teachers, as well as paying them competitive salaries. With the exception of teachers' salaries, it is difficult to estimate the costs of employing teachers and to compare them between countries.

Figure 2.4 shows an estimate of the impact of the changes in the demand for teachers in primary to upper secondary education on expenditure on

Figure 2.4
Change in expenditure on educational institutions due to
in/decreases in the expected number of teachers at the primary and
secondary levels of education, 1998-2010
*Assuming changes in the number of teachers lead to equal increases in all current
and capital expenditure*

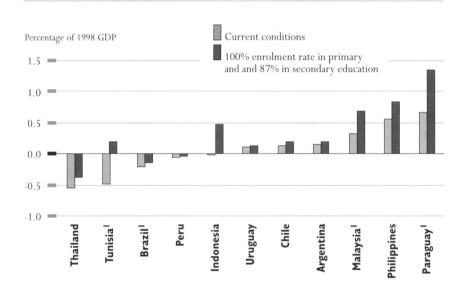

*Enrolment rates at the secondary level of 87% represent the rates reached by the three WEI countries
with the highest rates.*

1. Public institutions only.
Source: OECD/UNESCO WEI, Table 11 in Annex A4.

educational institutions (1998-2010), based on the assumption that changes in the numbers of teachers will affect current and capital expenditure equally.

The projected increase in the demand for teachers, due mainly to the expansion in the population of secondary-school age, is expected to lead to a rise in spending on education in the majority of WEI countries. For example, Paraguay would have to increase expenditure on education from 3.5 to 4.5 per cent of its 1998 GDP in order to maintain current enrolment rates for the populations of primary and secondary-school age, and to 4.9 per cent of its 1998 GDP in order to achieve universal primary education and to achieve the secondary enrolment rate of the three best-performing WEI countries (87 per cent) (see Table 11 in Annex A4).

Similarly, in 2010 the Philippines would have to spend 5.5 per cent of its 1998 GDP on education (compared with 4.9 in 1998) in order to respond to the increased demand for teachers due to the growth in the school-age population, and 5.8 per cent of its 1998 GDP in order to provide enough teachers to enrol all children of primary-school age and 87 per cent of young people of secondary-school age.

Finally, Malaysia would have to increase expenditure on education between 1998 and 2010 from 3 to 3.7 per cent of its 1998 GDP in order to expand the supply of teachers to match the growth in the populations of primary and secondary-school age and to enrol 87 per cent of the population of secondary-school age.

While these estimates are based on the assumption that all conditions other than enrolment numbers and rates remain constant (including teachers' salaries), several other factors may have an impact. During the 1990s, many countries in South Asia and in sub-Saharan Africa made a trade-off in order to enrol more students at lower cost, for example by appointing untrained teachers at lower salaries, raising student-teacher ratios, and/or increasing teaching hours while reducing instruction time for students. Conversely, in Latin America and even more so in Eastern Asia and the Pacific, despite the expansion in enrolment of the school-age population, expenditure per student as a percentage of GDP also increased in response to the demand for new teachers and buildings (Siniscalco, 2000).

Improving quality

Despite an increasing population of secondary-school age, the next few decades will provide a unique window of opportunity for many WEI countries to improve the quality of educational provision. Because of demographic changes, which are already having an impact on the size of the cohorts of primary-school age, the proportion of people of working age (15-64 years) will grow faster over the next few decades than that of children (aged under 15) in many WEI countries. Before the declining ratio of children to active workers is eventually overtaken by the rising ratio of retired people to workers, countries will have an increased ability to mobilise resources for services including education, making it easier to fund better education systems. It will therefore be possible to shift the focus of educational policy from expanding the coverage of the education system to improving the quality of educational provision.

In many WEI countries, current demographic changes provide a unique window of opportunity for improving educational quality.

One of the issues that need to be addressed is the high proportion of over-age students, repeaters or late entrants enrolled in primary education (see Table 15 in Annex A4). High rates of repetition and drop-out impair the efficiency of education systems, increase the cost of education and cause wastage.

In addition, education cannot be defined narrowly to mean merely enrolment in school. While the emphasis on putting more children into school may be an essential step in the development of education systems, it is by no means sufficient. In the next few decades, the development of a well-trained and motivated teaching force will be a major challenge facing many WEI countries, which will need to be reflected in the priority given to education within national budgets.

2 THE EXPECTATIONS PLACED ON TEACHERS

Recent educational reforms throughout the WEI and OECD countries have focused on improving students' educational outcomes, in order to ensure that young adults have acquired both knowledge and skills in key subject areas, and the capacity and motivation to continue learning throughout life. The success of educational reforms will critically depend on the ability of teachers to incorporate these goals into their daily teaching and to move from a self-contained model of school education to a model in which school education is seen as the foundation for a learning process which is meant to continue throughout life.

These high demands made of teachers need to be weighed against what teachers are offered in terms of pre-service education and training, continuing training, salaries and working conditions.

Today more than ever, schools and teachers face high expectations.

Policy-makers and society at large have high expectations of teachers as professionals, role models, experts in a wide range of areas, substitute parents and community leaders. Teachers are asked to manage the far-reaching changes that are taking place in and outside schools, and to implement the complex reforms of education systems that are under way in most countries. In the words of two WEI programme representatives:

> *"Teachers are asked to be major agents of the profound structural and curricular transformation taking place"(Argentina).*

> *"The teacher is the most important agent in the implementation of the innovations introduced through the reform of the education system"(Paraguay).*

The future role of teachers depends not just on the specifics of how teaching is organised, but also on the future role of the school itself (OECD, 2001*b*). Will it remain a key social institution or is it likely to decline? Those who suggest a declining role for schools and teachers argue that:

* the growth in alternative sources of information and knowledge, including the media, and in peer and youth culture, is leading to a decline in the monopoly of schools over information and knowledge, and is reducing the impact of schools and teachers;

* economic, political and cultural globalisation is tending to render obsolete the locally based, culturally bound institution of the school (and with it the teacher);

- even within schools, greater individualisation in modes of learning, made possible partly through the spread of ICT and human resources other than teachers, is displacing supply-dominated models and implies a decline in the importance of teachers.

However, it would be an oversimplification to regard schools as being exclusively about the transmission of knowledge and to conclude that this task can now simply be transferred to other technologies. Schools have always had wider roles, including social functions, which are likely to become more rather than less important. There is a strong sense of schooling as a "public good", and a marked upward shift in the general status and level of support for schools. The individualisation of learning needs to be tempered by a clear collective emphasis. Greater priority needs to be accorded to the social, community role of schools, with more explicit sharing of programmes and responsibilities with the other settings of further and continuing education and training.

In some respects, therefore, the role of the school is expanding, at times perhaps unrealistically. The consequent expectations of teachers have many dimensions:

Teachers need to develop a new type of professionalism that draws on both old and new models of what it means to be a good teacher.

- *Expertise*. This traditional characteristic of a good teacher will not be the only attribute needed, but its importance should not therefore be underestimated. In the words of one of the WEI programme representatives: "*Teachers are asked to be not only knowledgeable and innovative, but also highly disciplined, strongly motivated and dedicated*" (Malaysia). The importance of teachers' expertise is shown, among other things, in the increasing level of academic qualifications required of them. However, the way in which teachers themselves access knowledge must change, since they will need to update their expertise continually.

- *Pedagogical know-how*. This characteristic continues to be central as well, although it should focus on the transmission of a range of high-level skills, including motivation to learn, creativity and co-operation, rather than on information recall and performance in tests. The increasing pedagogical training requirements for teachers at all levels indicate recognition of the importance of this aspect.

- *Understanding of technology*. This is a new key feature of professionalism in teaching, requiring an understanding of the pedagogical potential of technology and the ability to integrate it into teaching strategies. "*Teachers and headteachers need to become familiar with distance education and new technologies*" (Uruguay).

- *Organisational competence and collaboration*. Professionalism in teaching can no longer be seen as an individual competence, but must include the ability to function as part of a "learning organisation". The ability and willingness to learn from and to teach other teachers is an essential aspect of this attribute.

- *Flexibility.* Teachers have to accept that professional requirements may change several times in the course of their careers, and must not interpret professionalism as an excuse to resist change. "*Teachers must be lifelong learners*" (Thailand).

- *Mobility.* A particular form of flexibility is mobility, that is, the capacity and willingness to move in and out of other careers and experiences that can enrich teaching ability.

- *Openness.* This ability means being able to work with parents and other non-teachers in ways that complement the teacher's professional role. "*The role of the teacher is changing and comprises aspects such as (…) working in a team, not only with other teachers but also with the educational community, since the organisation of the teaching/learning process is an integrated whole, based on interaction between the various elements*" (Paraguay). "Teachers' openness to work with other stakeholders, including parents, teachers' associations and the community, promotes a harmonious relationship that can result in better teaching/learning processes" (Philippines).

Whether schools can start to meet these expectations will depend to a high degree on their ability to develop a central position in society, as more "open" organisations serving a wide range of interests and a broad clientele. This, in turn, means that teachers will have to develop a new type of professionalism which will need to draw on both old and new models of what it means to be a good teacher.

Pre-service training requirements for new teachers

Policy-makers are faced with the questions of how much to invest in pre-service as opposed to in-service training, and of how to invest strategically in those levels of education that justify higher qualification requirements.

Pre-service training is typically a combination of academic education, professional training and teaching practice.

Increasing expectations of schools and teachers, together with the current spread of knowledge-based societies and economies, call for higher levels of specialised training in the teaching profession. Policy-makers are faced with the questions of how much to invest in pre-service as opposed to in-service and on-the-job training, and of how to invest strategically in those levels of education that justify higher qualification requirements.

As in the OECD countries, pre-service training in WEI countries is typically a combination of academic education (*i.e.*, subject-matter teaching) and professional training (*i.e.*, pedagogical studies), often accompanied by periods of work experience (*i.e.*, practical training). Limited research evidence suggests that the number of years of teachers' education is generally positively correlated with their students' performance, although there is a debate about the threshold at which the returns from additional teacher training declines.

Figure 2.5
Number of years of tertiary training required for prospective teachers by level of education, 2000

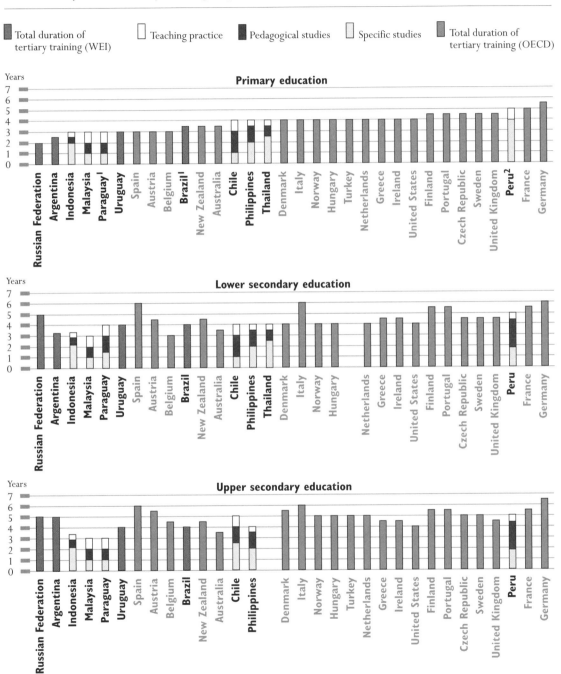

1. Prospective primary teachers have the choice of attending either a secondary-level programme leading to an ISCED 3 qualification, or a tertiary-level programme leading to an ISCED 5 (A or B) qualification.

2. Pedagocial studies are included in specific studies.

Source: OECD/UNESCO WEI, Table 34 in Annex A4.

Figure 2.5 shows the number of years of post-secondary education required of prospective teachers by level of education taught, with a distinction between subject-matter teaching, professional training and work experience.

In all WEI countries, a tertiary qualification is required for entry into the teaching profession at all levels of education.

In the same way as OECD countries, all the WEI countries supplying data train their prospective primary teachers at tertiary level, either in universities, other post-secondary non-university institutions or special teacher training institutes (see Table 34 in Annex A4). The only partial exceptions are Brazil and Paraguay, where primary teachers have the choice of a secondary-level programme leading to an ISCED 3 qualification, or tertiary-level training. In Brazil, this secondary-level programme will however disappear by 2007 according to the reforms in progress.

Some countries have the same qualification requirements from primary to upper secondary education: in Uruguay, an ISCED 5B qualification is required for entry to the teaching profession at all levels of education, while in Chile, the Philippines and the Russian Federation, primary, lower and upper secondary teachers must have obtained an ISCED 5A qualification (see Table 34 in Annex A4).

Other countries have higher qualification requirements for secondary teachers: in Brazil and Malaysia, an ISCED 5B qualification may be sufficient at the primary level, while prospective secondary teachers have to obtain an ISCED 5A qualification, and in Argentina an ISCED 5B qualification is required for primary and lower secondary teachers, whereas upper secondary teachers have the choice of either an ISCED 5B or a 5A qualification. Finally, Indonesia, Peru and Thailand allow prospective teachers at all levels of education to complete their training by means of different paths leading to either ISCED 5B or ISCED 5A qualifications.

As compared to this, all OECD countries require an ISCED 5A qualification for entry to teaching in upper secondary education. At the primary level, Austria, Belgium, Denmark, and Hungary are the only countries where an ISCED 5B qualification is sufficient for entry to the profession at both the primary and the lower secondary level of education, and in Portugal a tertiary-type B qualification is sufficient in primary education.

The duration of pre-service training tends to increase with the level of education taught...

While WEI countries, like OECD countries, generally require a qualification at the tertiary level, the duration of pre-service training is usually shorter in WEI countries. For primary teachers, this varies from a minimum of two years in the Russian Federation to five years in Peru, with three to four years of training in the majority of countries (see Table 34 in Annex A4). In OECD countries, the duration of pre-service training for primary teachers varies from three years in Austria, Belgium and Spain to 5.5 years in Germany.

The average duration of pre-service training for secondary teachers in general programmes ranges from 2.5 years in Argentina and three years in Malaysia to five years in Peru, the Russian Federation, Argentina (upper secondary level only) and Chile (upper secondary level only). In half of the WEI countries, the duration of training for lower secondary teachers is higher than that for primary teachers, the largest difference being in the Russian Federation.

Pre-service training requirements are higher for upper secondary teachers than for primary teachers in one third of the countries (see Table 34 in Annex A4). However, the duration of pre-service training at the upper secondary level in the WEI countries remains considerably below that in the OECD countries. Among the WEI countries, the duration of pre-service training for upper secondary teaching exceeds five years only in Argentina, Chile, Paraguay, Peru and the Russian Federation, but only six OECD countries are below this level (Australia, Greece, Ireland, New Zealand, the United Kingdom and the United States).

The choice to invest more heavily in the training of teachers working at the higher levels of education is, from an educational point of view, not an obvious one given that important foundations for learning are laid in the early years. And in fact, though predominant in both WEI and OECD countries, this choice is not universal. In Malaysia, for example, the duration of pre-service training is three years for the primary level, while for the secondary level it is either three or four years depending on the choice of the teacher training programme. In Peru and the Philippines, the duration of pre-service training is the same for all levels (see Table 34 in Annex A4).

… but that choice is not an obvious one.

In more than half of the countries supplying data, pre-service teacher training is clearly structured into subject-matter teaching, pedagogical studies and teaching practice (see Table 34 in Annex A4).

Upgrading the educational and training requirements for prospective teachers means that new teachers obtain the knowledge and skills considered suitable before they enter the profession. While greater professionalism in the teaching force requires more resources for institutions of tertiary education and specialised teacher-training establishments, together with higher salaries at entry levels, these requirements for additional investment may be offset by a reduction in the burden on administrative, training and supervisory budgets.

Some of the returns to investment in the professionalisation of the teaching force accrue in the form of savings on guidance and supervision.

Not all members of existing teaching forces meet the requirements that governments have set for new entrants to the profession. The discrepancies are most notable in those countries which have upgraded qualification requirements for teachers only recently. Comparing the requirements for new teachers with the actual level of qualifications of existing teaching forces provides an indication of the efforts which countries will need to make in

Some countries still have a long way to go before the entire teaching force meets current qualification requirements.

order to bring all their teachers up to the level of today's standards. Figure 2.6 shows the proportions of existing teaching forces that do not meet current pre-service requirements, by level of education.

Figure 2.6
Percentage of the existing teaching force that does not meet current pre-service requirements for new teachers, 1999

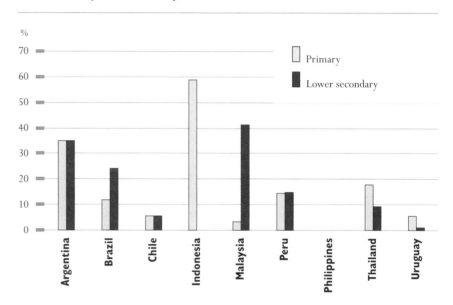

Source: OECD/UNESCO WEI, Tables 32 & 34 in Annex A4.

The Philippines is the only country where the whole employed teaching force, at both primary and lower secondary level, has obtained the requisite ISCED 5A qualification, including necessary teacher training (see Table 32 in Annex A4). In Malaysia, all employed teachers also have an ISCED 5A qualification, but a small percentage of these do not hold the required teaching certificate.

At the other end of the scale, between 58 and 78 per cent of active primary teachers in Indonesia, and Brazil and more than 40 per cent of lower secondary teachers in Malaysia have not completed the tertiary-level education required of prospective teachers today. These countries have recently made a decision to upgrade teachers' qualifications, but making this a reality for the entire teaching force will require substantial in-service training.

In many WEI countries, the demand for teachers accounts for a high proportion of tertiary graduates...

New qualification requirements place current tertiary education systems under some pressure. Figure 2.7 compares the demand for new teachers over the period 1998-2010 with the number of tertiary graduates over the same period, on the basis of current graduation rates.

Figure 2.7
Primary and secondary teachers to be employed by 2010 as a percentage
of tertiary graduates, 1999
Annual graduate output estimated by educational attainment of 25 to 34-year-olds

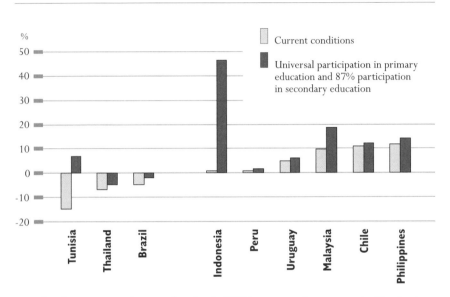

Note: Enrolment rates at the secondary level of 87% represent the rates reached by the three
WEI countries with the highest rates.
Source: OECD/UNESCO WEI, Tables 19 & 37 in Annex A4.

If tertiary graduation rates remain at current levels until 2010, more than
7 per cent of the total supply of graduates in Chile and the Philippines will be
required merely to sustain the current size of the teaching force. If the
projected growth in student populations is taken into account, this figure will
rise to more than 11 per cent in both countries. If, in addition, Chile and the
Philippines attain universal enrolment at the primary level and reach the
average secondary-level enrolment rate of the three best-performing WEI
countries (87 per cent), then more than 12 per cent of tertiary graduates in
Chile and more than 14 per cent of tertiary graduates in the Philippines will
need to go into teaching.

In Malaysia and Indonesia, the "best practice" enrolment scenario (87 per
cent) means that 19 and 46 per cent of current tertiary graduates, respectively, would need to go into teaching. These are unrealistic objectives which
illustrate the enormous efforts that will be required in many WEI countries
to ensure access to qualified teaching for all students.

*... which underlines the
enormous efforts required
in many WEI countries.*

In the OECD countries, the comparable figures tend to be much smaller,
since tertiary qualifications have, in most OECD countries, been an entry
requirement for teachers for a long time.

> ### Box 2.2
> ### The role of professional development for teachers
>
> In-service training, continuing education, further training and the upgrading of teachers are different terms used to refer to continuing professional development of teachers. Although the main focus of teacher education continues to be on pre-service training, the need for in-service upgrading, updating and renewal of knowledge, skills and capabilities in now widely acknowledged as a high priority.
>
> In both OECD and WEI countries, the speed of reform and the scale of expectations of schooling continue to rise, placing new responsibilities on all teachers, including the requirement for continuing professional learning. In the OECD countries, for example, the age structure of the teaching force indicates that 15 to 20 years have passed since the large majority of teachers received their initial training. In many WEI countries, substantial proportions of teachers have received virtually no training or do not meet newly introduced qualification and training requirements.
>
> As in other highly skilled professional occupations, the pace of change means that continual updating of knowledge and skills is required. In-service training is therefore an essential component of career development.
>
> While there is no shortage of in-service training in many OECD countries, it is noted that much of what passes for professional development is fragmented and fleeting, is not sufficiently focused and is too "top-down" to give teachers any real sense of ownership. Finally, the analysis undertaken by the OECD shows that relatively few resources out of the total education budget are spent on in-service training. However, other evidence, for example on the ways in which teachers spend their time within schools, needs to be considered, in order to include the invisible costs of professional learning that is integrated into day-to-day school life.
>
> In most WEI countries, in-service training aimed at upgrading teachers' qualifications is currently a high priority that has a significant impact on educational budgets. Not all of this upgrading occurs in educational institutions. Brazil, for example, is carrying out extensive in-service training programmes, mainly by means of distance education, in order to upgrade the qualifications of the entire pre-primary and primary teaching force by 2007, in accordance with the new requirements of the 1996 National Educational Guidelines and Framework Law. This law increases the minimum requirement for basic education teachers from a secondary to a tertiary qualification.

Teachers' workload

Working hours and the number of students per class are important factors in the workload of teachers.

Significant indicators of the workload of teachers include class size and student-teacher ratios, teaching hours and the extent of non-teaching duties. Moreover, as students' family structures and background change and the impact of the media grows, teachers will have to spend more time handling behavioural problems associated with these changes. This is an additional requirement that is difficult to quantify.

A teacher's work does not end with statutory teaching hours but includes all the working hours (whether specified or not in the teacher's contract or conditions of service) that are devoted to other activities related to teaching, such as the preparation of lessons, correction of assignments and tests, professional development, counselling of students, meetings with parents, staff meetings and general school tasks. Working patterns for teachers vary widely between countries, making it difficult to undertake international comparisons. Table 2.1 depicts the structure of a teacher's working week. Note that working time, as reported here, refers to the normal working hours of a full-time teacher. According to the formal policy in a given country, working time may refer solely to the time directly spent teaching (and in

Table 2.1
Structure and organisation of teachers' working time
in public institutions, 1998

1 *In the following countries, full-time teachers are required to work a specific number of hours per week in order to earn their full-time salary. They include teaching and non-teaching activities.*

	Pre-primary	Primary	Lower secondary	Upper secondary General	Upper secondary Vocational
Argentina	20.0	22.5	25.0	25.0	29.0
Indonesia	15.0	30.0	18.0	18.0	18.0
Malaysia	32.5	32.5	32.5	32.5	32.5
Philippines	40.0	40.0	40.0	40.0	
Thailand	35.0	35.0	35.0	35.0	35.0
Czech Republic	42.5	42.5	42.5	42.5	42.5
Denmark	37.0	37.0	37.0	37.0	
Greece	37.5	37.5	37.5	37.5	37.5
Hungary	40.0	40.0	40.0	40.0	40.0
Korea		44.0	44.0	44.0	44.0
Netherlands	38.0	38.0	38.0	38.0	38.0
Norway		44.0	44.0	44.0	44.0
Spain	37.5	37.5	37.5	37.5	37.5
Sweden		40.0	40.0	40.0	40.0

2 *In the following countries, full-time teachers are required to be at school for a specific number of hours per week. They include teaching and non-teaching activities.*

	Pre-primary	Primary	Lower secondary	Upper secondary General	Upper secondary Vocational
Brazil	40.0	40.0	40.0	40.0	40.0
Chile	30.0	38.0	38.0	42.0	42.0
Indonesia	6.0	6.0	4.0	4.0	4.0
Malaysia	34.5	40.5	40.5	40.5	40.5
Philippines	40.0	40.0	40.0	40.0	
Thailand	40.0	40.0	40.0	40.0	40.0
Uruguay	20.0	20.0	20.0	20.0	20.0
Australia		38.0	38.0	38.0	
England		33.3	33.3	33.3	
Ireland	28.3	28.3			
Mexico	20.0	25.0			
New Zealand		25.0			
Scotland		27.5	27.5		

3 *In the following countries, full-time teachers are only required to teach a specified number of hours per week. There is no set time to be spent in non-teaching activities.*

	Pre-primary	Primary	Lower secondary	Upper secondary General	Upper secondary Vocational
Indonesia			1.0	1.0	1.0
Peru	22.5	22.5	18.0	18.0	18.0
Thailand	30.0	25.0	20.0	20.0	15.0
Uruguay	Yes	Yes	Yes	Yes	Yes
Belgium (Fl.)	21.7	21.7	19.2	17.9	26.3
Belgium (Fr.)	21.7	21.7	19.2	17.9	26.3
Finland		17.3	17.3	17.3	17.3
France	27.0	27.0	18.4	18.4	18.4
Ireland			22.0	22.0	
Italy	a	a	a	a	a
Portugal	30.0	28.0	31.3	31.6	31.6

4 *In the following countries, there is no mandatory or formal amount of time that full-time teachers must spend working, but there is a customary number of working hours for all civil servants.*

	Pre-primary	Primary	Lower secondary	Upper secondary General	Upper secondary Vocational
Thailand	40.0	40.0	40.0	40.0	40.0
Australia	37.5				
Germany	38.5	38.5	38.5	38.5	38.5

5 *In the following countries, teachers' working hours are set at the individual, local or school level. They include teaching and non-teaching activities.*

	Pre-primary	Primary	Lower secondary	Upper secondary General	Upper secondary Vocational
Russian Federation	m	20.0	18.0	18.0	m
New Zealand			25.0	26.0	

6 *In the following countries, teachers are employed under individual, local or school-level contracts for a specific number of teaching hours. There is no set time to be spent in non-teaching activities.*

	Pre-primary	Primary	Lower secondary	Upper secondary General	Upper secondary Vocational
Uruguay	Yes	Yes	Yes	Yes	Yes
Mexico			25.0		

Source: OECD/UNESCO WEI.

other curricular activities such as supervising assignments and tests, but excluding annual examinations), or both to the time directly spent teaching and to the hours devoted to the other activities related to teaching which are mentioned above. Working time in Table 2.1 does not include paid overtime.

Overall, teachers' working time varies between countries from 20 hours per week to over 40.

In some countries, such as Indonesia, Peru, Thailand and Uruguay, only teaching hours are fixed and it is assumed that teachers will carry out their other duties without the need for the requisite extra time to be laid down in their contracts.

In other countries, such as Argentina, Indonesia, Malaysia, the Philippines and Thailand, teachers are required to be at school for a specific number of hours per week. They include teaching and non-teaching activities.

In some countries, including Indonesia, Peru, Thailand and Uruguay, teachers are only required to teach a specified number of hours per week. There is no set time to be spent in non-teaching activities. And in yet other countries, such as the Russian Federation, teachers' working hours are set at the local or school level.

Taking only the countries where statutory working time comprises both teaching and non-teaching activities, the 40-hour working week of a teacher in Brazil, Malaysia, the Philippines or Thailand is twice as long that of a teacher in Indonesia or Uruguay. In general, the non-teaching component of teachers' work appears to account for between 10 and 50 per cent of teachers' weekly working hours in WEI countries.

Although the statutory number of hours for which teachers are required actually to teach only measures part of a teacher's work, it is more easily compared between countries than are total working hours. Figure 2.8 shows average annual teaching hours by level of education. The number of teaching hours is defined here as the net contact hours of teaching. It is calculated on the basis of the annual number of teaching weeks multiplied by the number of periods which a teacher is supposed to spend teaching a class or group, multiplied by the length of a period in minutes, and divided by 60. Periods of time formally allowed for breaks between lessons or groups of lessons, and days when schools are closed for public holidays and festivities, are excluded.

Teaching hours are more easily compared between countries than working hours.

At the primary level, Paraguay and the Russian Federation, with less than 700 hours of teaching per year – around 100 hours below the OECD average – are at the low end of the spectrum in WEI countries, while Indonesia, the Philippines and Sri Lanka, with some 1 200 or more annual hours of teaching, are at the high end, between 400 and 600 hours above the OECD average (see Table 33 in Annex A4). In the remaining nine countries, the designated number of teaching hours per year ranges from 732 in Uruguay to 975 in Zimbabwe.

In Indonesia, the Philippines and Sri Lanka, teachers teach almost twice as many hours as teachers in Paraguay and the Russian Federation.

Given the high costs of training teachers for higher levels of education, countries need to ensure that they maximise the returns on this investment. Unlike the situation in the large majority of the OECD countries, where teaching hours decrease at higher levels of education, teaching hours in two thirds of the WEI countries remain the same between primary and upper secondary education, and even increase in Argentina, Paraguay and, to a lesser extent, Malaysia (see Table 33 in Annex A4). The countries where secondary teachers have a lighter teaching load are Indonesia, Peru, Thailand and Tunisia.

Unlike the situation in the OECD countries, teaching hours are similar in most WEI countries at all levels of education, or increase at higher levels.

Figure 2.8
Statutory number of teaching hours per year in public institutions, by level of education, 1999

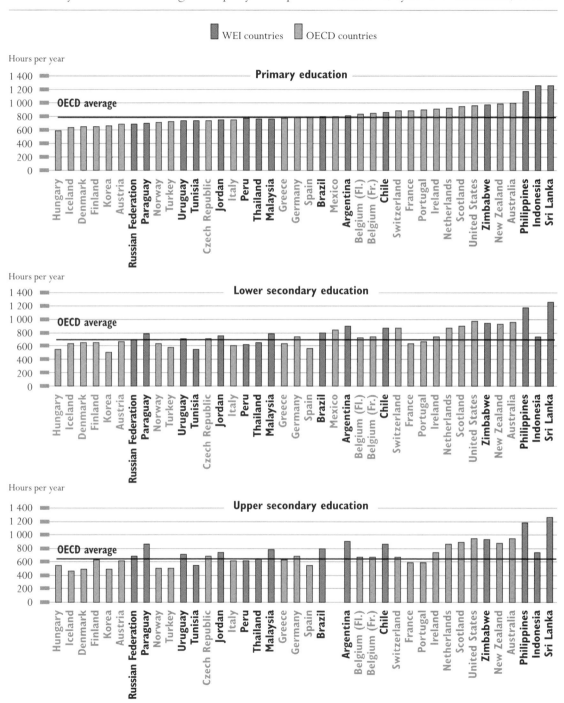

Countries are ranked in ascending order of the teaching time in primary education.
Source: OECD / UNESCO WEI, Table 33 in Annex A4.

In Indonesia, teaching time drops from 1 260 hours in primary education to 738 in secondary education, and in the other three countries secondary teachers teach between 104 and 187 hours fewer than their primary colleagues.

In WEI countries, upper secondary teachers teach on average only some 50 hours fewer than primary teachers, while the average difference in the OECD countries is about 140 hours, although fewer teaching hours at the upper secondary level may in some cases be offset by an increase in the time allocated to non-teaching activities.

Higher teaching hours at higher levels of education, where students' hours of instruction are usually longer, reduce costs but increase the burden placed on teachers.

Reducing teaching hours at the secondary level, where students tend to have more hours of instruction, clearly implies an increase in student-teacher ratios, with a direct impact on the costs of teaching per student. Many WEI countries have opted to keep teachers' working hours constant at all levels. One of the consequences of this strategy is that teachers' workload increases at the secondary level, both as a result of larger classes and because the non-teaching working time needed for preparing lessons and marking, for example, is likely to be longer at higher levels of education.

There is no single answer to the question of how big or how small classes should be in order to optimise educational outcomes. Ultimately, appropriate class size is dependent on management techniques which, in turn, depend on cultural values and attitudes (*e.g.* discipline and group behaviour), on physical facilities (*e.g.* size of classroom) and on adequate teaching materials. In a recent review of international research evidence on the effect of class size on student achievement (Hanushek, 1998), only 15 per cent of the 250 studies examined were found to reveal a statistically significant relationship favouring smaller classes. Research in OECD countries over the last decade has shown that it is not sufficient to focus attention on class size without also considering changes in teaching methods and classroom organisation. In general, however, smaller classes allow teachers to spend more time teaching, to use alternative teaching approaches, to be more innovative, to evaluate students more frequently and to manage classes better. There is evidence that the main advantage of smaller classes is often that teachers' attitudes and teaching behaviour improve, and that both teachers and learners suffer less stress.

While the debate on optimal class sizes continues, the costs associated with reducing class sizes must be weighed against other policy goals.

At the same time, smaller classes are more expensive, and the decision to reduce class sizes must be weighed against other policy goals, including improved access to education, competitive salaries for teachers, and investment in school infrastructure, equipment and supplies.

An indirect estimate of class size can be obtained by weighting student-teacher ratios by the number of hours for which teachers and students meet during the year.

Figure 2.9 shows average class sizes in primary and lower secondary education, class size being estimated as hours of instruction divided by statutory teaching hours times student-teacher ratios. This measure is equivalent to weighting student-teacher ratios by the number of hours for which teachers and students meet during the year, and it can be used as a proxy for class size if the assumption is made that all classroom teachers are fully occupied with teaching duties.

Primary teachers teach classes of between 13 and 35 students, while at the secondary level the number of students per class ranges from 12 to 50.

Using this methodology for estimating class sizes, a primary-school teacher teaches, on average, a class three times as large in Chile (35 students) as in Uruguay (13 students) (see Table 36 in Annex A4). Classes in the remaining 12 countries have average numbers of students ranging from 20 (Paraguay) to 32. In the OECD countries, however, the majority of countries, including Australia, Austria, Belgium, the Czech Republic, Denmark, Finland, France, Germany, Greece, Iceland, Italy, Ireland, Hungary, New Zealand, Norway and Spain, have an average primary class size of 20 or fewer students.

In all WEI countries except Argentina, Paraguay and the Russian Federation, lower secondary teachers teach classes that are on average larger than those of their primary colleagues, ranging from below 20 in those three countries to 50 students per class in the Philippines. In seven out of 13 countries for which data are available, there are on average more than 30 students per class, and in Thailand and Tunisia, besides the Philippines, teachers are faced with more than 40 students per class (see Table 36 in Annex A4).

These figures may underestimate real class sizes in both primary and secondary education since they are based on the total number of full-time equivalent

Figure 2.9
Average class sizes for public primary and lower secondary education

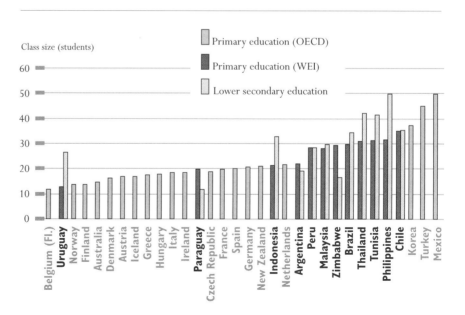

Source: OECD/UNESCO WEI, Table 36 in Annex A4. For year of reference see Table 36.

teachers, which may include teaching personnel not actually engaged in teaching, *e.g.* teachers on maternity or training leave. However, the direct estimates of class size provided by the Third International Mathematics and Science Study Repeat (TIMSS-R) conducted by the International Association for the Evaluation of Educational Achievement (IEA), are larger than the WEI estimates in only two out of eight WEI countries with available data. These are Malaysia and Indonesia, where mathematics teachers are faced with classes averaging 38 and 44 students respectively.

Figure 2.10
Class size and teaching hours, 1999

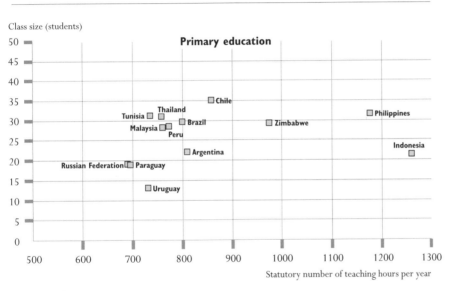

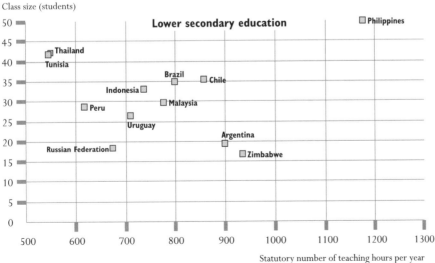

Source: OECD/UNESCO WEI, Tables 33 & 36 in Annex A4.

Looking at hours of teaching and class size together provides a better picture of teachers' workload and reveals possible trade-offs.

The burden of a large number of teaching hours may be alleviated by smaller classes, just as a light load in terms of teaching hours may be made heavier by large classes. For a more comprehensive picture of teachers' workload, teaching hours and class sizes therefore need to be considered jointly. Figure 2.10 compares differences in annual teaching hours and class sizes between primary and upper secondary levels.

In some countries, there appears to be a trade-off between class size and teaching hours. In Indonesia, for example, primary teachers have the heaviest teaching load (see Table 33 in Annex A4) but relatively few students per class (see Table 36 in Annex A4). And in Tunisia, lower secondary teachers have relatively large classes, but the number of teaching hours is the third lowest in the WEI group. Other countries, however, do not exhibit these trade-offs. Lower secondary teachers in the Philippines, for example, have the longest teaching hours among the WEI countries, combined with the largest classes, while at the other extreme, primary teachers in Uruguay have the second shortest teaching hours and the smallest classes.

In some cases, the trade-off is restricted to a particular level of education. Thailand and Tunisia, for example, compensate for the increase in the number of students per class from primary to lower secondary level with a lighter teaching load. In other countries, such as the Philippines, Uruguay and, to a lesser extent, Brazil, larger classes in lower secondary than in primary education are not accompanied by fewer teaching hours. In yet another group of countries, including Chile, the teaching hours and class sizes of primary and lower secondary teachers are, on average, the same. These differences between countries may indicate the relative priority given to students' access to teaching staff and exposure to teaching at a particular level of education, but they may also reflect the impact of rapidly changing demographic and/or enrolment factors.

Overall, the analysis of teachers' working hours and class sizes reveals that teachers have widely differing working conditions in the WEI countries. In the Philippines, a lower secondary teacher is in classes with an average of 50 students for more than 29 hours per week and 40 weeks per year, totalling 1 176 hours of teaching per year (see Table 33 in Annex A4). At the other extreme, a primary teacher in Uruguay teaches fewer than 20 hours per week for 38 weeks per year, totalling 732 hours per year, with fewer than 13 students per class on average. Conclusions from these figures about the relative standing of the teaching profession in different countries must, however, be drawn with care since the situation of teachers is often influenced by other local circumstances not accounted for by the data.

Teachers' workload and national income

Policy decisions on class sizes and teaching hours are made within budgetary constraints. While there is no clear relationship between teaching hours and income per capita in the WEI countries, student-teacher ratios and national income seem to be more closely connected (Figure 2.11).

At both the primary and the lower secondary level of education, student-teacher ratios (and by extension, class sizes) are broadly correlated with levels of GDP per capita. However, some countries, such as Indonesia and Uruguay, have smaller classes than would be expected from average per-capita national income. Conversely, in Chile at the primary level, and in the Philippines at the lower secondary level, class sizes are larger than might be expected from the level of national income per capita. The large number of statutory teaching hours for primary teachers in Indonesia, and the small number of hours of

Figure 2.11
Student-teacher ratios and GDP per capita, 1999

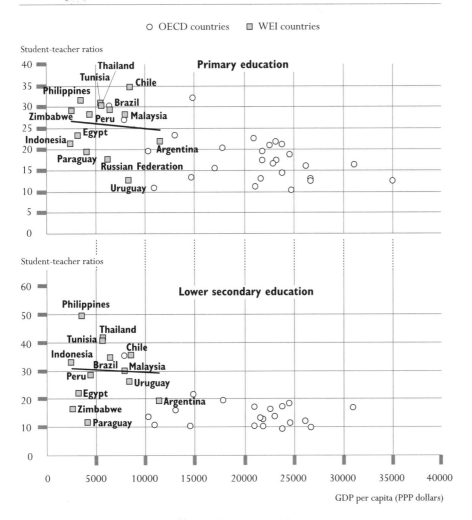

Source: OECD/UNESCO WEI, Tables 1 & 21 in Annex A4.

instruction for primary students in Uruguay, may help to explain why class sizes at the primary level are smaller than expected in those two countries. On the other hand, the large number of hours of instruction for primary students in Chile, and for lower secondary students in the Philippines, may help to explain the larger than expected class sizes observed in those two countries.

Overall, the deviation of several countries from a linear relationship between class sizes and GDP per capita indicates that there is room for policy choices. These may involve according high economic priority to education, charging teachers with smaller working loads, increasing intended instruction time for students, or paying teachers higher salaries.

As can be seen when OECD countries are taken into account, the relationship between student-teacher ratios and GDP per capita levels off as GDP per capita increases and factors other than national income tend to predominate in the choice of class sizes.

3 WHAT IS OFFERED TO TEACHERS

Salaries and career prospects are, broadly speaking, the material incentives offered to teachers. The balance between what is required of teachers and what is offered to them has a significant impact on the composition of the teaching force and the quality of teaching. Attempts to reduce costs by increasing class sizes and teaching hours, and reducing qualifications and pay, have often proved to impair educational development. Attracting skilled individuals and retaining them in the teaching profession is an essential prerequisite for ensuring high-quality education in the future.

Teachers' salaries

Teachers' salaries relate closely to the quality of the teaching force. But they are also the largest single factor in educational expenditure.

The relative level of teachers' salaries and the availability of salary increases during the course of teachers' careers can affect the decision by qualified individuals to enter or to remain in the teaching profession. At the same time, the pressure to improve the quality of education is often subject to tight fiscal constraints, and teachers' salaries and allowances are the largest single factor in the cost of providing education, accounting for two thirds or more of public expenditure on education in most countries.

The level of compensation includes not only teachers' take-home pay, but also fringe benefits. In certain circumstances, qualified individuals may be attracted to teaching, even when salaries are relatively low, because job security in teaching is greater than in private-sector jobs, because working conditions are advantageous (*e.g.* a short working day, week or year), or because it provides them with access to national medical insurance and pension schemes.

In almost all WEI countries, market forces determine the attractiveness of teaching. The impact of various elements of the total compensation package varies from country to country and, within a given country, over time. If the compensation package is too generous there will be a surplus of qualified applicants for the profession. In addition, teaching is sometimes one of the few occupations in developing countries designed for individuals with a high level of education. In such cases, there is no effective market alternative, and even low levels of compensation will attract qualified applicants. As other areas of the economy begin to develop, however, there is likely to be a sudden exodus of the best- qualified teachers from teaching into more attractive new positions.

Market forces determine the attractiveness of the teaching profession.

Most governments use a standard salary scale which they set directly or agree through negotiations with teachers' organisations. Often there is one salary scale for primary teachers and a second scale (with higher levels of compensation) for secondary-school teachers. The main feature of a uniform salary scale is usually that a teacher's pay depends upon educational qualifications and years of experience.

Most governments use a standard salary scale to pay the teachers whom they employ.

Figure 2.12 shows, for each WEI country with available data, annual statutory teachers' salaries (including bonuses) at the beginning of the career, after 15 years' experience and at the top of the scale, by level of education taught. "Statutory" means that salary data are reported in accordance with formal policies for public institutions. The salaries reported are defined as gross salaries (the total sum of money that is paid by the employer for the labour supplied) minus the employer's contribution to social security and pension (according to existing salary scales). Salaries are "before tax", *i.e.*, before deductions for income taxes. The starting salaries reported refer to the average scheduled gross salary per year for a full-time teacher with the minimum training necessary for certification at the beginning of his or her teaching career. Salaries after 15 years' experience refer to the scheduled annual salary of a full-time classroom teacher with the minimum training necessary for certification and with 15 years' experience. The maximum salaries reported refer to the scheduled maximum annual salary (top of the salary scale) of a full-time classroom teacher with the minimum training for certification for his or her job.

Salaries are converted into purchasing power parities (PPPs) and incremented by the maximum bonuses that teachers may receive, in order to assess their maximum potential income and allow comparison between countries of teachers' ability to purchase a common set of goods and services.

Mid-career teachers' salaries in Indonesia are about one fifth of those in Chile at the primary level, even after adjustment for differences in purchasing power parities.

There are significant differences between countries in the salaries paid to teachers. The statutory salary of an experienced primary-school teacher with the minimum training required for certification ranges from below 3 000 PPP dollars in Indonesia to almost 16 000 PPP dollars in Chile (see Table 25*a* in Annex A4).

Figure 2.12
Annual starting, mid-career and maximum statutory teachers' salaries (including all possible bonuses) by level of education and years of service, 1999 (PPP dollars)

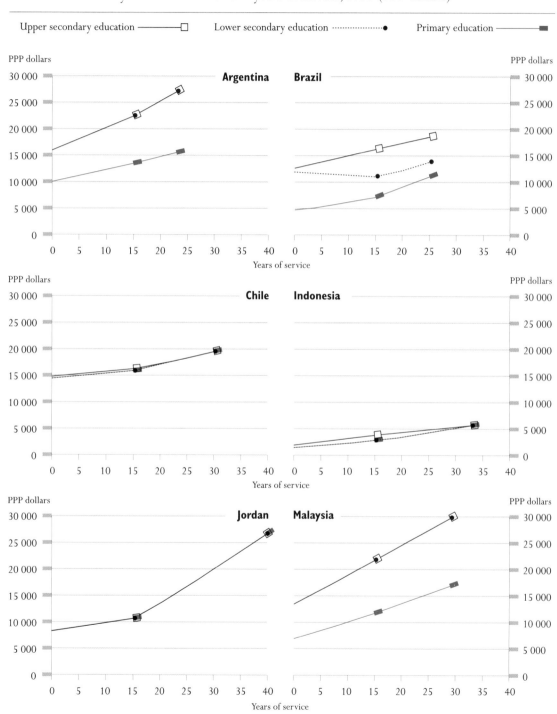

Source: OECD/UNESCO WEI, Tables 25*a*, 26*a* & 27*a* in Annex A4.

Figure 2.12 *(continued)*
Annual starting, mid-career and maximum statutory teachers' salaries (including all possible bonuses)
by level of education and years of service, 1999 (PPP dollars)

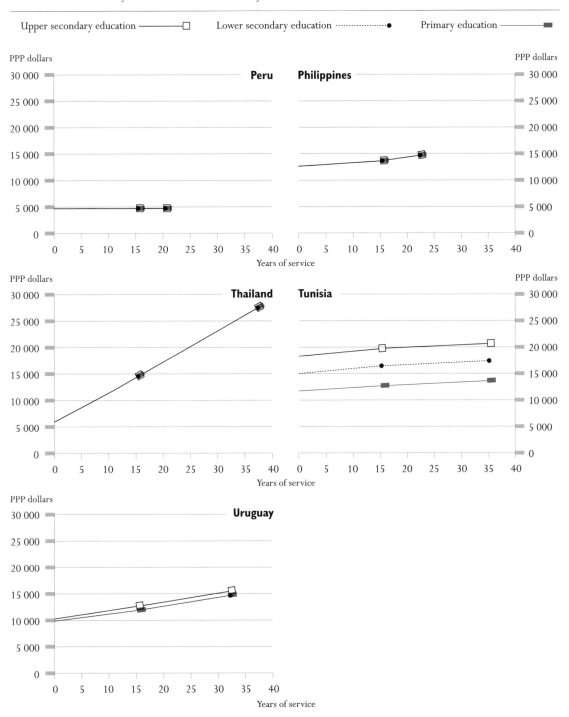

Upper secondary education ———□   Lower secondary education ·············●   Primary education ———■

Source: OECD/UNESCO WEI, Tables 25*a*, 26*a* & 27*a* in Annex A4.

However, even the salary levels in Chile are more than 10 000 PPP dollars below the average in OECD countries, where salary levels range from between 8 000 and 13 000 PPP dollars in the Czech Republic, Hungary, Mexico and Turkey to between 30 000 and 52 000 PPP dollars in Australia, Belgium, Denmark, Germany, Ireland, Korea, the Netherlands, New Zealand, Spain, Switzerland, the United Kingdom and the United States.

At the secondary level, salaries including all bonuses after 15 years' experience range from 2 900 and 3 500 PPP dollars in Indonesia (depending on the level of education) to over 20 000 PPP dollars in Argentina and Malaysia. At the secondary level also, WEI average statutory salaries are less than half of the average salaries among the OECD countries.

Some countries value and reward teachers' experience...

In Thailand, an experienced primary teacher at the top of the salary scale earns almost five times as much as a teacher at the beginning of his or her career (see Table 25 in Annex A4). Other countries with large increases in salaries during service are Brazil, Malaysia, Indonesia and Jordan, where maximum salaries are between 2.3 and 3.4 times starting salaries. These differences are an indication of the value attached to teaching experience and the incentives for experienced teachers to remain in the profession. It should be noted that the differentials between maximum and starting salaries in WEI countries tend to be considerably larger than those in OECD countries, reflecting a higher premium for staying in the teaching profession.

... but not all do.

However, there are also WEI countries with small differentials or even no differentials at all. For example, in Peru, salaries do not change over the course of a teacher's career for those with minimum training (*i.e.* without pedagogical title), and in Chile, the Philippines and Tunisia, they increase by only about 15-50 per cent from the beginning of the career to the top of the salary scale. It should also be noted that the number of years required to reach the top of the salary scale from the starting salary varies considerably, ranging from around 20 years in Argentina or the Philippines to more than 40 years in Jordan.

In some countries, upper secondary teachers are paid up to two thirds more than primary-school teachers.

Teachers' salaries may also be higher for teachers in the higher levels of education. In seven out of eleven countries, the statutory salaries of teachers with 15 years' experience and minimum qualifications are the same or do not differ by more than 20 per cent between primary and upper secondary (general) levels. By contrast, in Argentina, Brazil, Malaysia and Tunisia, the statutory salaries of experienced upper secondary teachers are 69 per cent, 124 per cent, 88 per cent and 54 per cent, respectively, higher than those of their counterparts in primary schools. One of the reasons for the variation in teachers' salaries between levels of education in these countries is undoubtedly the higher qualifications required to enter the profession at the secondary level.

It should be noted that the differentials between the salaries of primary and secondary teachers tend to be much larger in WEI countries than in OECD countries, which may reflect the greater demand for highly skilled teachers, and the lower supply.

While uniform salary scales are transparent and simple to administer, they do not help to motivate teachers to perform at their best, nor do they help to solve problems of shortages of teachers in certain subjects (such as mathematics and science) or in rural areas.

Bonuses may be paid on top of basic salary scales, ranging among WEI countries from 6 to 49 per cent of total salaries.

Additional bonuses are a means of adjusting the remuneration of teachers without altering the basic government scales. Such adjustments may serve different aims, such as rewarding teachers who take on responsibilities or duties beyond statutory norms, attracting better candidates to the teaching profession, encouraging teachers to improve their performance, or attracting teachers into subject areas where demand is greater than supply, for example science and mathematics, or to rural locations where there is a scarcity of applicants.

In seven out of 12 WEI countries, teachers may receive bonuses on top of their gross salaries. These range from 7 to 86 per cent of total salaries, exceeding 30 per cent in Chile (51), Indonesia (60) and Uruguay (86) (see Tables 25*a*, 26*a* and 27*a* in Annex A4). Table 2.2 shows the criteria governing the award of bonuses to teachers. An enhancement to basic salary is defined here as any difference in salary between what a particular teacher actually receives as payment for work performed at a school and the amount that he or she would be expected to receive on the basis of level of experience alone (*i.e.*, number of years in the teaching profession). Adjustments may be temporary (indicated by "T" in Table 2.2) or permanent (indicated by "P"), and they may effectively move a teacher "off-scale", on to a different salary scale, or on to a higher step on the same salary scale. They may be awarded to all teachers who satisfy the relevant conditions (indicated by ●), with discretion to some teachers (indicated by ■) or in exceptional circumstances only (indicated by ▲).

All WEI countries, with the exception of Zimbabwe, provide monetary incentives to teachers working in difficult circumstances, including disadvantaged, remote or high-cost areas. Half of the countries award additional salary increments on the basis of teachers' family status. Several countries apply task-based criteria in awarding additional bonuses, the most frequent being management duties in addition to teaching duties, followed by the teaching of more classes or hours than those required by the statutory full-time contract. About two thirds of the countries reward teachers holding an initial educational qualification higher than the minimum required to enter the teaching profession, as well as teachers who obtain such a qualification or pursue more

Table 2.2

Criteria for salary increments (bonuses) for teachers in primary and secondary schools

	Management responsibilities in addition to teaching duties	Teaching students with special educational needs	Special tasks	Teaching more classes or hours than required by a full-time contract	Educational qualification higher than minimum	Location allowances	Other	Special activities	Holding a higher than minimum level of teaching certification	Outstanding performance in teaching	Age (independent of years of teaching)
WEI participants[1]											
Argentina						●	●				
Brazil		●			●	●	●		■		
Chile	●					●	●			●	
Indonesia		▲			●	▲					●
Jordan	●	■	●		●	●			●	●	
Malaysia		●			●				■		
Paraguay		●				●			●	●	
Peru		●			●	●	●				
Philippines		■				▲			●	●	
Thailand		■			●	▲	▲		●		
Uruguay		■		■		●					
Zimbabwe	●				●					●	
OECD countries											
Australia	●	●	●	●	●	▲ ●		●	■	● ●	▲
Austria	●	●	●		●			●			
Belgium (Fl.)			●						●		
Belgium (Fr.)			●								
Czech Republic		●	●	●	●			●	●		●
Denmark			●	●					■		
England	●	■	● ▲	■	●	●		■		■	
Finland	●	●		●	●	●		●	●	▲	●
France		●	●	●	●	●					
Germany											
Greece			●		●	●					
Hungary	●	●	●	●	●	●		●	■		
Iceland	●	●	●	●	●	■		●			●
Ireland	●				●			●	●		
Italy		●		●					●		
Mexico	●				●		●	●	●	●	
Netherlands			●								
New Zealand	●	●	●		●			●	●	●	
Norway	●			◐	●						
Portugal		●		●	●					▲	
Scotland					■		■				
Spain		●				▲					
Sweden		●	■	■	●	■	■	●	■	■	
Switzerland	■		■	■		●	▲		■		
Turkey				●	●	●	●				
United States	●				●			●	●		

● Adjustment is given all the time or most of the time
■ Adjustment is given occasionally
▲ Adjustment is rarely given
  Permanent salary adjustment
  Temporary salary adjustment

1. Year of reference 1998 for all WEI countries.
Source: OECD / UNESCO WEI.

extensive training than the required minimum on the job. Finally, four countries (Chile, Malaysia, Paraguay and the Philippines) award bonuses on the basis of merit, rewarding teachers with outstanding performance.

Box 2.3
Economic incentives to improve teaching

The ultimate goal of most salary differentials is to provide students with effective teachers in all disciplines and in all areas of a country. However, the payment of bonuses should be considered carefully and its impact evaluated from case to case since there is evidence that it may elicit responses from teachers that have an effect opposite to that which is intended, impairing school effectiveness and hence student achievement.

For example, merit pay is intended to encourage teachers to work harder. However, merit pay schemes frequently place individual teachers in competition with each other; they may then be reluctant to share with their colleagues the new ideas and successful practices which they discover. They may also compete among themselves for the best classes, or may encourage slow learners to drop out of school. Finally, many teachers who do not receive merit pay may respond by reducing their effort and willingness to co-operate with other teachers, feeling that they have been treated unfairly. In many cases, when merit pay schemes have been implemented they have quickly been abandoned, and those that have survived tend not to be based on true merit.

An alternative approach consists of singling out entire schools for their achievement, rather than individuals, thus encouraging co-operative work among teachers. One example of this approach is offered by Chile's national system of performance evaluation for government-funded schools (Sistema Nacional de Evaluación del Desempeño de los Establecimientos Educacionales Subvencionados, SNED), which provides merit awards to all teachers in a school on the basis of student outcomes. Student outcomes are assessed by means of a comprehensive standardised testing system (Sistema de Medición de la Calidad de la Educación, SIMCE) which assesses Spanish and mathematics skills every two years among students in grades 4 and 8 alternately and allows the calculation of changes in average SIMCE scores in schools between successive applications.

The SNED evaluation programme, established in 1995, has carried out two rounds of measurement and awards since its inception (1996-97 and 1998-99) and is conducting the third round of measurement and awards in 2000-2001. It provides financial merit awards to schools, which are then used to pay bonuses to teachers. Awards are made to the schools that achieve the best performance in each of a number of socio-economic strata, so that competition is between relatively comparable schools. Any municipal or government-dependent school is eligible to win an award, and may win in successive evaluations. That is to say, SNED awards are fully competitive, but the competition is between schools rather than between teachers, thus promoting a co-operative effort within schools. Moreover, the competition is viewed as "fair", because it compares schools that are roughly comparable in terms of the student populations that they serve, the socio-economic levels of the communities in which they are located, and other external factors that affect student outcomes.

The awards are based on a school's performance on an index that includes the absolute levels of SIMCE test scores and improvements since the last SIMCE tests, as well as other indicators of educational outcomes and some process measures. Data come from the SIMCE tests and from questionnaires administered to parents at the time when the tests are administered, a special survey carried out for the purpose of SNED, a report associated with subvention or subsidy payments to the school, and the Ministry of Education statistics unit. The index of school excellence includes six factors (effectiveness, improvement, initiative, improvement in working conditions, equality of opportunity, and involvement of teachers, parents and guardians) in which outcomes are heavily weighted through the combined effect of the effectiveness and improvement factors in the SNED index. Award funds can be used only for bonuses for teachers (including headteachers or school directors). Ninety per cent of the funds are distributed on the basis of the number of hours that a teacher works in the school. The school director may allocate the remaining 10 per cent to the teachers who have made the most "outstanding" contribution to professional performance. Some documents indicate that the distribution of this final 10 per cent is based on decisions of "the education professionals in the school".

The number of schools winning awards was 2 285 during the first two-year period, decreasing to 1 826 during the 1998-99 SNED exercise, and approximately 31 000 teachers received bonuses in each of the rounds. Virtually all directors approve the system of awards to schools rather than to individual teachers, on the ground that this strengthens teamwork among teachers in a school.

Another alternative approach to the assignment of merit pay to individual teachers consists of providing small grants to teachers who want to experiment with innovative methods and projects. To this end, Thailand has recently introduced an award that comprises a significant salary increment for the teacher who proposes the innovation, a project grant for carrying out the proposed innovation, and a grant to the school to facilitate the implementation of the teacher's innovation throughout the school.

Paying additional bonuses to mathematics and science teachers is another option, but it may be perceived as unfair by other teachers, who work as hard in the same schools, teach the same students and work hours that are as long, thereby jeopardising co-operation between colleagues. Moreover, the benefits are quickly incorporated into salaries and, once the shortage of teachers disappears, these bonuses are very hard to change. An alternative approach that can be used to attract mathematics and science graduates to the teaching profession is to provide for differential training costs for students who train to become mathematics and science teachers, offering them loans repayable through service as teachers, with institutional mechanisms to collect loan repayments from students who choose not to teach.

Finally, the payment of premiums to teachers working in rural areas has sometimes proved insufficient to convince teachers to leave more attractive locations. An alternative solution is to recruit potential teachers from rural areas, to train them as teachers and to encourage them to return as teachers to the rural areas where they grew up.

In general, it is important to bear in mind that policies cannot dictate outcomes. Outcomes will depend on responses to policies. Policy-makers need to monitor the range of responses to policies in a given country, in order to detect as soon as possible any dysfunctional behaviour which may jeopardize student outcomes, and must then introduce the necessary corrections to the original strategies.

Teachers' salaries and national income per capita

Ultimately, whether salaries are perceived as low or high in a country depends on how well other workers are paid. Even though teachers' salaries may be low in comparison with those of other countries, if they are high in relation to what might be paid in similar jobs in their own country, teachers are likely to consider themselves well paid. In general, teachers' salary scales reflect government policies towards public servants. If these are disadvantageous in comparison with the private sector or other employment opportunities, the public labour force tends to be of lower quality, although the entire package of fringe benefits should be taken into account when teachers' compensation conditions are compared (Figure 2.13).

The competitiveness of teachers' salaries is mainly determined by the salaries of other workers.

Measuring statutory salaries for teachers against GDP per capita provides an indication of the extent to which a country invests in teachers, bearing in mind its ability to fund educational expenditure. High salaries relative to GDP per capita suggest that a country is making more of an effort to invest its financial resources in teachers. In the absence of comparable information on the salaries of other highly skilled professions that could be used as points of comparison with teachers' salaries, GDP per capita is often also used to create a proxy for the financial standing of teachers. However, it must be remembered that the ratio of teachers' salaries to GDP per capita reflects patterns of relative productivity that vary greatly between sectors in accordance with a country's level of development. This ratio is generally higher in developing than in more developed countries, because of the greater productivity in the service sector than in the rest of the economy.

Comparing statutory salaries relative to GDP per capita indicates the extent to which a country invests in teachers.

While only a minority of OECD countries pay initial teachers' salaries at all levels of education at or above GDP per capita, this is the case in the large majority of WEI countries. Starting salaries for teachers with the minimum requisite qualifications are above GDP per capita in seven out of 11 WEI countries at the primary level (see Table 25 in Annex A4), and at the secondary level in all countries, except Indonesia, Uruguay and Peru (upper-secondary only) (see Table 26 in Annex A4), and they rise to 3 times GDP per capita in the Philippines at all levels of education. By contrast, among the 27 OECD countries for which comparable data are available, starting salaries are below GDP per capita in 16 countries, and only in Germany, Greece, Korea and Spain are starting salaries higher than 1.3 times GDP per capita at all levels.

In most WEI countries, starting salaries are at or above GDP per capita, unlike the situation in OECD countries.

Mid-career salaries for teachers with the minimum qualifications exceed GDP per capita at all levels of education in all countries except Indonesia and Uruguay, where the salary of a primary-school teacher with 15 years' experience is about 30 per cent lower than average per capita income. Finally, salaries at the top of the pay scale range from the equivalent of GDP per capita in Brazil (primary level) to 400 per cent or more of GDP per capita in the Philippines and Thailand, respectively.

Figure 2.13
Statutory teacher salaries relative to GDP per capita by level of education, 1999

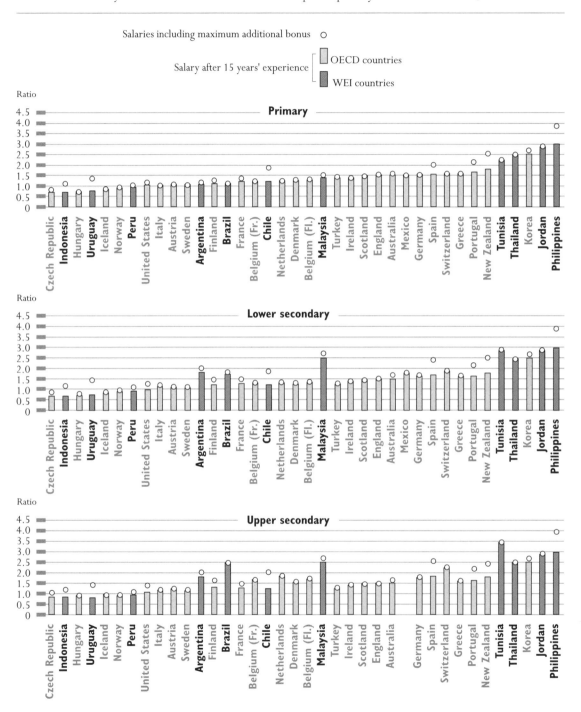

Countries are ranked by salaries in primary education after 15 years of experience without bonuses.

Source: OECD/UNESCO WEI, Tables 25, 25a, 26, 26a, 27 & 27a in Annex A4.

The Philippines has comparatively high teachers' salaries relative to GDP per capita, which is itself relatively low, while Argentina, Chile, Malaysia and Uruguay have comparatively high GDP per capita and lower ratios of teachers' salaries to GDP per capita. This confirms that countries at lower stages of development have higher ratios of teachers' salaries to GDP per capita.

The relationship between a country's level of development, teachers' salaries can be seen in Figure 2.14, which compares teachers' salaries (including bonuses) with GDP per capita.

4 POLICY CHOICES

If the future working conditions for the teaching force and their associated costs are to be judged accurately, the various indicators discussed in the preceding section need to be considered in combination rather than in isolation. When governments decide on their education budgets, they need to make trade-offs between factors such as the level of teachers' salaries, the size of classes, the number of teaching hours required of teachers and the intended instruction time for students.

When establishing future working conditions and incentives for the teaching force, policy-makers need to consider a combination of many factors.

Figure 2.14
Mid-career salaries for primary teachers (including all bonuses)
relative to GDP per capita, 1999

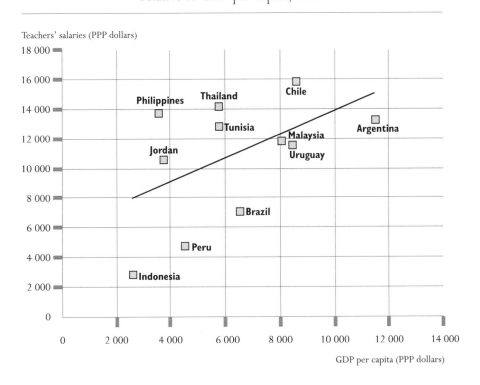

Source: OECD/UNESCO WEI, Tables 1 & 25*a* in Annex A4.

- How much does it cost an education system, for example, to have a teaching force that teaches fewer hours per year than in other countries, if all other characteristics of the education system remain unchanged?

- By how much do higher statutory salary levels, which are likely to be related to higher qualifications, increase costs per student?

- By how much do higher student-teacher ratios reduce costs per student?

These are questions that are difficult to answer from a solely national point of view because it is difficult to find points of comparison for many of the determinants of cost. International comparisons can widen the perspective by showing how other countries make different trade-offs and policy choices between the determinants of the costs of the teaching force.

In order to address these questions, this section first reviews teachers' salary costs per student at both the primary and the lower secondary levels of education. The section then analyses what factors account for differences between countries in teachers' salary costs per student. To accomplish this, the difference between the statutory teachers' salary costs per student in each country and the average over all WEI countries is decomposed into four components that measure how much more (or less) than the average is spent per student on the major determinants of educational costs: the level of statutory salaries for teachers after 15 years' experience, hours of instruction per student per year, designated number of teaching hours per year, and class size.

On average, teachers' salary costs per student are about 50 per cent higher in lower secondary education than in primary education.

The overall comparison between patterns of spending at different levels of education shows that a general trade-off is made between levels of education. The average teachers' salary costs per student (see Table 36 in Annex A4) are 138 PPP dollars higher in lower secondary education than in primary education: while a primary teacher costs 368 PPP dollars per student per year, a lower secondary teacher costs 506 PPP dollars (Figure 2.15).

Teachers' salary costs per secondary student also vary much more between countries than similar costs at the primary level. At the primary level, the highest ranking country, which is Thailand, has teachers' salary costs per student that are about 622 PPP dollars higher than those of Indonesia, which is the lowest ranking country (see Table 36 in Annex A4). At the lower secondary level, the difference in teachers' salary costs per student between the countries at the top and bottom ends of the scale, which are Argentina and Indonesia respectively, is 990 PPP dollars.

In Argentina, teachers' salary costs per student double, rising from 504 PPP dollars per student at the primary level to 1 083 PPP dollars at the lower secondary level (see Table 36 in Annex A4). These increased costs are mainly an effect of higher salary levels in themselves: the statutory salary of a lower secondary teacher after 15 years' experience, 20 903 PPP dollars, is almost 1.7 times the corresponding statutory salary of a primary teacher (12 377 PPP dollars). Smaller class sizes in lower secondary education also contribute to this effect. Similarly, in Malaysia, the higher teachers' salary costs per student at lower secondary level are due first to higher salary levels and, second, to a larger number of hours of instruction for lower secondary students. Conversely, in Uruguay, teachers' salaries are the same at all levels of education, and the higher teachers' salary costs per student are due to a sharp increase in the amount of instruction time for students at lower secondary level, which almost trebles, rising from 455 hours per year for primary students to 1 369 hours per year for lower secondary students (see Table 28 in Annex A4).

Argentina, Malaysia and Uruguay have teachers' salary costs per student at the lower secondary level that are twice those at the primary level.

Figure 2.15
Statutory salary costs per student, 1999

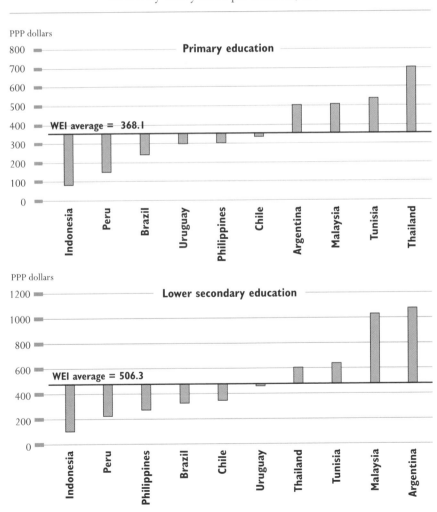

Source: OECD/UNESCO WEI, Table 36 in Annex A4.

Other countries, such as Thailand and the Philippines, give comparatively high financial priority to primary education.

Other countries, however, exhibit a more marked commitment to primary education. In Thailand and the Philippines, for example, teachers' salaries are the same at all levels, but the number of students per class is much lower at the primary level (31 and 32 students per class respectively) than at the lower secondary level (42 and 50 students respectively), thus causing the teachers' salary costs per student to be higher in primary than in lower secondary education in the latter.

Countries with similar teachers' salary costs per student make different policy choices about other matters.

Table 2.3
Statutory salaries, teaching hours per year and class size

	Statutory salary (after 15 years' experience)	Students' hours of instruction	Teachers' teaching hours	Student-teacher ratio	Class size	Statutory salary costs per teaching hour	Statutory salary costs per student enrolled
	A	B	C	D	E= (B*D)/C	F= A/C	G= A/D
Primary							
Argentina	12 377	729	810	24.6	22.1	16	504
Brazil	7 191	800	800	29.7	29.7	9	242
Chile	10 476	980	860	30.7	34.9	18	342
Egypt	m	913	965	23.5	22.3	m	m
Indonesia	1 836	1 187	1 260	22.8	21.4	2	81
Malaysia	11 017	991	762	21.6	28.1	15	510
Paraguay	m	690	696	19.9	19.7	m	m
Peru	4 282	774	774	28.4	28.4	6	151
Philippines	10 640	1 067	1 176	34.8	31.6	12	306
Russian Federation	m	756	686	17.6	19.4	m	m
Thailand	14 208	1 160	760	20.2	30.9	19	703
Tunisia	12 877	960	735	23.9	31.3	18	538
Uruguay	6 281	455	732	20.6	12.8	16	304
Zimbabwe	m	753	975	37.9	29.3	m	m
Lower secondary							
Argentina	20 903	896	900	19.3	19.2	25	1083
Brazil	11 180	800	800	34.6	34.6	14	323
Chile	10 476	990	860	30.7	35.3	18	342
Egypt	m	1 034	724	21.8	31.2	m	m
Indonesia	1 836	1 231	738	19.7	32.9	4	93
Malaysia*	20 076	1 189	778	19.4	29.6	28	1037
Paraguay	m	860	774	10.5	11.7	m	m
Peru	4 235	903	619	19.5	28.5	8	217
Philippines	10 640	1 467	1 176	39.8	49.7	12	267
Russian Federation	m	892	686	14.1	18.3	m	m
Thailand	14 208	1 167	652	23.5	42.1	22	605
Tunisia	16 467	880	548	25.8	41.4	30	638
Uruguay	6 281	1 369	712	13.7	26.3	16	458

Source: OECD/UNESCO WEI, Table 36 in Annex A4.

Box 2.4 How to read Table 2.3

This box provides the definitions and methods underlying the analysis in this section.

Intended instruction time for students measures the number of hours of instruction to be received by students as defined in the national curriculum guidelines, regulations or other official statements governing the education system.

The *designated teaching hours required from teachers* measure the total number of hours for which a full-time teacher is expected to teach groups or classes of students per year, according to formal policy.

The *ratio of students to teaching staff (the student-teacher ratio)* measures the number of students enrolled relative to the number of teachers employed at a given level of education. This ratio should not be confused with *class size*, which takes into account the respective amounts of time that teachers and students spend in the classroom.

Class size is estimated by dividing the total number of hours of instruction received by students by the total number of hours of teaching delivered by teachers. The formula below shows how class size depends on the three factors mentioned above, increasing with higher *student-teacher ratios*, longer *intended annual hours of instruction* for students, and lower *teaching loads* for teachers.

$$\text{Class size} = \frac{\text{annual total of hours of instruction received by students}}{\text{annual total of hours of instruction delivered}}$$

$$= \frac{\text{number of students * intended annual hours of instruction per student}}{\text{number of teachers * designated annual hours of teaching required from teachers}}$$

$$= \text{student-teacher ratio} * \frac{\text{intended annual hours of instruction per student}}{\text{designated annual hours of teaching required from teachers}}$$

As shown by the data in Table 2.3, countries differ widely in their treatment of the basic determinants of educational costs.

- At the lower secondary level, for example, Brazil, Indonesia and Peru offer low salaries, which tends to reduce educational costs.

- In Argentina and Uruguay, small class sizes tend to increase educational costs.

- Tunisia has high salaries and low teaching hours but large classes.

- The Philippines are characterised by high numbers of hours of instruction for students, a heavy teaching load and large classes (with higher salaries at primary level).

- Peru has low salaries, low student instruction hours and low teaching hours (with smaller classes at secondary level).

- Brazil has low salaries and low student instruction hours.

- In Thailand, low teaching hours are compensated by large classes (with higher salaries and longer instruction time at primary level).

The following shows how these basic structural characteristics of education systems translate into higher or lower teaching costs per student. In order to assess national policy choices, some sort of benchmark is needed for the purposes of comparison. In the analysis which follows, the average of the WEI countries has been chosen as this benchmark, not because it has any inherent normative value, but simply because education systems in WEI countries are sufficiently diverse for the average to provide a convenient reference point from which to assess national policy choices.

Using the WEI average as a benchmark, the difference between the statutory teachers' salary costs per student in each of the countries and the average of all the WEI countries is decomposed into four components that measure how much more (or less) than the average is spent per student on significant determinants of educational costs: the level of statutory salaries for teachers after 15 years' experience, hours of instruction per student per year, designated number of teaching hours per year, and class size. Statutory salaries after 15 years' experience are then used as the basis for examining the effects on teachers' salary costs of the various structural characteristics of national education systems. Class size has been estimated as described above. A fifth component ("two or more of the other factors taken together") summarises the joint effects of two or more of the preceding four factors.

Uruguay compensates small primary-level class sizes with a low number of hours of instruction.

At the primary level, the Philippines and Uruguay are countries with similar teachers' salary costs per student (306 and 304 PPP dollars per year respectively). While the number of hours of instruction for students is much higher in the Philippines than the average (1 067 hours per year) and the number of students per class is around the WEI average (31 compared to 29), in Uruguay the number of hours of instruction for students is the lowest among the WEI countries (455 hours), which reduces the cost per student in Uruguay by about 176 PPP dollars. On the other hand, average class sizes in Uruguay are the lowest in the WEI countries (13 students per class), which reduces the workload of teachers but adds 396 PPP dollars to costs per student.

Thailand compensates a high number of hours of instruction with bigger class sizes.

Argentina and Thailand, which have annual teachers' salary costs per primary student of more than 500 PPP dollars, are at the higher end of the scale of costs. The two countries make different decisions, however, about the number of hours of instruction for students, and about class sizes. While annual hours of instruction for students, 1 080 hours, are comparatively high in Thailand (increasing the salary costs per student by 97 PPP dollars), in Argentina, they are comparatively low (729 hours), reducing the salary costs per student by 70 PPP dollars. The pattern of class sizes has the reverse effect on costs. In Thailand, class sizes are slightly above the WEI average, helping to reduce the salary costs per student by more than 40 PPP dollars, while in Argentina class sizes are well below the WEI average (22 students per class), increasing the salary costs per student by 81 PPP dollars.

Figure 2.16
Contributions of various factors to in/decreasing statutory teachers' salary
cost per student relative to the WEI average, 1999

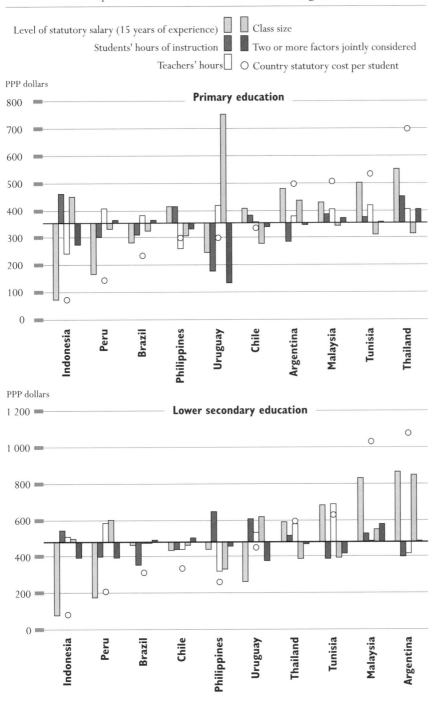

Countries are ranked by country statutory cost per student.
Source: OECD/UNESCO WEI, Table 35 in Annex A4.

Table 2.4

Contributions of various factors to in/decreasing statutory teachers'
salary costs per student relative to the WEI average
(after 15 years' experience, in PPP dollars, 1999)

| | WEI average statutory salary costs per student enrolled | Incremental or decremental effect of each specified factor (in US dollars per student converted using PPPs) | | | | | Statutory salary costs per student enrolled |
		Statutory salary (after 15 years' experience)	Students' hours of instruction	Teachers' teaching hours	Class size	Two or more of the other factors taken together	
	1	2	3	4	5	6	1+2+3 +4+5
Primary							
Argentina	352	126	-70	24	81	-10	504
Brazil	352	-75	-43	29	-30	8	242
Chile	352	53	27	2	-78	-15	342
Indonesia	352	-282	107	-111	95	-82	81
Malaysia	352	73	31	47	-11	16	510
Peru	352	-187	-53	53	-24	9	151
Philippines	352	59	61	-93	-49	-24	306
Thailand	352	197	97	48	-42	49	703
Tunisia	352	145	19	62	-46	4	538
Uruguay	352	-110	-176	64	396	-222	304
Lower secondary							
Argentina	479	382	-85	-63	365	5	1083
Brazil	479	-19	-127	-11	-10	11	323
Chile	479	-48	-44	-44	-20	17	342
Indonesia	479	-404	62	28	14	-86	93
Malaysia	479	348	44	2	68	95	1037
Peru	479	-305	-82	98	117	-91	217
Philippines	479	-41	166	-161	-153	-24	267
Thailand	479	106	34	95	-94	-16	605
Tunisia	479	199	-92	204	-88	-64	638
Uruguay	479	-220	123	47	136	-106	458

Source: OECD/UNESCO WEI.

Argentina counterbalances high salaries with high teaching hours. At the lower secondary level, Argentina and Malaysia show the highest annual salary costs per student, 1 083 and 1 037 PPP dollars respectively. In Argentina, high salaries are counterbalanced by comparatively high teaching hours (900 hours per year), while in Malaysia, the teaching load is slightly below the WEI average (778 hours per year). In Malaysia, class sizes are smaller than the average (29 students per class compared with an average of 33), while in Argentina they are almost half the average (19 students per class), reducing the workload of teachers but adding 68 and 365 PPP dollars respectively to salary costs per student.

Box 2.5
How to read Table 2.4

Expenditure per student on teachers' salaries can be estimated from teachers' salaries, students' hours of instruction, teachers' hours of teaching, and class size, calculated on the basis of student-teacher ratios.

This figure shows how the different factors influence expenditure in each country. It illustrates the effect on salary costs of each individual factor in turn, by showing the national value for that factor and assuming that all other factors are at the WEI average level.

Column 1 shows expenditure on teachers' salaries per student, if all four factors are at WEI average level.

Column 2 shows the effect on teachers' salary costs per student if students' hours of instruction, teaching time and class size are at the WEI average, but teachers' salaries are at the national level. Since higher teachers' salaries lead to an increase in costs per student, a positive value indicates that salaries are above the WEI average. For example, Table 2.4 indicates that for lower secondary teachers in Argentina, higher than average teacher salaries add PPP dollars 382 to the WEI average of PPP dollars 479 of statutory teacher salary per student enrolled. Conversely, a negative value indicates that salaries are below the WEI average. In Brazil, for example, below-average statutory teacher salaries reduce the WEI average of PPP dollars 479 by PPP dollars 19.

Column 3 shows the effect on teachers' salary costs per student if the other three factors are at the WEI average, but the number of hours of instruction is at the national level. Since more hours of instruction per student lead to an increase in costs per student, a positive value indicates that hours of instruction are above the WEI average. While higher than average statutory teacher salaries add to the costs per lower secondary student in Argentina, fewer than average hours of instruction reduce the average costs per student by PPP dollars 85.

Column 4 shows the effect on teachers' salary costs per student if the other three factors are at the WEI average, but the number of teaching hours is at the national level. In this case, if teachers teach more hours, costs per student decrease. A positive value therefore indicates that teaching hours are below the WEI average.

Column 5 shows the effect on teachers' salary costs per student if the other three factors are at the WEI average, but class size is at the national level. Again, since costs increase if fewer students are in a class, a positive value indicates that class sizes are above the WEI average.

Column 6 shows the residual value due to the interaction of all four factors.

Column 7 shows the teachers' salary costs per student for each country. This is the sum of columns 1 to 6.

In Chile and the Philippines, comparatively high statutory salaries for primary teachers are compensated by a high number of teaching hours or larger than average classes, while in Thailand high salaries are combined with large classes and/or light teaching loads.

In Argentina, Thailand and Tunisia, annual statutory salaries for primary teachers (not including bonuses) are the highest in the WEI countries, between 12 377 and 14 208 PPP dollars. In Argentina, more than half of this effect on salary costs per student is compensated by lower than average hours of instruction for students, while in Thailand and Tunisia, one fifth and one third respectively of this effect is counterbalanced by slightly larger than average classes. Among other countries with relatively high salaries, Chile compensates its high salary costs by larger than average classes while in the Philippines large classes and higher than average teaching load balance the teachers' payroll effect. Conversely, in Thailand, high salary costs are compounded by higher than average hours of instruction and a lighter teaching load.

In Indonesia, Peru and Uruguay, the salary levels of primary teachers are the lowest in the WEI group (not including bonuses), between 1 836 and 6 281 PPP dollars. In Indonesia, low salaries are combined with a heavier than average teaching load (1 260 hours per year), which reduces salary costs per student by 111 PPP dollars, while in Peru and Uruguay, low salaries are counterbalanced by lower than average teaching loads.

In some countries, a lower than average teaching load is compensated by larger class sizes, while in other countries, smaller than average class sizes add to a light teaching load, increasing the salary costs per student.

In Thailand, Tunisia and Uruguay, annual teaching hours at both the primary and lower secondary level are relatively low (between 732 and 760 hours); as a result, more teachers are required to cover the total demand for teaching. This adds significantly to salary costs per student (at the primary level by between 48 PPP dollars in Thailand and 64 PPP dollars per student in Uruguay). In Uruguay, smaller than average class sizes add to this effect, whereas in Thailand and Tunisia larger class sizes compensate for the lower teaching load.

At the other end of the spectrum are Indonesia and the Philippines, where teachers are required to teach for more than 1 150 hours per year. This adds to the burden on teachers but releases resources for other purposes. In the Philippines, larger than average class sizes exacerbate the high teaching load.

In Chile, the Philippines, Thailand and Tunisia, larger class sizes reduce teachers' salary costs per student.

In Chile, the Philippines, Thailand and Tunisia, class sizes are comparatively high, above 30 students at the primary level and between 35 and 50 students at the lower secondary level. As a result, salary costs are reduced in all of these countries, in the case of Chile at the primary level by 78 PPP dollars and in the case of the Philippines at the lower secondary level by 153 PPP dollars. Resources are thus released for other purposes, including increasing the general salary level of teachers.

■ CONCLUSIONS

Rising enrolment rates, in some cases combined with an expanding population of school age, are increasing the demand for new teachers in many WEI countries, most significantly often in those with the lowest levels of economic development. This has significant implications not only for teacher training and recruitment but also for the financial resources which countries need to invest in education if they are to achieve universal education for all children of primary-school age and to increase, or merely to maintain, current enrolment rates in secondary education.

And yet, despite an increasing population of secondary-school age, the next few decades will provide a unique window of opportunity for many WEI countries to improve the quality of educational services. Because of demographic changes, which are already having an impact on the size of the cohorts of primary-school age, the proportion of people of working age will grow faster over the next few decades than that of children in many WEI countries. Before the declining ratio of children to active workers is eventually overtaken by the rising ratio of retired people to workers, countries will have an increased ability to mobilise resources for services including education, making it easier to fund better education systems. Policy makers can use this opportunity to shift the focus from expanding the coverage of the education system to improving the quality of educational provision and outcomes, including reducing the, in some WEI countries, still high proportion of over-age students, repeaters or late entrants enrolled in primary education.

To provide tomorrow's world with the knowledge and skills on which economic and social progress so critically depends, educational institutions will need to respond to change, and teachers will need to develop and deliver educational content in ways that meet the needs of tomorrow's citizens. The expectations on teachers are high and varied. They need to be experts in the field which is reflected, among other things, in the increasing level of academic qualifications required of them. The way in which teachers themselves access knowledge must also change, since they will need to update their expertise continually to respond to the changes in demands they face. Subject matter expertise must be complemented with pedagogical know-how, with a focus on the transmission of a range of high-level skills, including motivation to learn, creativity and co-operation. In some WEI countries, technology is beginning to become a new feature of professionalism in teaching, requiring an understanding of the pedagogical potential of technology and the ability to integrate it into the teaching-learning process. Finally, professionalism in teaching can also no longer be seen as an individual competence, but must include the ability to function as part of a "learning organisation" and the capacity and willingness to move in and out of other careers and experiences that can enrich teaching ability.

Educational policy-makers must ensure that the investment made in teachers is sufficient and proportionate to the demands placed upon them. This means both that the qualifications of the teaching force must be adequate and that the salaries and working conditions of teachers must be sufficiently competitive to attract people with the desired qualifications into the teaching profession.

This chapter has examined some of the challenges and policy choices that countries face in the striving for providing quality educational services for all.

Many countries seek to address these challenges through providing better and more advanced teacher training. In the same way as OECD countries, virtually all the WEI countries supplying data now train their prospective primary teachers at tertiary level, either in universities, other post-secondary non-university institutions or special teacher training institutes. However, in many WEI countries only a fraction of the existing teaching force meets the requirements that governments have set for new entrants to the profession, with discrepancies being most notable in those countries which have upgraded qualification requirements for teachers only recently. In many WEI countries, new qualification requirements will continue to place current tertiary education systems under some pressure.

Salaries and career prospects are, broadly speaking, the material incentives offered to teachers. The balance between what is required of teachers and what is offered to them has a significant impact on the composition of the teaching force and the quality of teaching. Attracting skilled individuals and retaining them in the teaching profession is an essential prerequisite for ensuring high-quality education in the future. While uniform salary scales are transparent and simple to administer, they do not help to motivate teachers to perform at their best, nor do they help to solve problems of shortages of teachers in certain subjects or in rural areas. Among the policy options that many WEI countries have not yet fully exploited are additional bonuses as a means of adjusting the remuneration of teachers without altering the basic government scales. Such adjustments may serve different aims, such as rewarding teachers who take on responsibilities or duties beyond statutory norms, attracting better candidates to the teaching profession, encouraging teachers to improve their performance, or attracting teachers into subject areas where demand is greater than supply, for example science and mathematics, or to rural locations where there is a scarcity of applicants.

At the same time, the payment of bonuses will have to be considered carefully and its impact evaluated from case to case since there is evidence that it may elicit responses from teachers that have an effect opposite to that which is intended, impairing school effectiveness and hence student achievement. For example, performance-based pay is intended to encourage teachers to work harder. However, performance-based pay schemes frequently place individual teachers in competition with each other; they may then be reluctant to share with their colleagues the new ideas and successful practices which they discover. They may also compete among themselves for the best classes, or may encourage slow learners to drop out of school. The examples for performance based pay that have been discussed in this chapter do, however, show that the challenges of designing effective salary schemes can be addressed.

Material incentives for teachers are not the only factors in the equation for improving the quality of education. If the working conditions for the teaching force and their associated costs are to be judged accurately, the various indicators discussed in this chapter need to be considered in combination rather than in isolation. In other words, when governments decide on their education budgets, they need to make trade-offs between factors such as the level of teachers' salaries, the size of classes, the number of teaching hours required of teachers and the intended instruction time for students.

Some countries seek to increase the competitiveness of teacher salaries and/ or to raise participation levels by increasing student-teaching staff ratios, sometimes in combination with the integration of new technologies in the teaching-learning process. However, while in some WEI countries this may be a viable option to improve the effectiveness of education systems, in other WEI countries student-teacher ratios already exceed 40 students per full-time equivalent teacher so that, in these countries at least, it will be difficult to respond to the increased demand for teachers by raising student-teaching staff ratios further without risking a deterioration in the quality of educational provision.

The chapter has illustrated that, even among countries with similar teachers' salary costs per student, there are different policy choices about other matters. Uruguay, for example, compensates small primary-level class sizes with a low number of hours of instruction. Thailand compensates a high number of hours of instruction with bigger class sizes. Argentina counterbalances high salaries with high teaching hours at the secondary level. In Chile and the Philippines, comparatively high statutory salaries for primary teachers are compensated by a high number of teaching hours or larger than average classes, while in Thailand high salaries are combined with large classes and/or light teaching loads. In some countries, a lower than average teaching load is compensated by larger class sizes, while in other countries, smaller than average class sizes add to a light teaching load, increasing the salary costs per student. Finally, in Brazil, Chile, Malaysia, Peru, the Philippines, Thailand and Tunisia, larger than average class sizes reduce teachers' salary costs per student.

These examples illustrate that there are a number of different "models" of how instruction is organised and what elements of instruction are to be emphasised. The question of which model is better is a natural one, but not entirely appropriate. Each education system is a working system, which to a greater or lesser degree has satisfied the requirements of its society. The different "models" discussed in this chapter represent a long history of decisions taken nationally and are subject to a certain inertia that makes it difficult to introduce substantial changes overnight, if for no other reason than that some features of the system are often subject to negotiation in the framework of collective bargaining agreements. The success of a "model" may also depend on less quantifiable characteristics of the education system, such as the teaching methods used or the extent of remedial help available. The interplay between, for example, class size and teaching methods is far from clear. Small classes may mean that more attention to individual students is possible, but in the absence of curriculum reform or of a change in teaching practices, for example, the expected benefits may not be forthcoming.

While it is difficult to assess the effectiveness of the different "models", the analysis has shown that there is room for policy choices and that international comparative analysis can be a useful instrument for informing the debate. To advance the debate and to determine which choices lead to optimal returns on educational investments, it will be important to link the structural features of education systems to the learning outcomes they produce. This remains one of the most important objectives for the future of the WEI programme. The OECD Programme for International Student Assessment (PISA), through which OECD countries and many WEI countries seek to monitor the outcomes of education systems on a regular basis and within a common international framework, is one of the efforts that may contribute to this goal and assist policy-makers in the preparation of young people for adult life at a time of rapid change and increasing global interdependence.

REFERENCES

Hanushek, E. A. (1998), "The evidence of class size", Occasional Paper No. 98-1, W. Allen Wallis Institute of Political Economy, University of Rochester, Rochester, NY.

ILO (1996), "Impact of structural adjustment on the employment and training of teachers", Joint Meeting on the Impact of Structural Adjustment on Educational Personnel, Geneva.

ILO (2000), *Lifelong Learning in the Twenty-first Century. The changing role of educational personnel*, Geneva.

OECD (1998*a*), *Education Policy Analysis*, Paris.

OECD (1998*b*), *Staying Ahead: In-service training and teacher professional development*, "What Works in Innovation in Education" series, Paris.

OECD (1999), *OECD Annual Data Collection on Education Statistics*, Paris.

OECD (2000*a*), *Investing in Education*, Paris.

OECD (2000*b*), *Education at a Glance – OECD Indicators 2000*, Paris.

OECD (2001*a*), *Education at a Glance – OECD Indicators 2001*, Paris.

OECD (2001*b*), *Education Policy Analysis*, Paris.

UNESCO (1996), "Strengthening the role of teachers in a changing world: Issues, prospects and priorities", International Conference on Education, Forty-fifth session, Geneva.

UNESCO (1998*a*), *World Education Report. Teachers and Teaching in a Changing World*, Paris.

UNESCO (1998*b*), *Wasted Opportunities: When school fails*, UNESCO EFA Forum Secretariat, Paris.

UNESCO (1999), *Statistical Yearbook 1999*, Paris.

Siniscalco, M. T. (2000), *Achieving Education for All: Demographic Challenges*, UNESCO, Paris.

United Nations (1999), *Population Growth and Demographic Structure*, Department of Economic and Social Affairs, Population Division, New York.

Chapter 3

COUNTRY PROFILES

Prepared by Andreas Schleicher, Michael Bruneforth,
Maria Teresa Siniscalco and Karine Tremblay
(OECD)
in co-operation with country representatives mentioned in the text

ARGENTINA

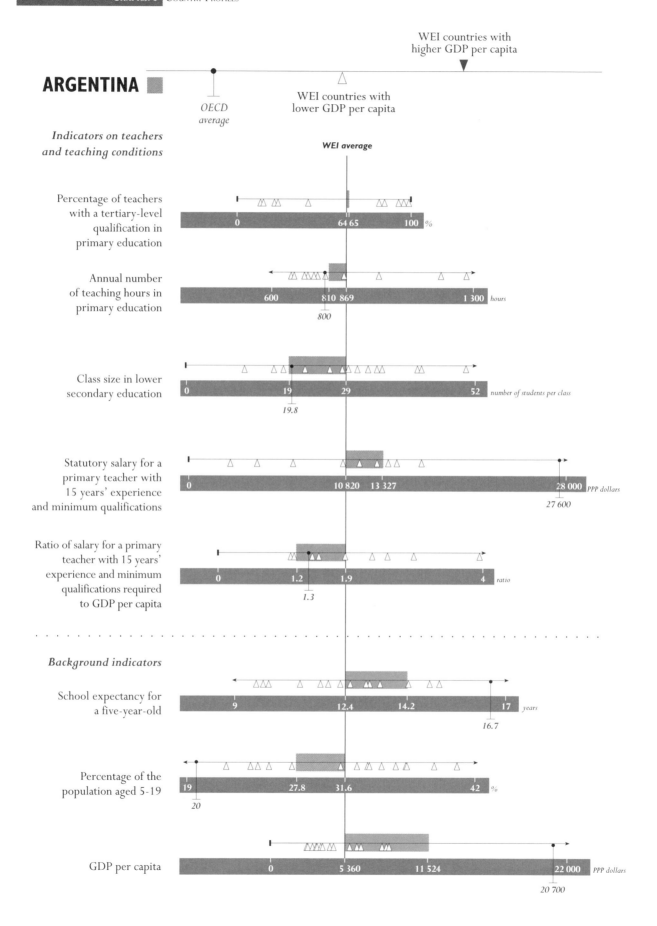

WEI countries with
higher GDP per capita

OECD average

WEI countries with
lower GDP per capita

*Indicators on teachers
and teaching conditions*

WEI average

Percentage of teachers
with a tertiary-level
qualification in
primary education

0   64 65   100 %

Annual number
of teaching hours in
primary education

600   810 869   1 300 hours

800

Class size in lower
secondary education

0   19   29   52 number of students per class

19.8

Statutory salary for a
primary teacher with
15 years' experience
and minimum qualifications

0   10 820   13 327   28 000 PPP dollars

27 600

Ratio of salary for a primary
teacher with 15 years'
experience and minimum
qualifications required
to GDP per capita

0   1.2   1.9   4 ratio

1.3

Background indicators

School expectancy for
a five-year-old

9   12.4   14.2   17 years

16.7

Percentage of the
population aged 5-19

19   27.8   31.6   42 %

20

GDP per capita

0   5 360   11 524   22 000 PPP dollars

20 700

ARGENTINA

*Prepared in co-operation between the OECD, UNESCO
and the Instituto para el Desarrollo de la Calidad Educativa (IDECE)*

In comparison with the situation in other WEI countries, economic and demographic conditions in Argentina should favour further educational improvement. GDP per capita, 11 524 PPP dollars, is about twice the WEI average and higher than that of some OECD countries. Argentina also has the fifth lowest school-age population ratio among WEI countries, with only 28 per cent of the total population in the age group 5 to 19 years. This means that investment in education translates into relatively high expenditure per student.

An Argentinian five-year-old child can currently expect 14.2 years of schooling (all levels of education combined), which is 1.5 years above the WEI average and only 2.5 years below the OECD average.

Teaching conditions in Argentina, as measured by the WEI indicators, are comparatively favourable. The average class size in lower secondary education is the third lowest among the WEI countries, 19 students per class. This is well below the WEI average of 29 students per lower secondary class and comparable to average class sizes in OECD countries. The teaching load in Argentinian primary education, 810 hours per year, is roughly comparable to the OECD average and well below the WEI average.

However, the indicators also reveal some significant challenges facing the Argentinian education system. There is still a wide discrepancy between current qualification requirements for new teachers and the qualifications of the existing teaching staff, with only 65 per cent of the teaching force at the primary level holding a tertiary-level qualification, the fifth lowest proportion among the WEI countries. This relatively low ratio of tertiary training is partly a result of the extension of compulsory education from seven to ten years and the subsequent increase in enrolments at the higher levels of education, which has tended to divert the most highly qualified teachers away from the lower levels of education.

The low level of teachers' qualifications is matched by comparatively low salaries. Statutory salaries, despite being relatively high in absolute terms in comparison with other WEI countries (13 327 PPP dollars including bonuses), are among the lowest in relation to GDP per capita. While Argentinian primary teachers receive statutory salaries that are only 1.2 times GDP per capita, the WEI average is 1.9 times GDP per capita.

For data see Annex A.4.

WEI countries with
higher GDP per capita

BRAZIL

*OECD
average*

WEI countries with
lower GDP per capita

*Indicators on teachers
and teaching conditions*

WEI average

Percentage of teachers
with a tertiary-level
qualification in
primary education

0   22   64   100   %

Annual number
of teaching hours in
primary education

600   800   869   1 300   *hours*

800

Class size in lower
secondary education

0   29   35   52   *number of students per class*

19.8

Statutory salary for a
primary teacher with
15 years' experience
and minimum qualifications

0   7 191   10 820   28 000   *PPP dollars*

27 600

Ratio of salary for a primary
teacher with 15 years'
experience and minimum
qualifications required
to GDP per capita

0   1.1   1.9   4   *ratio*

1.3

Background indicators

School expectancy for
a five-year-old

9   12.4   14.9   17   *years*

16.7

Percentage of the
population aged 5-19

19   31.6   32.6   42   *%*

20

GDP per capita

0   5 360   6 524   22 000   *PPP dollars*

20 700

BRAZIL

Prepared in co-operation between the OECD, UNESCO, Ivan Castro DE ALMEIDA
and Maria Helena GUIMARAES DE CASTRO

Brazil underwent striking demographic changes during the last quarter of the 20th century. The annual rate of population growth halved during this period, with the result that the school-age population is expected to decline over the period 2000 to 2010 by 3 percentage points in the age group 5 to 14 years and by 8 percentage points in the age group 15 to 19 years. Brazil should thus see its school-age population, at 33 per cent currently above the WEI average, decrease in the medium term. In the meantime, with GDP per capita at 6 524 PPP dollars, Brazil has a comparatively high level of national income at its disposal to respond to the above-average demand for education.

The decrease in the number of children, coupled with policies aimed at improving enrolment rates, has led to a significant increase in school expectancy: A Brazilian five-year-old child can expect an average of 14.9 years of schooling (all levels of education combined), well above the WEI average (12.7 years) and only 1.5 years below the OECD average. However, high levels of enrolment are accompanied by very high rates of repetition – 25 per cent at the primary level, and 15 and 18 per cent at the lower and upper secondary levels, respectively.

One challenge facing the Brazilian education system is the comparatively low level of qualifications among the teaching force. Fewer than 22 per cent of primary teachers hold a tertiary qualification, the third lowest rate among the WEI countries and well below the WEI average of 64 per cent. The situation looks somewhat better at the secondary levels, with 76 per cent of lower secondary teachers and 89 per cent of upper secondary teachers holding a tertiary-level qualification.

Brazilian teachers face comparatively demanding working conditions. The average class size, 35 students, is high compared with the averages of 32 in the WEI countries and 20 in the OECD countries. The teaching load, despite being at the OECD average level (800 hours per year), is the fifth highest among the WEI countries.

Teachers' salaries in Brazil are among the lowest in the WEI group, both in absolute terms and relative to GDP per capita. In absolute terms, primary teachers' salaries after 15 years' experience, 7 191 PPP dollars, are two thirds of the WEI average and only a quarter of the OECD average. Similarly, the average salary after 15 years' experience is only 1.1 times GDP per capita, just over half of the WEI average (1.9 times GDP per capita), and close to the ratio of 1.3 in the OECD countries.

For data see Annex A.4.

WEI countries with
higher GDP per capita

CHILE

*OECD
average*

WEI countries with
lower GDP per capita

*Indicators on teachers
and teaching conditions*

WEI average

Percentage of teachers
with a tertiary-level
qualification in
primary education

0   64   94 100 %

Annual number
of teaching hours in
primary education

600   860 869   1 300 *hours*

800

Class size in lower
secondary education

0   29   35   52 *number of students per class*

19.8

Statutory salary for a
primary teacher with
15 years' experience
and minimum qualifications

0   10 820   15 868   28 000 *PPP dollars*

27 600

Ratio of salary for a primary
teacher with 15 years'
experience and minimum
qualifications required
to GDP per capita

0   1.8 1.9   4 *ratio*

1.3

Background indicators

School expectancy for
a five-year-old

9   12.4   14.3   17 *years*

16.7

Percentage of the
population aged 5-19

19   27.5   31.6   42 *%*

20

GDP per capita

0   5 360   8 612   22 000 *PPP dollars*

20 700

CHILE

Prepared in co-operation between the OECD, UNESCO, Paula DARVILLE and Vivian HEYL

Chile has the second highest GDP per capita (8 765 PPP dollars) among the WEI countries and a below-average proportion of the population of school age (5 to 19 years): 27 per cent. Given this comparatively favourable situation of demand and available national income, it is not surprising that participation rates, expressed in school expectancy, are above the WEI average. However, at 14.3 years, school expectancy in Chile is still two years below the OECD average and also lower than those of three WEI countries with lower GDP per capita. Furthermore, school expectancy does not provide a measure of the quality of educational provision, and it should be noted that the mathematics achievement of students at the 8th-grade level in Chile is lower than that in OECD and WEI countries with comparable data, except the Philippines and Indonesia.

The Chilean teaching force has a high level of pre-service training. Over 90 per cent of all teachers at primary to upper secondary levels hold a tertiary qualification. New teachers are required to possess a tertiary-type A degree. Special emphasis is given to pedagogical studies, particularly for primary and lower secondary teachers. In fact, four out of 4.5 years of tertiary studies for teachers are devoted to pedagogical studies and teaching practice, far more than in any other WEI and OECD country.

Teaching conditions in Chile are characterised by a combination of comparatively high salaries, average teaching hours and above-average class sizes. The underlying determinants are comparatively high student-teacher ratios, combined with an above-average number of hours of instruction. These factors result in class sizes of around 35 in lower secondary education, well above the OECD average of 19.8. Only three WEI countries show higher class sizes.

Salaries are uniform for primary and secondary teachers. After 15 years' experience, the average teacher's salary is 15 868 PPP dollars (including bonuses), the highest among the WEI countries. However, this needs to be seen in the context of a high level of national income. The statutory salary after 15 years' experience is no higher than the WEI average, 1.9 times GDP per capita.

Merit awards for teachers can form a significant element of teachers' salaries in Chile, however, accounting for increases of up to 51 per cent over the basic salary. The national system of performance evaluation for public schools (SNED) provides merit awards for teachers on the basis of the school's performance on an index of achievement. This index chiefly includes test scores obtained in Spanish and mathematics, but takes account of improvements since previous tests. An annual award scheme has also been introduced for outstanding teachers. Finally, there is a hardship allowance for teachers in schools with particular difficulties, such as remote locations, an unsafe environment, or a particularly high proportion of students with social problems.

For data see Annex A.4.

CHINA

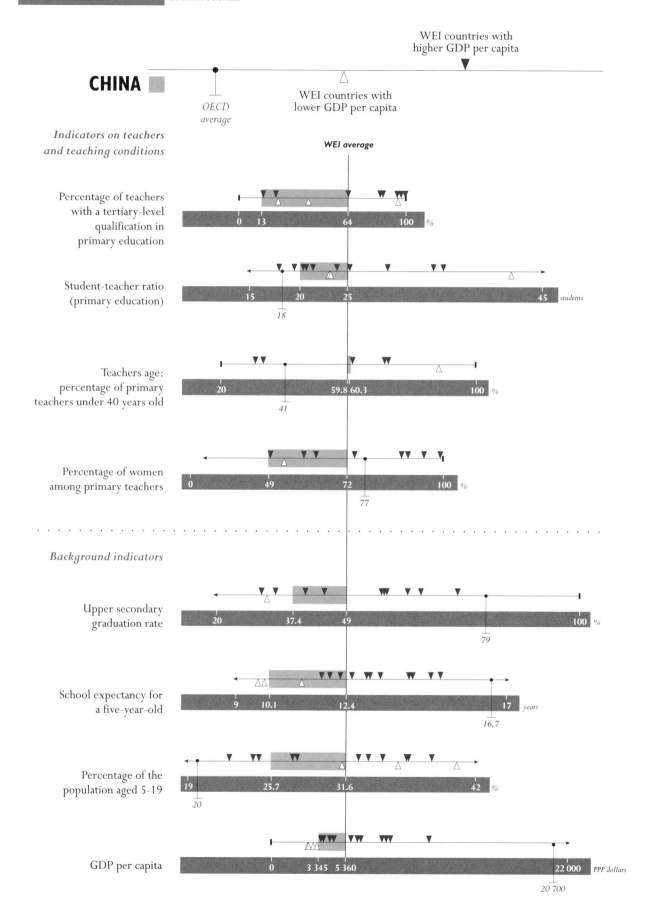

WEI countries with
higher GDP per capita

OECD average

WEI countries with
lower GDP per capita

*Indicators on teachers
and teaching conditions*

WEI average

Percentage of teachers
with a tertiary-level
qualification in
primary education

0   13   64   100 %

Student-teacher ratio
(primary education)

15   20   25   45 students

18

Teachers age:
percentage of primary
teachers under 40 years old

20   59.8 60.3   100 %

41

Percentage of women
among primary teachers

0   49   72   100 %

77

Background indicators

Upper secondary
graduation rate

20   37.4   49   100 %

79

School expectancy for
a five-year-old

9 10.1   12.4   17 years

16.7

Percentage of the
population aged 5-19

19   25.7   31.6   42 %

20

GDP per capita

0   3 345 5 360   22 000 PPP dollars

20 700

CHINA

Prepared in co-operation between the OECD, UNESCO and Zhi Hua LIN

Despite a comparatively low level of national income (GDP per capita is 3 345 PPP dollars, about 40 per cent below the WEI average), China has shown the fastest economic growth of all WEI countries, with an annual growth rate of 7.8 per cent in 1998. At the same time, China's school-age population ranks third lowest among WEI countries, only 26 per cent of the total population being in the age group 5 to 19 years. The number of children of primary-school age is expected to decrease by a further 15 per cent in the next decade.

Rising national income, together with declining demographic demand, will provide an opportunity to improve access to education at the secondary levels of education. Currently, a Chinese five-year-old child can only expect 10.1 years of schooling (all levels of education combined), and gross entry rates in secondary education are the second lowest among the WEI countries. In China, only 80 per cent of an age cohort move on to lower secondary education, 43 per cent enter upper secondary programmes, and as few as 13 per cent reach the tertiary level of education.

At the same time, China's education system shows a high degree of internal efficiency, with very low grade repetition rates (0.8 per cent at the primary level and 0.1 per cent at the lower secondary level), and a graduation rate in upper secondary education, 37 per cent, that is very close to the entry rate of 43 per cent. It should also be noted that 56.6 per cent of secondary students are enrolled in vocational programmes, making China's education system the second most vocationally oriented among the WEI countries, after that of Egypt.

Currently, only 12.8 per cent of primary teachers, and just over half of lower secondary teachers, hold a tertiary qualification. However, upper secondary teachers almost all have a tertiary qualification. In the WEI and OECD group, China is the only country with a majority of male primary and lower secondary teachers. This current gender balance appears to be changing, however, women being in the majority among younger teachers. A high proportion of teachers are below 30 years of age, one third at the primary level and almost half at the lower secondary level.

For data see Annex A.4.

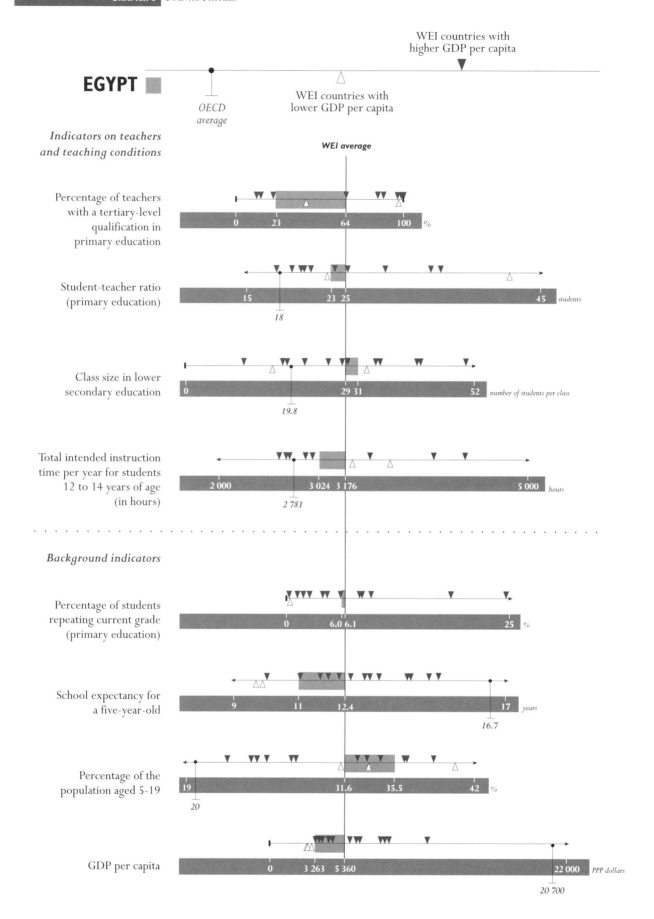

WEI countries with
higher GDP per capita

EGYPT

OECD average

WEI countries with
lower GDP per capita

Indicators on teachers and teaching conditions

WEI average

Percentage of teachers
with a tertiary-level
qualification in
primary education

0   23   64   100   %

Student-teacher ratio
(primary education)

15   23 25   45   *students*

18

Class size in lower
secondary education

0   29 31   52   *number of students per class*

19.8

Total intended instruction
time per year for students
12 to 14 years of age
(in hours)

2 000   3 024 3 176   5 000   *hours*

2 781

Background indicators

Percentage of students
repeating current grade
(primary education)

0   6.0 6.1   25   *%*

School expectancy for
a five-year-old

9   11   12.4   17   *years*

16.7

Percentage of the
population aged 5-19

19   31.6   35.5   42   *%*

20

GDP per capita

0   3 263 5 360   22 000   *PPP dollars*

20 700

EGYPT

Prepared in co-operation between the OECD, UNESCO and Mohamed Abdul Salam RAGHEB

A comparatively low level of national income (3 263 PPP dollars, about 42 per cent lower than the WEI average), coupled with an above-average school age population (36 per cent of the total population being in the age group 5 to 19 years), represents a challenging economic and demographic environment for educational improvement. However, the school-age population is expected to stabilise in the coming years in the age range 5 to 14, and to increase only slightly, by 3 per cent, in the age group 15 to 19 years. As a result, Egypt's recent efforts to expand educational access and participation should allow school expectancy for five-year-old children to rise from its current level of 11 years, which is 1.7 years below the WEI average and 5.7 years below the OECD average.

A major challenge ahead for Egypt is to enhance the training of its primary teachers, fewer than a quarter of whom currently hold a tertiary qualification (the WEI average being 64 per cent). This issue is already being addressed: an extensive in-service training programme was introduced during 1999 and 2000, mainly by means of distance learning, with the aim of updating the pedagogical skills of teachers and introducing them to the use of technologies in the classroom.

The internal efficiency of the education system rises markedly with the level of education. Repetition rates drop from 9.7 per cent at the lower secondary level to 3.5 per cent at the upper secondary level.

The vocational orientation of Egypt's upper secondary education also affects the qualifications structure of the teaching force. A higher proportion of Egyptian teachers have a tertiary qualification at the lower secondary level (89 per cent) than at the upper secondary level (76.3 per cent). Disaggregation by programme orientation shows that in upper secondary general programmes, 97.4 per cent of teachers possess a tertiary qualification, whereas this rate drops to 64.8 per cent in pre-vocational and vocational programmes.

Primary teachers have a teaching load of 965 hours per year. This is higher than both the WEI average and the required hours of teaching for secondary teachers. The average class size at the primary level, 22.3 students, is comparatively low, but this national average hides considerable variations between areas of the country and between subjects. Secondary teachers have a smaller teaching load (724 hours per year) but larger classes, 31.2 students on average.

For data see Annex A.4.

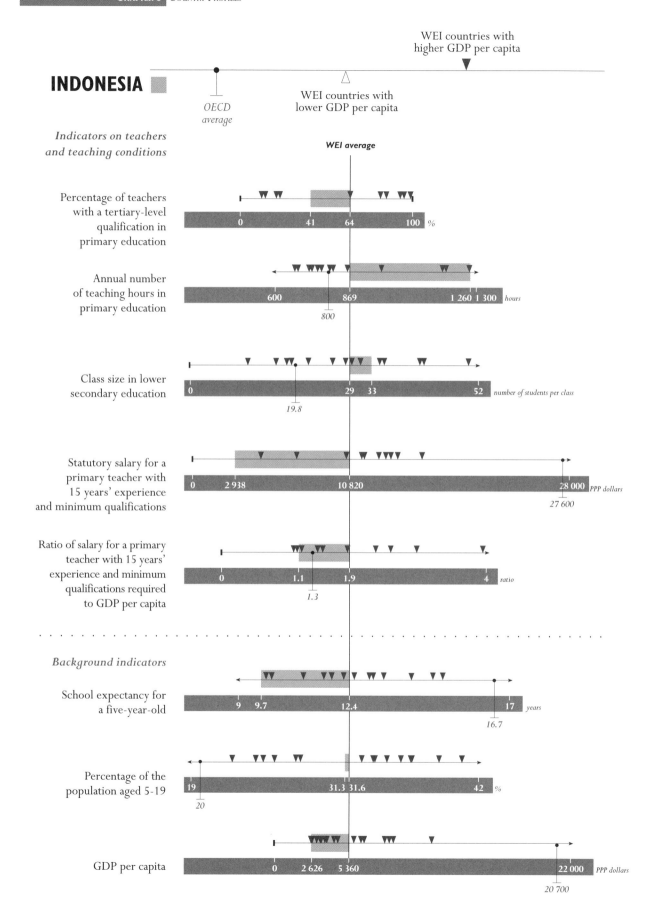

INDONESIA

WEI countries with
higher GDP per capita

OECD average

WEI countries with
lower GDP per capita

*Indicators on teachers
and teaching conditions*

WEI average

Percentage of teachers
with a tertiary-level
qualification in
primary education

0   41   64   100   *%*

Annual number
of teaching hours in
primary education

600   869   1 260   1 300   *hours*

800

Class size in lower
secondary education

0   29   33   52   *number of students per class*

19.8

Statutory salary for a
primary teacher with
15 years' experience
and minimum qualifications

0   2 938   10 820   28 000   *PPP dollars*

27 600

Ratio of salary for a primary
teacher with 15 years'
experience and minimum
qualifications required
to GDP per capita

0   1.1   1.9   4   *ratio*

1.3

Background indicators

School expectancy for
a five-year-old

9   9.7   12.4   17   *years*

16.7

Percentage of the
population aged 5-19

19   31.3   31.6   42   *%*

20

GDP per capita

0   2 626   5 360   22 000   *PPP dollars*

20 700

INDONESIA

Prepared in co-operation between the OECD, UNESCO and Ade CAHYANA

After a phase of steadily declining population growth in Indonesia between 1970 and 2000, the proportion of the population at the age of primary and lower secondary education has now reached the WEI average. However, while decreasing demographic pressure opens up opportunities to improve the education system, financial resources remain limited. The Asian economic crisis and the ensuing political instability in the country contributed to a decline in GDP per capita between 1997 and 1999 from 3 091 to 2 626 PPP dollars, one of the lowest among the WEI countries.

The most pressing issue is to widen access to education. School expectancy is the lowest among all WEI and OECD countries. A five-year-old child can expect to enrol in formal education for only 9.7 years, three years less than the WEI average. Besides this, mathematics achievement, as measured in the TIMSS 1999 assessment, is comparatively low (403 points), although still higher than in Chile and the Philippines.

At the primary level of education, the percentage of teachers holding a tertiary qualification in Indonesia, 41 per cent, is below the WEI average of 64 per cent. By contrast, virtually all secondary teachers hold a tertiary qualification. Furthermore, all new teachers at the primary level are now required to hold a tertiary-level qualification (ISCED 5A or 5B), earned after a three or four-year programme provided by a teacher training institute and including subject-matter instruction, pedagogical instruction and six months of teaching practice.

Teachers' salaries, which were already relatively low before the 1997 economic crisis, have dropped further in recent years. With annual statutory mid-career salaries (including bonuses) of 2 938 PPP dollars in primary and lower secondary education, and 3 537 PPP dollars in upper secondary education, Indonesian teachers' salaries are the lowest among the WEI countries. Starting salaries show an even wider gap. Teachers' salaries are also low when compared with national income, teachers with 15 years' experience being paid the equivalent of 1.1 times GDP per capita.

Whereas salaries are relatively uniform across the levels of education, the working conditions of primary and secondary teachers differ markedly. While the workload of primary teachers (1 260 hours per year) is by far the highest among the WEI and OECD countries, it is below the WEI average in the case of secondary teachers (738 hours per year). On the other hand, primary teachers teach classes that are one third smaller than those of their lower secondary colleagues (class sizes at the lower secondary level being around the WEI average).

The Indonesian teaching force is very young compared with those of most WEI and OECD countries. Fifty-two per cent of primary-school teachers are younger than 30 years of age, and 85 per cent are under 40 years of age. The situation is similar at the secondary level.

For data see Annex A.4.

JORDAN

WEI countries with
higher GDP per capita

*OECD
average*

WEI countries with
lower GDP per capita

*Indicators on teachers
and teaching conditions*

WEI average

Percentage of teachers
with a tertiary-level
qualification in
primary education

0   64   99 100 %

Annual number
of teaching hours in
primary education

600   745   869   1 300 *hours*

800

Class size in lower
secondary education

0   22   29   52 *number of students per class*

19.8

Statutory salary for a
primary teacher with
15 years' experience
and minimum qualifications

0   10 652 10 820   28 000 *PPP dollars*

27 600

Ratio of salary for a primary
teacher with 15 years'
experience and minimum
qualifications required
to GDP per capita

0   1.9   2.9   4 *ratio*

1.3

Background indicators

School expectancy for
a five-year-old

9   11.6 12.4   17 *years*

16.7

Percentage of the
population aged 5-19

19   31.6   38.5   42 %

20

GDP per capita

0   3 714 5 360   22 000 *PPP dollars*

20 700

JORDAN

Prepared in co-operation between the OECD, UNESCO, Jehad Jamil Abu EL-SHAAR and Maen MUHAISIN

Jordan faces a sharply rising demographic demand for education. An already high proportion of school-age children (38.5 per cent of the total population are in the age group 5 to 19 years) is expected to increase by more than 25 per cent, with a significant impact at both the primary (+26 per cent) and secondary (+28 per cent) levels of education. At the same time national income, 3 714 PPP dollars, is 33 per cent below the WEI average.

A Jordanian five-year-old child can expect 11.6 years of schooling (all levels of education combined), one year below the WEI average. Jordan provides comparatively good learning conditions, with a qualified teaching force and relatively small classes. More than 99 per cent of primary and lower secondary teachers hold a tertiary qualification, more than in many other WEI countries with higher GDP per capita. An average of 22 students per class at the lower secondary level takes Jordan closer to the OECD average (20) than to the WEI average (32).

Besides teaching small classes, Jordanian teachers have the fourth lowest workload among WEI countries, 745 teaching hours per year at all levels, significantly below the OECD (800 hours) and WEI (869 hours) averages.

Teachers' salaries are close to the WEI average (10 800 PPP dollars) at the primary level, but 19 to 25 per cent below the WEI average at the secondary level. However, Jordanian teachers' salaries compare well in terms of GDP per capita, being 2.9 times average GDP per capita, more than in most WEI countries.

Teachers' salaries are uniform across levels of education in Jordan, averaging 10 652 PPP dollars. They increase with experience, but not with level of qualifications, although qualifications can still speed up the promotion process. For example, a Master's degree allows a teacher to reach the top of the scale two years earlier than a teacher holding only the minimum Bachelor's degree.

For data see Annex A.4.

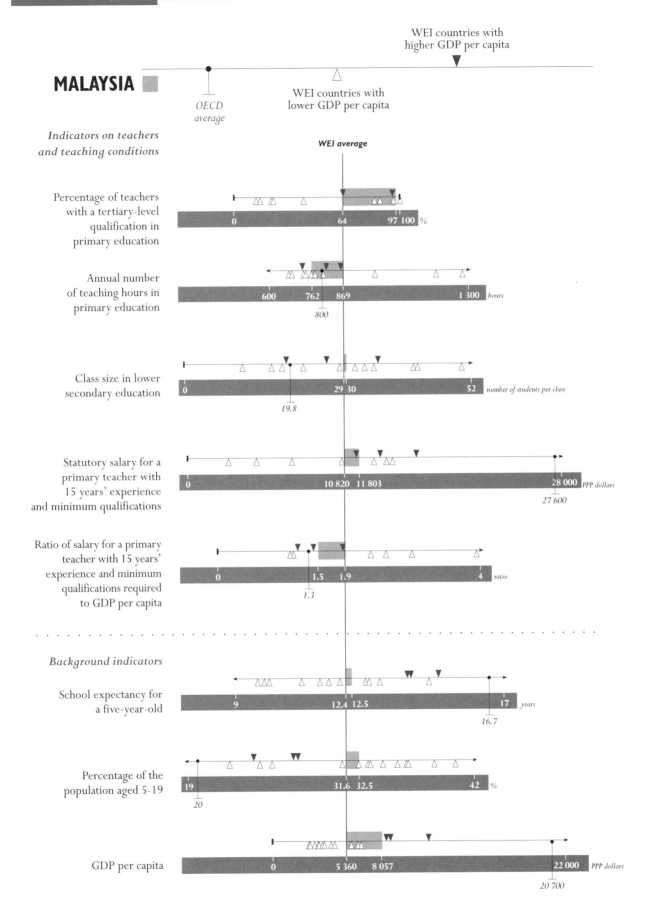

WEI countries with
higher GDP per capita

MALAYSIA

WEI countries with
lower GDP per capita

*OECD
average*

*Indicators on teachers
and teaching conditions*

WEI average

Percentage of teachers
with a tertiary-level
qualification in
primary education

0   64   97 100 %

Annual number
of teaching hours in
primary education

600   762 869   1 300 *hours*

800

Class size in lower
secondary education

0   29 30   52 *number of students per class*

19.8

Statutory salary for a
primary teacher with
15 years' experience
and minimum qualifications

0   10 820 11 803   28 000 *PPP dollars*

27 600

Ratio of salary for a primary
teacher with 15 years'
experience and minimum
qualifications required
to GDP per capita

0   1.5 1.9   4 *ratio*

1.3

Background indicators

School expectancy for
a five-year-old

9   12.4 12.5   17 *years*

16.7

Percentage of the
population aged 5-19

19   31.6 32.5   42 %

20

GDP per capita

0   5 360 8 057   22 000 *PPP dollars*

20 700

MALAYSIA

Prepared in co-operation between the OECD, UNESCO and Khalijah MOHAMMAD

With GDP per capita 45 per cent above the WEI average (8 057 PPP dollars), Malaysia has the financial resources to respond to rising demand for education, much of which is due to demographic growth. An already above-average proportion of school-age children in the population is expected to increase sharply. The number of children at the age of upper secondary schooling, for example, is expected to rise in the next ten years by 19 per cent.

A five-year-old child can expect to be enrolled in schooling for 12.5 years, just below the WEI average. At the same time, the achievement of 8th-grade students in mathematics is higher than the TIMSS 1999 international average (519 points compared with the average score of 487 points), with Malaysia outperforming all but one of the WEI countries that participated in the TIMSS 1999 study.

Almost all Malaysian teachers have received a tertiary-level education. At the primary level, 97 per cent of the existing teaching force hold a tertiary-type B qualification, and 96 per cent of teachers in lower and upper secondary education are university-level graduates.

With a teaching load of between 762 teaching hours per year at the primary level and 778 hours at the secondary level, Malaysian teachers not only teach fewer hours than the WEI average, but also fewer than the OECD average. Class sizes of between 28 and 30 students are just above the WEI average in primary education and below the WEI average at the lower secondary level. Although they are higher than the OECD average, they are much lower than those in Korea, one of the two Asian OECD countries.

There are significant differences in teachers' salaries between the primary and secondary levels of education. While the average salary for Malaysian primary teachers, 11 803 PPP dollars (including bonuses), is just above the WEI average, their lower and upper secondary colleagues earn almost twice as much, 21 568 PPP dollars, the second highest salary for upper secondary teachers among the WEI countries. Measures aimed at enhancing teachers' status and motivation include the revision of remuneration and promotion schemes, appropriate allowances and facilities for teachers teaching specific subjects and for those working in remote areas, and rewards for outstanding performance (up to 7 per cent). The policy emphasis on rural schools results in more incentives being provided to teachers serving in rural and remote areas.

The teaching profession in Malaysia is becoming more and more a female domain. While older cohorts of teachers are predominately male, the gender pattern has changed over time, and 70 per cent of younger teachers and of those newly appointed are now female.

For data see Annex A.4.

WEI countries with
higher GDP per capita

PARAGUAY

OECD average

WEI countries with
lower GDP per capita

WEI average

*Indicators on teachers
and teaching conditions*

Educational personnel
as percentage of the
labour force (primary and
secondary education)

0   4.1 4.5   9   %

4.6

Annual number
of teaching hours
in primary education

600 696 869   1 300 *hours*

800

Class size in lower
secondary education

0   12   29   52   *number of students per class*

19.8

Total intended instruction
time per year for students
12 to 14 years of age
(in hours)

2 000 2 736 3 271   5 000 *hours*

2 781

Background indicators

Percentage of students
repeating current grade
(primary education)

0   6.1 8.6   25   %

School expectancy for
a five-year-old

9   11 12.4   17   *years*

16.7

Percentage of the
population aged 5-19

19   31.6 36.4 42   %

20

GDP per capita

0   4 249 5 360   22 000 *PPP dollars*

20 700

PARAGUAY

Prepared in co-operation between the OECD, UNESCO, Hilda GONZALEZ GARCETE and Dalila Noemi ZARZA PAREDES

The demographic demand for education in Paraguay is considerable. The proportion of 5 to 19 year-olds in the total population, 36 per cent, is already the third highest among WEI and OECD countries and is expected to rise by a further 14 per cent by 2010. Changes in demand will be most significant at the upper secondary level, where the relevant age cohort is expected to increase by 21 per cent. These figures represent the second highest growth rate among the WEI countries. With GDP per capita of 4 337 PPP dollars, the national resources available to respond to rising demand are limited.

A five-year-old can expect to be enrolled for only 11 years in formal education. Furthermore, Paraguay has the lowest upper secondary graduation rate among the WEI and OECD countries. Besides participation rates, hours of instruction are also comparatively low. According to the curriculum, children aged 9-11 years (in primary education) receive just 660 hours of instruction per year, the second lowest total among the WEI countries. This is due to a double shift system, whereby students are enrolled for only four hours per day at the primary level. The hours of instruction increase at the lower secondary level, but remain well below the WEI average.

Primary teachers in Paraguay have the second lowest number of statutory teaching hours among the WEI countries, 696 hours per year, over 100 hundred hours less than the WEI average. However, this low teaching load does not fully reflect reality since most primary teachers hold two positions within the double shift system, thus doubling their teaching hours. One implication of this double shift system is that the teaching load in Paraguay increases with the level of education, contrary to the pattern in the majority of WEI countries. Lower secondary teachers are required to teach 774 hours per year, between the OECD and WEI averages, while upper secondary teachers are required to teach 870 hours, 50 hours more than the WEI average.

The comparatively low teaching load is matched by comparatively low student-teacher ratios, 19.7 at the primary level and 9.9 at the secondary level. At the lower secondary level, this ratio is the lowest among the WEI countries and lower than in all but two OECD countries. Average class sizes in primary education are estimated at 19.7, and in lower secondary at 11.7, by far the smallest among the WEI countries.

Given the rapid growth in the student population and the extensive use of the existing teaching force and infrastructure (due to the double shift system), it is likely that the extension of compulsory education from six to nine years will result in an even more acute shortage of teachers in the future.

For data see Annex A.4.

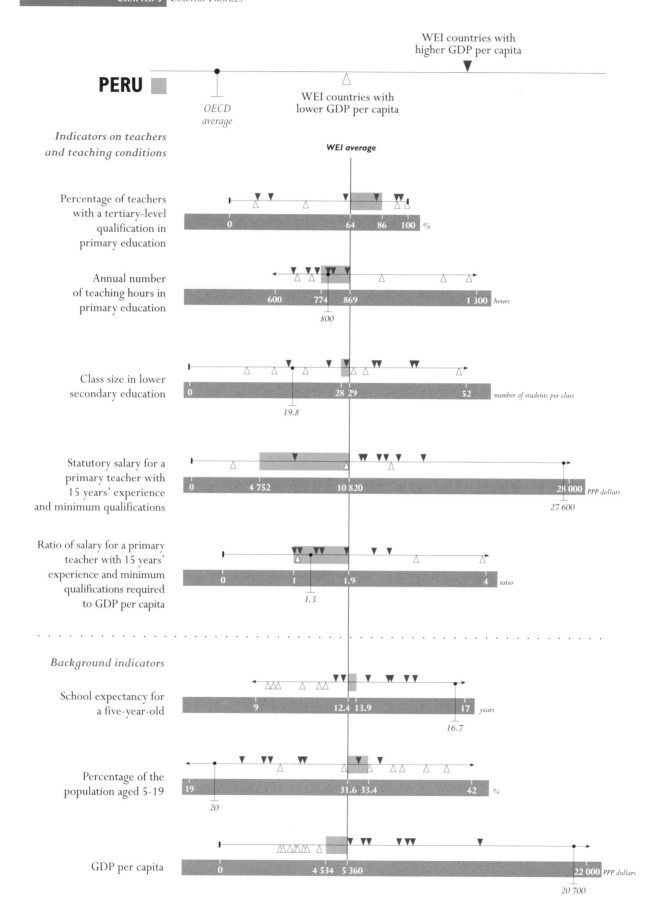

PERU

WEI countries with higher GDP per capita

OECD average

WEI countries with lower GDP per capita

Indicators on teachers and teaching conditions

WEI average

Percentage of teachers with a tertiary-level qualification in primary education

0   64   86   100 %

Annual number of teaching hours in primary education

600   774 869   1 300 hours

800

Class size in lower secondary education

0   28 29   52 number of students per class

19.8

Statutory salary for a primary teacher with 15 years' experience and minimum qualifications

0   4 752   10 820   28 000 PPP dollars

27 600

Ratio of salary for a primary teacher with 15 years' experience and minimum qualifications required to GDP per capita

0   1   1.9   4 ratio

1.3

Background indicators

School expectancy for a five-year-old

9   12.4 13.9   17 years

16.7

Percentage of the population aged 5-19

19   31.6 33.4   42 %

20

GDP per capita

0   4 534 5 360   22 000 PPP dollars

20 700

PERU

Prepared in co-operation between the OECD, UNESCO, José RODRIGUEZ and
Gloria María ZAMBRANO ROZAS

With GDP per capita at 4 534 PPP dollars, and 33 per cent of the population in the age group 5 to 19 years, Peru has limited resources to respond to higher than average demand for education. Nevertheless, school expectancy is above the WEI average. A Peruvian five-year-old child can expect to stay enrolled in education for 13.9 years, longer than in any other WEI country with similar or lower GDP per capita, and longer than in two other countries with higher per capita resources.

The Peruvian primary-level teaching force is among the best educated among the WEI countries, with 84.7 per cent of all primary teachers holding a tertiary qualification. Lower secondary and upper secondary teachers have equally high levels of education. Besides a comparatively high level of formal education, more than three out of four primary teachers have received teacher training. The proportion of teachers without tertiary education or teacher training is expected to diminish further in the future, since five years of tertiary education, including at least 1.1 years of teaching practice, are now a requirement for entry into the teaching force at the primary level of education.

Teachers at the primary level work significantly fewer hours per year than the WEI average (774 teaching hours per year compared with an average of 869 teaching hours). Teaching hours are even lower than in most countries with higher GDP per capita. Class sizes are also smaller than in most WEI countries, with an average of 28.5 students per lower secondary class.

Primary and secondary teachers make up 3.8 per cent of the total labour force, a larger proportion than in other countries with similar school-age populations and similar or higher GDP per capita, such as Brazil and Paraguay. Other types of educational personnel account for a further 1.1 per cent of the labour force.

However, the relatively small class sizes and low level of teaching hours go together with below-average salaries. Primary teachers earn an average of 4 752 PPP dollars, less than half of the WEI average. Moreover, teachers' salaries do not increase with years of experience for those with minimum training. In the case of teachers with an educational qualification (70 per cent of the public teaching force), salaries increase by 28 per cent over the career, and reach the top of the scale after 20 years. Even though the earnings premium for experience is small, teachers seek to obtain educational qualifications because they are a requirement for recruitment in public schools that provide a higher degree of employment stability.

For data see Annex A.4.

PHILIPPINES

WEI countries with
higher GDP per capita

OECD
average

WEI countries with
lower GDP per capita

*Indicators on teachers
and teaching conditions*

WEI average

Percentage of teachers
with a tertiary-level
qualification in
primary education

0   64   100   %

Annual number
of teaching hours in
primary education

600   869   1 176   1 300   hours

800

Class size in lower
secondary education

0   29   51 52   number of students per class

19.8

Statutory salary for a
primary teacher with
15 years' experience
and minimum qualifications

0   10 820   13 715   28 000   PPP dollars

27 600

Ratio of salary for a primary
teacher with 15 years'
experience and minimum
qualifications required
to GDP per capita

0   1.9   3.8 4   ratio

1.3

Background indicators

School expectancy for
a five-year-old

9   11.8 12.4   17   years

16.7

Percentage of the
population aged 5-19

19   31.6   36.3   42   %

20

GDP per capita

0   35 80 5 360   22 000   PPP dollars

20 700

PHILIPPINES

Prepared in co-operation between the OECD, UNESCO, Ramon BACANI and Lilia ROCES

The education system in the Philippines has to cope with a large and rapidly increasing client base. In 1999, the school-age population accounted for 36 per cent of the total population, and it is projected that the number of 5 to 19-year-olds will increase by a further 10 per cent over the period 2000 to 2010. Resources to deal with the growing demand for education are limited. The Philippines has one of the lowest GDPs per capita in the WEI sample, 3 580 PPP dollars, far below the WEI average of 5 550 PPP dollars.

It is thus not surprising that school expectancy in the Philippines is around one year below the WEI average. In addition, the country's achievement in mathematics at the 8th-grade level, as assessed by TIMSS 1999, is the lowest among the WEI countries.

At the same time, upper secondary graduation rates are well above the WEI average, with 57 per cent of a given age cohort completing upper secondary education. This high graduation rate may be enhanced in part by the relatively short duration of lower and upper secondary education in the Philippines.

The level of qualifications of the existing teaching force demonstrates the national commitment to education. The Philippines is the only WEI country where, throughout primary and secondary education, virtually all members of the existing teaching force have completed university-level education.

The working conditions of teachers in the Philippines are characterised by an above-average annual teaching load, above-average class sizes and comparatively high salaries. Teaching time in the Philippines, 1 176 hours at all levels of education, is between 33 and 44 per cent higher than the WEI average, depending on the level of education, and is above the OECD average. The regulations stipulate that teachers shall deliver six hours of actual teaching per day. Class sizes are the second highest in primary education (32 students per primary class, on average) and by far the highest in lower secondary education (50 students).

With a mid-career statutory salary of 13 715 PPP dollars (including bonuses), teachers in the Philippines earn well above the WEI average. For primary teachers, earnings are around 30 per cent above the WEI average and far higher than in many countries with higher levels of GDP per capita. Expressed as a percentage of GDP per capita, teachers' salaries are the highest among the OECD and WEI countries. Additional compensation is paid for extra teaching hours, out-of-school activities and any other activities outside what is defined as normal duties. Such bonuses may increase the basic salary by up to 30 per cent.

The Philippines' primary teaching force has the highest proportion of older teachers among the WEI and OECD countries. Forty-four per cent of primary teachers are older than 50 years of age. This proportion is much smaller at the secondary level.

For data see Annex A.4.

RUSSIAN FEDERATION

Indicators on teachers and teaching conditions

WEI countries with
higher GDP per capita

OECD average

WEI countries with
lower GDP per capita

WEI average

Student-teacher ratio
(primary education)

| 15 | 17.6 | 25 | 45 | students |

18

Annual number
of teaching hours
in primary education

| 600 | 686 | 869 | 1 300 | hours |

800

Class size in lower
secondary education

| 0 | 18 | 29 | 52 | number of students per class |

19.8

Total intended instruction
time per year for students
12 to 14 years of age
(in hours)

| 2 000 | 2 952 | 3 271 | 5 000 | hours |

2 781

Background indicators

Percentage of students
repeating current grade
(primary education)

| 0 | 1.2 | 6.1 | 25 | % |

School expectancy for
a five-year-old

| 9 | 12.2 | 12.4 | 17 | years |

16.7

Percentage of the
population aged 5-19

| 19 | 22.4 | 31.6 | 42 | % |

20

GDP per capita

| 0 | 5 360 | 6 271 | 22 000 | PPP dollars |

20 700

RUSSIAN FEDERATION

Prepared in co-operation between the OECD, UNESCO and Alexander SAVELYEV

The education system in the Russian Federation, unlike the other WEI countries, is seeing a dramatic decline in its client base. Between 1995 and 2000 the number of children of primary-school age decreased by one sixth, and it is expected to fall by a further quarter over the next decade. The proportion of children of primary-school age is currently 22.4 per cent, the smallest proportion among WEI countries, although still above the OECD average.

A Russian five-year-old child can expect 12.2 years of schooling (all levels of education combined), which is at the WEI average. However, the TIMSS achievement tests in 1995 and 1999 indicated that the quality of educational outcomes is comparatively high in the Russian Federation. The Russian Federation recorded the highest score in 8th-grade mathematics achievement of all the eight WEI countries that participated in TIMSS 1999, and came very close to the OECD average. Low rates of grade repetition are a further indicator of a high degree of internal efficiency in the education system.

The number of hours that primary teachers are required to teach, 686 hours per year, is the lowest among the WEI countries and well below the OECD average of 800 hours. Limited instruction time for students is counterbalanced by comparatively small class sizes. The average class size of 18 students is around 10 students lower than the WEI average. Student-teacher ratios, 15 students per teacher at the primary level, are the lowest among the WEI countries and below the OECD average.

Teaching in Russia is almost exclusively a female occupation. Almost all primary teachers, 98 per cent, are women, and even at the secondary level, no other WEI or OECD country has a higher proportion of women in the teaching force. Eighty per cent of all upper secondary teachers are women.

For data see Annex A.4.

WEI countries with
higher GDP per capita

THAILAND

*OECD
average*

WEI countries with
lower GDP per capita

*Indicators on teachers
and teaching conditions*

WEI average

Percentage of teachers
with a tertiary-level
qualification in
primary education

0   64 82 100   %

Annual number
of teaching hours in
primary education

600 760 869   1 300   *hours*

800

Class size in lower
secondary education

0   29   42   52   *number of students per class*

19.8

Statutory salary for a
primary teacher with
15 years' experience
and minimum qualifications

0   10 820 14 208   28 000   *PPP dollars*

27 600

Ratio of salary for a primary
teacher with 15 years'
experience and minimum
qualifications required
to GDP per capita

0   1.9 2.5   4   *ratio*

1.3

Background indicators

School expectancy for
a five-year-old

9   13.1 12.4   17   *years*

16.7

Percentage of the
population aged 5-19

19 24.9   31.6   42   %

20

GDP per capita

0   5 360 5 757   22 000   *PPP dollars*

20 700

THAILAND

Prepared in co-operation between the OECD, UNESCO and Sirivarn SVASTIWAT

After the Russian Federation, Thailand has the lowest proportion of the population at school age, with 25 per cent of the population in the age group 5 to 19 years, midway between the OECD (20) and WEI (31.6) averages. In addition, the school-age population is expected to decrease by a further 10 per cent in the age group 5 to 14 years and by 13 per cent in the age group 15 to 19 years during the period 2000-2010. Despite a continuing economic downturn, Thailand's GDP per capita, 5 757 PPP dollars, is still above the WEI average.

School expectancy in Thailand is high, 13.1 years of full-time participation, compared with the WEI average of around 12 years. In addition, Thailand provides a significant amount of part-time education for adults, which accounts for nearly another five years of school expectancy. Thailand's score in the 1999 TIMSS assessment of 8th-grade mathematics achievement, 467 points, ranked below the international average (487 points), but placed the country in third position among the eight WEI countries participating in the study.

Thailand's teaching force is well educated, with 82 per cent of primary teachers holding a tertiary qualification. This is well above the WEI average, and the regulations require four years of tertiary training (including 1.5 years of pedagogical studies and teaching practice) for new entrants to the profession.

Teachers' pay is relatively attractive. At 14 208 PPP dollars, primary teachers' salaries are the second highest among the WEI countries, 31 per cent above the WEI average and much higher than in many countries with higher per capita national income. When compared with GDP per capita, teachers' salaries in Thailand rank third among the WEI countries, with salaries for primary teachers with 15 years' experience equalling 2.5 times GDP per capita, well above both the OECD average (1.3 times) and the WEI average (1.9 times). Teachers' salaries in Thailand show little variation with the level of education taught, but increase with both experience (a 250 per cent increase over the first 15 years) and qualifications (a 41 per cent differential between minimum and maximum qualifications).

These relatively high salaries appear all the more attractive given the comparatively low workload of teachers, 760 teaching hours per year in primary education, compared with an average of 800 hours in OECD countries, and 869 hours in WEI countries.

These attractive working conditions are, however, offset by large classes. The average class size is 42 students at the lower secondary level, more than double the OECD average (19.8), and around one third higher than the WEI average (32). These large classes are mainly the result of the high number of hours of instruction, 3 500 hours per year, and the low teaching load of teachers.

For data see Annex A.4.

WEI countries with
higher GDP per capita

TUNISIA

OECD average

WEI countries with
lower GDP per capita

*Indicators on teachers
and teaching conditions*

WEI average

Percentage of teachers
with a tertiary-level
qualification in
primary education

0   14   64   100   %

Annual number
of teaching hours in
primary education

600   735   869   1 300   *hours*

800

Class size in lower
secondary education

0   29   41   52   *number of students per class*

19.8

Statutory salary for a
primary teacher with
15 years' experience
and minimum qualifications

0   10 820 10 877   28 000   *PPP dollars*

27 600

Ratio of salary for a primary
teacher with 15 years'
experience and minimum
qualifications required
to GDP per capita

0   1.9 2.2   4   *ratio*

1.3

Background indicators

School expectancy for
a five-year-old

9   12.4 13.4   17   *years*

16.7

Percentage of the
population aged 5-19

19   31.6 34.4   42   %

20

GDP per capita

0   5 360 5 732   22 000   *PPP dollars*

20 700

TUNISIA

Prepared in co-operation with OECD and UNESCO

While the current proportion of the population in the age group 5 to 19 years, 34 per cent, is still well above the WEI average, the number of children in this age group is expected to fall over the next decade. This decrease began in the mid-1990s and is expected to amount to a further 5 per cent between 2000 and 2010. In terms of available national resources, Tunisia stands slightly above the WEI average, with a GDP per capita of 5 731 PPP dollars.

Tunisia shows an above-average school expectancy of 13.4 years, outperforming all the WEI countries with lower GDP per capita and, by a full year, two countries with higher GDP per capita. This high level of school expectancy is, however, due not only to high participation rates at primary and lower secondary levels, but also to high rates of grade repetition. At the secondary level, the Tunisian repetition rate is the highest among the WEI countries. Among other effects, high repetition rates tend to increase class sizes, which in Tunisia are already among the largest among the WEI countries. Mathematics achievement in Tunisia, as measured in the TIMSS 1999 assessment, stands around the average among the participating WEI countries, but is lower than the TIMSS 1999 international average.

Tunisia's investment in human and financial resources is among the highest in the WEI countries. Public expenditure on primary and secondary education, as a percentage of GDP, is the second highest among the WEI countries (5.4 per cent). Similarly, Tunisia has the highest proportion of the labour force in all OECD and WEI countries working in primary and secondary education, 6 per cent.

The level of tertiary qualifications of the current teaching force is relatively low at the primary level (15 per cent), but rises to 84 and 96 per cent at the lower and upper secondary levels of education respectively. In 1999, the Ministry of Education introduced a new entrance examination for secondary teachers (CAPES), requiring teachers to have at least a university Master's degree. In addition, continuing training for the existing teaching force is being given high priority in Tunisian reform efforts. Since 1991, an extensive in-service training programme has provided an average of 30 hours of training per year free of charge for all teachers.

Teachers' working conditions are characterised by a below-average teaching load combined with above-average class sizes. Teachers are required to teach 735 hours per year in primary education and 548 hours in secondary education, the latter figure being the lowest among the WEI countries at the secondary level. This comparatively low teaching load partly explains why class sizes are above the WEI average despite average student-teacher ratios. Class sizes are estimated at 31 students in primary education and 41 in secondary education.

The remuneration of teachers is high in comparison with both the WEI average and GDP per capita. A primary teacher with 15 years' experience earns 12 877 PPP dollars, which is 19 per cent above the WEI average and 2.2 times GDP per capita. This ratio increases to 2.9 for experienced lower secondary teachers, and to 3.4 for experienced upper secondary teachers. Teachers' salaries have recently been raised to match those of administrative staff with equivalent qualifications, while teachers in rural areas have been given additional financial aid.

For data see Annex A.4.

URUGUAY

WEI countries with
higher GDP per capita

OECD average

WEI countries with
lower GDP per capita

*Indicators on teachers
and teaching conditions*

WEI average

Student-teacher ratio
(primary education)

15   21   25   45   *students*

17.5

Annual number
of teaching hours in
primary education

600   732   869   1 300   *hours*

800

Class size in lower
secondary education

0   26   29   52   *number of students per class*

19.8

Statutory salary for a
primary teacher with
15 years' experience
and minimum qualifications

0   10 820   11 675   28 000   *PPP dollars*

27 600

Ratio of salary for a primary
teacher with 15 years'
experience and minimum
qualifications required
to GDP per capita

0   1.4   1.9   4   *ratio*

1.3

Background indicators

School expectancy for
a five-year-old

9   12.4   15.2   17   *years*

16.7

Percentage of the
population aged 5-19

19   24.3   31.6   42   *%*

20

GDP per capita

0   5 360   8 418   22 000   *PPP dollars*

20 700

URUGUAY

Prepared in co-operation between the OECD, UNESCO and Mara PEREZ TORRANO

Uruguay has the third highest GDP per capita (8 602 PPP dollars) among the WEI countries and the smallest school-age population. Only 24 per cent of the total population are in the age group 5 to 19 years, which is closer to the OECD average (20 per cent) than to the WEI average (32 per cent).

A five-year-old child can expect to participate in formal education for 15.2 years, the second highest figure among the WEI countries and only 1.5 years below the OECD average.

High levels of participation are achieved despite comparatively low expenditure on primary and secondary schools. Only 2.1 per cent of GDP is spent on educational institutions, well below the WEI and OECD averages.

The generally favourable economic and demographic conditions are reflected not only in high participation rates but also in better than average working conditions for teachers. Classes are particularly small in primary education, with fewer than 13 students on average (about half the WEI average). They are still below the WEI figure in lower secondary education, with an average of 26 students per class. Teaching hours are also below the OECD and WEI averages, 732 hours per year for primary teachers and 712 hours for secondary teachers.

The comparatively small class sizes at the lower secondary level of education are mainly explained by low student-teacher ratios, the lowest among the WEI countries. At the primary level, however, the main factor behind small classes is the small number of hours of instruction. The intended number of hours of instruction for primary students (455 hours per year) is around half the WEI average.

Enhancing the initial and continuing training of teachers is one of the priorities for improving the quality of education. The aim is to build a system of initial training and to update and upgrade the training of existing classroom teachers, headteachers and supervisory staff.

A tertiary qualification (ISCED 5B) is required for entry to the teaching profession at all levels of education. Its duration varies from three years for prospective primary teachers to four years for prospective secondary teachers.

Mid-career statutory salaries for teachers are at similar levels for primary and secondary teachers (11 675 PPP dollars including bonuses), 1.4 times GDP per capita at the primary and lower secondary levels, and 1.5 times GDP per capita at the upper secondary level. These ratios are close to the OECD average and below the WEI average. Bonuses are an essential part of teachers' remuneration in Uruguay, and may increase the basic salary by up to 85 per cent.

For data see Annex A.4.

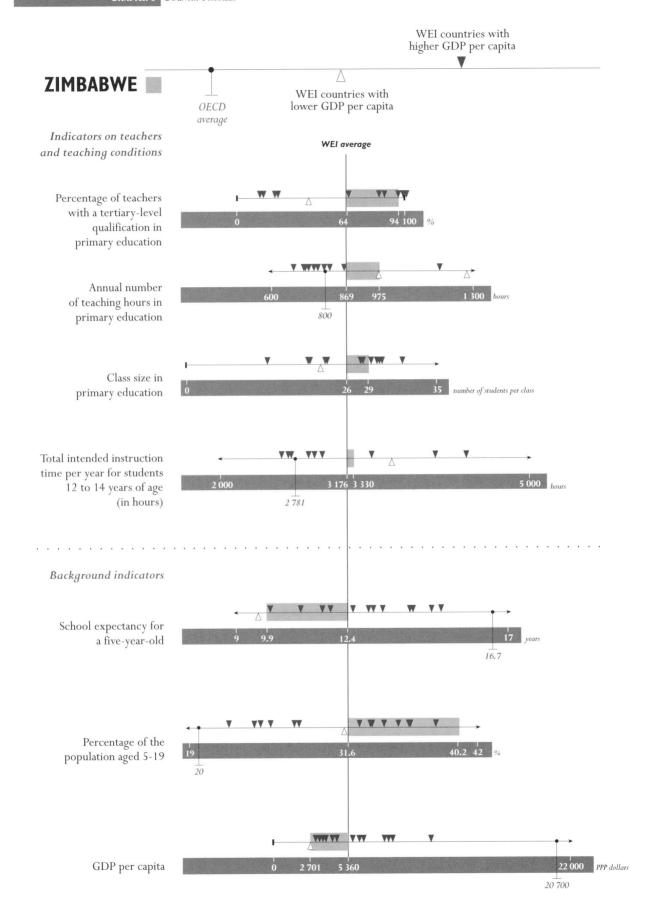

WEI countries with
higher GDP per capita

ZIMBABWE

OECD average

WEI countries with
lower GDP per capita

*Indicators on teachers
and teaching conditions*

WEI average

Percentage of teachers
with a tertiary-level
qualification in
primary education

0   64   94 100   %

Annual number
of teaching hours in
primary education

600   869   975   1 300   *hours*

800

Class size in
primary education

0   26   29   35   *number of students per class*

Total intended instruction
time per year for students
12 to 14 years of age
(in hours)

2 000   3 176 3 330   5 000   *hours*

2 781

· ·

Background indicators

School expectancy for
a five-year-old

9   9.9   12.4   17   *years*

16.7

Percentage of the
population aged 5-19

19   31.6   40.2 42   *%*

20

GDP per capita

0   2 701 5 360   22 000   *PPP dollars*

20 700

ZIMBABWE

Prepared in co-operation between the OECD, UNESCO and Farai CHOGA

With the second lowest GDP per capita among the WEI countries, 2 701 PPP dollars, and the largest proportion of the population at school age, 40 per cent, Zimbabwe's education system faces major challenges if it is to improve provision.

It is therefore not surprising that participation in education in Zimbabwe is low. School expectancy is only 9.9 years (all levels of education combined) for a five-year-old child, almost three years below the WEI average. In addition, school expectancy is one year lower for girls.

At the same time, Zimbabwe spends a higher proportion of national income on educational institutions (11.6 per cent) than any other WEI country. Expenditure per student, 768 PPP dollars at primary level, is more than six times that of Indonesia, for example, a country with similar GDP per capita. At the secondary level, expenditure per student, 1 179 PPP dollars, is also more than double that of Indonesia.

The main challenge facing Zimbabwe is to expand participation in education. For that purpose, it already has a well-qualified teaching force, with 94 per cent of its primary and 99 per cent of its secondary teachers holding a tertiary qualification.

Teachers' working conditions in Zimbabwe are characterised by above-average teaching hours (975 hours per year at primary, and 936 at secondary level) and small classes. Zimbabwe has the smallest average class size of the WEI countries at the lower secondary level, 16.5 students, which is below the OECD average of 19.8 and only just over half the WEI average. At the primary level, the average class size in Zimbabwe (29.3) is slightly higher than the WEI average (25.9).

For data see Annex A.4.

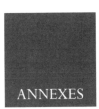

ANNEXES

These annexes provide the data used in this publication as well as important information on the definitions and methods underlying these data. The full documentation of national data sources and calculation methods is published in the 2001 edition of OECD's *Education at a Glance* and is also available on the Internet:

http://www.oecd.org/els/education/ei/index.htm

Five annexes are presented below:

- **ANNEX A1** provides general notes pertaining to the coverage of the data, the reference periods and the main sources for the data;

- **ANNEX A2** provides definitions and notes that are important for the understanding of the indicators presented in this publication (the notes are organised alphabetically);

- **ANNEX A3** provides a cross-reference between tables and notes;

- **ANNEX A4** provides the full set of data used in this publication;

- **ANNEX A5** documents the classification of 18 WEI countries' educational programmes according to the 1997 International Standard Classification of Education (ISCED97).

■ ANNEX A1 – GENERAL NOTES

Coverage

Although a shortage of data still limits the scope of some indicators in many WEI countries, the coverage extends, in principle, to the entire national education system regardless of the ownership or sponsorship of the institutions concerned and regardless of education delivery mechanisms. With one exception described below, all types of students and all age-groups are meant to be included: children (including those classified as exceptional), adults, nationals, foreigners, as well as students in open distance learning, in special education programmes or in educational programmes organised by ministries other than the Ministry of Education, provided the main aim of the programme is the educational development of the individual. However, vocational and technical training in the workplace, with the exception of combined school and work-based programmes that are explicitly deemed to be parts of the education system, is not included in the basic education expenditure and enrolment data. Educational activities classified as "adult" or "non-regular" are covered, provided that the activities involve studies or have a subject-matter content similar to "regular" education studies or that the underlying programmes lead to potential qualifications similar to corresponding regular educational programmes. Courses for adults that are primarily for general interest, personal enrichment, leisure or recreation are excluded.

Reference periods

The reference year for data on entry, enrolment, completion and education personnel is the school year 1997/1998 for WEI countries and the school year 1998/1999 for OECD countries. The reference year for the financial data is the calendar year 1998 for both WEI and OECD countries. GDP consumer price deflators are used to adjust the data on expenditure where the national financial year does not coincide with the calendar year. In order to make this adjustment, the data on educational finance are multiplied by the ratio of GDP price levels between the calendar year for which data are published and those of the preceding calendar year, in proportion to the fraction of the national financial year that overlaps with the previous calendar year. The following two limitations of the use of such deflators should be recognised: i) the adjustments relate to changes in the general (GDP) price level but not to the price level for educational services (the assumption is made that educational costs are measured in terms of national income forgone); ii) no allowance has been made for real growth in educational expenditure (increases in excess of inflation or smaller increases) that might have taken place during the corresponding period of adjustment. Special adjustments are made for the calculation of indicators in which both financial and enrolment data are used (see below).

Data on national expenditure in this publication have been converted using purchasing power parities (PPPs).

Sources

Most numerical data used in this report are based on the annual WEI/UOE data collection. Government officials in OECD and WEI countries provide these data annually to the OECD and UNESCO in detailed and highly structured electronic questionnaires. These questionnaires consist of several electronic workbooks organised by topic – demographic background, education finance, enrolment, entrants, graduates, curriculum, personnel.

Sources used by government officials to complete the electronic questionnaires consist most often of labour force surveys, population censuses, or population projections based on censuses in the case of the demographic background and educational attainment data. Education system records, such as school censuses provide the data on enrolments, entrants, graduates, curriculum, and personnel in most cases. Education finance data often come from sources outside education ministries, most often government ministries that specialise in finance.

Additional financial and economic background data used in this report come from World Bank databases, some of which are published in its *World Development Indicators* publication. Specific indicators borrowed from World Bank databases include purchasing power parity indices and gross domestic product (GDP) per capita.

National sources are :

Argentina

Ministry of Education, 1998 School Census and University Statistics.

Brazil

Ministry of Education, 1998 School Census and 1998 Higher Education Census.

National Institute for Educational Studies and Research (Instituto Nacional de Estudos e Pesquisas Educacionais/INEP).

Coordination for the Improvement of Tertiary Education Personnel (Fundação Coordenação de Aperfeiçoamento de Pessoal de Nível Superior).

Office of National Accounting / National Bureau of Statistics (DECNA/IBGE – Departamento de Contas Nacionais/Instituto Brasileiro de Geografia e Estatística).

Chile

Ministry of Education , Enrolment and Achievement databases (ISCED 1-3), Higher Education Division (ISCED 5-7), JUNJI and INTEGRA (ISCED 0).

Central Bank, National Accounts.

China

Ministry of Education, Statistics Division.

Egypt

Ministry of Education, 1998 School Census.

India

Ministry of Human Resource Development.

Indonesia

Ministry of Education, School Statistics 1999/2000 and Planning Division, Directorate General of Higher Education.

Statistics, Finance Bureau, MONE.

Jordan

Ministry of Education, *The Educational Statistical Report 1998/99*.

Malaysia

Education Planning & Resources Division (EPRD), Teacher Education Division (TED), Technical & Vocational Education Department (TVED), Higher Education Department (HED), Private Education Department (PED), Royal Military College (RMC), ManPower Department (MPD), Council of Trust of the Indigenous People (MARA), Social Welfare Department (KEMAS).

Paraguay

Direction of Planning, Statistics and Information, Statistic Data Base Year 1998 (Anuario 1998 Estadistica Educativa).

Peru

Ministry of Education, 1998 School Census (database).

National Association of University Rectors (ANR), *Annual Report* (several years).

Ministry of Finance (MEF), 1998 Public Sector Budget.

National Statistics and Information Institute (INEI), 1997 National Household Survey (ENNIV).

Philippines

DECS, *CHED Statistical Bulletin*, school year 1997/98.

General Appropriations Act of 1997/Annual Financial Report of the Local Government. Local Government Audit Office, Commission on Audit/Census.

Russia

Institute for Higher Education.

Sri Lanka

Ministry of Education, School census, 1998.

Thailand

Office of the National Education Commission.

Tunisia

Ministry of Economic Development.

Uruguay

Ministry of Education and Culture, Education Division, Statistics Department.

Ministry of Economics and Finance.

National Administration of Public Education (Administración Nacional de Educación Pública).

Zimbabwe

Ministry of Education, Sport and Culture.

For a full documentation of national data sources and calculation methods for the OECD countries, refer to the 2001 edition of OECD's *Education at a Glance* or the Internet (http://www.oecd.org/els/education/ei/index.htm). Data for Korea refer to the Republic of Korea.

■ ANNEX A2 – DEFINITIONS, METHODS AND TECHNICAL NOTES

Class size (Tables 35, 36)

The class size presented in the indicators is not an empirical class size, but a theoretical constructed figure. It represents the class size or group size to be expected under the formal regulations in the educational systems given observed *student / teacher ratios*. It is estimated as student / teacher ratio multiplied by the *intended instruction time* for students divided by the statutory *teaching time*. Additional explanations on class size may be found in Box 2.4 (Chapter 2).

Current and capital expenditure (Table 7)

Current expenditure is **expenditure on educational institutions** consumed within the current year, which needs to be made recurrently to sustain the production of educational services. Minor expenditure on items of equipment, below a certain cost threshold, are also reported as current spending.

Capital expenditure represents the proportion of **expenditure on educational institutions** on capital acquired or created during the year in question – that is, the amount of capital formation – regardless of whether the capital outlay was financed from current revenue or by borrowing. Capital expenditure includes outlays on construction, renovation, and major repair of buildings and expenditure for new or replacement equipment. Although capital investment requires a large initial expenditure, the plant and facilities have a lifetime that extends over many years. Capital expenditure does not include debt-servicing.

Expenditure on compensation of personnel includes gross salaries plus expenditure on retirement and on other non-salary compensation (fringe benefits).

The category *teachers* includes only personnel who participate directly in the instruction of students. Under expenditure on compensation of teachers, countries report the full compensation of full-time teachers plus appropriate portions of the compensation of staff who teach part-time. In addition to headteachers and other administrators of schools, *non-teaching staff* includes supervisors, counsellors, school psychologists, school health personnel, librarians or educational media specialists, curriculum developers, inspectors, educational administrators at the local, regional, and national level, clerical personnel, building operations and maintenance staff, security personnel, transportation workers, food service workers, etc. The exact list of occupations included in this category varies from one country to another.

The proportions of current expenditure allocated to compensation of teachers (**teacher**), compensation of other staff, total staff compensation and other (non-personnel) current outlays are calculated by expressing the respective amounts as percentages of total current expenditure.

Decision-making in education

The indicators on the locus and mode of decision making in education are derived from the OECD-WEI locus of decision making questionnaire and refer to the school year 1998/1999.

Territorial decentralisation is concerned with the distribution of powers between levels of government. This concept encloses two different dimensions: i) the locus of decision-making, that is, it identifies which level has the decision-making authority; and ii) the mode of decision-making, which distinguishes between degrees to which levels are autonomous or "sharing" in decision-making authority.

When interpreting the indicators, it is important to recognise that the results are based on the 35 decision items included in the survey which are described below. The survey items were selected to be typical of the range of decisions taken in education systems and reviewed on this basis in participating countries. Each of the decision domains was given equal weight – and thus equal importance – in calculating the indicators.

The questionnaire was completed by panels of national experts in order to avoid problems with ambiguities and differences of opinion. For each level of education, a panel comprising one member from each of the following three decision-making levels was constituted: highest level (central government), middle levels (state governments, provincial/regional authorities or governments, sub-regional or inter-municipal authorities or governments, local authorities or governments), lowest level (individual school). This group completed the questionnaire and arrived at consensus on all questions. For each level of education, a second expert panel comprising representatives of the three decision-making levels was constituted and the process repeated. The WEI co-ordinator then reviewed and compared the results of the two surveys to identify differences in responses to the questionnaire. In cases where the responses differed, the WEI co-ordinator used source documents to reconcile disagreements between the two panels.

Levels of decision-making

With respect to the levels of decision-making the questionnaire distinguished between six levels:

Central Government: The central government consists of all bodies at the national level that make decisions or participate in different aspects of decision-making, including both administrative (government bureaucracy) and legislative bodies (*e.g.* parliament).

State Governments: The state is the first territorial unit below the nation in "federal" countries or countries with similar types of governmental structures. State governments are the governmental units that are the decision making bodies at this governmental level.

Provincial/Regional Authorities or Governments: The province or the region is the first territorial unit below the national level in countries that do not have a "federal" or similar type of governmental structure and the second territorial unit below the nation in countries with a "federal" or similar types of governmental structures. Provincial/regional authorities or governments are the decision making bodies at this governmental level.

Sub-Regional or Inter-Municipal Authorities or Governments: The sub-region is the second territorial unit below the nation in countries that do not have a "federal" or similar type of governmental structure. Sub-regional or inter-municipal authorities or governments are the decision-making bodies at this governmental level.

Local Authorities or Governments: The municipality or community is the smallest territorial unit in the nation with a governing authority. The local authority may be the education department within a general-purpose local government or it may be a special-purpose government whose sole area of authority is education.

School, School Board or Committee: The school attendance area is the territorial unit in which a school is located. This level applies to the individual school level only and includes school administrators and teachers or a school board or committee established exclusively for that individual school. The decision-making body – or bodies – for this school may be: i) an external school board, which includes residents of the larger community; ii) an internal school board, which could include headmasters, teachers, other school staff, parents, and students; and iii) both an external and an internal school board. Parents and teachers were considered as an element of the school level.

The descriptions of "at what level" and "how" educational decisions are made reflects the actual decision-making process. In some cases, a higher level of government may have formal or legal responsibility for decision-making, but in practice, that level of government delegates its decision-making authority to a lower level of government. In describing the actual decision making process, the lower level of government is identified as the decision-maker. Similarly, a higher level of government may provide a lower level of government with choices in a particular area of decision-making, (e.g., the selection of textbooks for particular courses). In that case too, the lower level of government is the actual decision-maker, but within a framework established by a higher level of government. Finally, there are cases in which one level of government may have the responsibility for an individual decision, but inaction by the higher level results in a decision being made by a lower level within the educational system. If a decision is left to the discretion of a lower level through the lack of determination of higher levels, then the level that actually makes the decision was indicated.

Mode of decision-making

The mode of decision-making refers to the issues as to how autonomously decisions are taken. The following categories were used:

Full autonomy: subject only to any constraints contained in the constitution or in legislation outside the education system itself.

After consultation with bodies located at another level within the education system.

Independently, but within a framework set by a higher authority (e.g., a binding law, a pre-established list of possibilities, a budgetary limit, etc.).

Other mode.

Decision-making items

Organisation of instruction: bodies determining the school attended; decisions affecting school careers; instruction time; choice of textbooks; grouping pupils; assistance to pupils; teaching methods; assessment of pupils' regular work.

Personnel management: hiring the principal; dismissal of the principal; hiring a teacher; dismissal of a teacher; hiring a person for a non-teaching post; dismissal of a person for a given non-teaching post. duties and conditions of service of principal; duties and conditions of service of teaching staff; duties and conditions of service of non-teaching staff. Fixing of salary scales for principals; fixing of salary scales for teaching staff; fixing of salary scales for non-teaching staff. Influence over the career of the principal; influence over the career of teachers; influence over the career of non-teaching staff.

Planning and structures: creation or closure of schools; creation or abolition of a grade level; designing programmes of study; selection of programmes of study offered in a particular school/selection of subjects taught in a particular school; definition of course content; setting of qualifying examinations for a certificate or diploma; credentialling.

Resource allocation and use: allocation of resources to the school for teaching staff; allocation of resources to the school for non-teaching staff; allocation of resources to the school for capital expenditure; allocation of resources to the school for operating expenditure; use of resources for staff; use of resources for capital expenditure; use of resources for operating expenditure.

Educational attainment (Tables 32, 34)

The levels of educational attainment used in Tables 32 and 34 to classify teacher training present the highest level of education, defined according to ISCED97 (Annex A5) completed, or to be completed by current teachers or newly recruited teachers. Note that many educational programmes cannot be easily classified and the content of a specific ISCED level may differ between countries, and even within countries over time between different age groups.

Educational institution

Educational institutions are defined as entities that provide instructional or education-related services to individuals and other educational institutions. Whether or not an entity qualifies as an educational institution is not contingent upon which public authority (if any) has responsibility for it.

Educational institutions are sub-divided into Instructional Educational Institutions and Non-Instructional Educational Institutions, the latter being of special importance for comparable coverage of the data on educational finance. The term "instructional" is used simply to imply the direct provision of teaching and learning.

Instructional Educational Institutions are those that provide individuals with educational programmes that fall within the scope of the WEI/UOE data collection. In this report, the generic term "school" is often used to refer to instructional institutions at the primary, secondary, and post-secondary non-tertiary levels, and "universities" to those at the tertiary level.

Non-Instructional Educational Institutions are educational institutions that provide administrative, advisory or professional services, frequently for other educational institutions. Non-Instructional Educational Institutions include the following entities:

a) Entities administering educational institutions include institutions such as national, state, and provincial ministries or departments of education; other bodies that administer education at various levels of government and analogous bodies in the private sector (*e.g.* diocesan offices that administer Catholic schools, and agencies administering admissions to universities).

b) Entities providing support services to other educational institutions include institutions that provide educational support and materials as well as operation and maintenance services for buildings. These are commonly part of the general-purpose units of public authorities.

c) Entities providing ancillary services cover separate organisations that provide such education-related services as vocational and psychological counselling, placement, transportation of students, and student meals and housing. In some countries, housing and dining facilities for tertiary students are operated by private organisations, usually non-profit, which may be subsidised out of public funds.

d) Institutions administering student loan or scholarship programmes.

e) Entities performing curriculum development, testing, educational research and educational policy analysis.

Educational institutions are subdivided in *public and private educational institutions*.

Educational personnel (Table 31)

Educational personnel include staff employed in both public and private schools and other institutions. Educational personnel is subdivided into *teacher* and *other personnel*. Other educational personnel comprises teachers' aides, teaching/research assistants and non-instructional personnel.

Teachers' aides and teaching/research assistants include non-professional personnel or students who support teachers in providing instruction to students.

Non-instructional personnel comprises four categories:

i) *Professional support* for students includes professional staff who provide services to students that support their learning. This category also includes all personnel employed in education systems who provide health and social support services to students, such as guidance counsellors, librarians, doctors, dentists, nurses, psychiatrists and psychologists and other staff with similar responsibilities. ii) *School and higher level management* includes professional personnel who are responsible for school management and administration and personnel whose primary responsibility is the quality control and management of higher levels of the education system. iii) *School and higher level administrative personnel* includes all personnel who support the administration and management of schools and of higher levels of the education system. iv) *Maintenance and operations personnel* includes personnel who support the maintenance and operation of schools, the transportation of students to and from school, school security and catering.

Expenditure on educational institutions (Tables 4, 5, 6)

Expenditure on educational institutions covers expenditure on *public and private educational institutions*. It covers expenditure by institutions from all sources, *public, private and international*. However, expenditure on educational institutions need to be defined by the functions of the specific expenditure, since in many countries educational institutions are embedded in wider institutional arrangements, *e.g.* general purpose units of local governments or institutions that provide both, education related services as well as child-care services. Those functions are: i) Instruction (*i.e.*, teaching); ii) Educational goods (books, materials, etc.) provided by institutions; iii) Training of apprentices and other participants in mixed school and work-based educational programmes at the workplace; iv) Administration; v) Capital expenditure and rent; vi) Student transportation, school meals, student housing, boarding; vii) Guidance, student health services, special educational needs; viii) Services for the general public provided by educational institutions; ix) Educational research and curriculum development; and x) Research and development performed at higher education institutions.

The following list provides an indication of what expenditure by educational institutions need to be excluded: i) Child care or day care provided by schools and other instructional institutions; ii) Expenditure on educational activities outside the scope of the WEI/UOE data collection; iii) Teaching hospitals; and iv) Debt servicing.

Direct public expenditure on educational institutions may take one of two forms: i) purchases by the government agency itself of educational resources to be used by educational institutions (*e.g.* direct payments of teachers' salaries by a central or regional education ministry); ii) payments by the government agency to educational institutions that have responsibility for purchasing educational resources themselves (*e.g.* a government appropriation or block grant to a university, which the university then uses to compensate staff and to buy other resources).

Direct private expenditure on educational institutions include tuition payments received from students (or the families) enrolled in public schools under that agency's jurisdiction, even if the tuition payments flow, in the first instance, to the government agency rather than to the institution in question. It also includes payments by other private entities to educational institutions, either as support for educational institutions or paid as rent for the use of resources by educational institutions. *Direct private expenditure on educational institutions* are net of subsidies received from public sources. Those are accounted as indirect public expenditure and included in public expenditure.

Indirect public expenditure on educational institutions are subsidies to students, families or other private entities that are used by the recipients for payments to educational institutions.

Expenditure per student (Tables 8, 9)

The data used in calculating expenditure per student include only direct public and private *expenditure on educational institutions*. Public subsidies for students' living expenses have been excluded.

For some countries, expenditure data for students in private educational institutions were not available (indicated by notes in the tables). Many of the WEI countries that do have data for independent private institutions only cover a very small number of them. In such cases, only the expenditure in public and government-dependent private institutions are accounted for.

Expenditure per student on a particular level of education is calculated by dividing the total expenditure at that level by the corresponding *full-time equivalent enrolment*. Only those types of educational institutions and programmes for which both enrolment and expenditure data are available are taken into account. The enrolment data are adjusted by interpolation so as to match either the financial year or the calendar year of each country (see explanation below). The result in national currency is then converted into equivalent PPP dollars by dividing the national currency figure by the *purchasing power parity* (PPP) index.

For countries for which the financial year and/or the school year does not match the calendar year, corresponding adjustments are made. The size of the overall adjustment is minimised by adjusting either the enrolment or the financial data, as appropriate, to accord with the calendar year.

For countries in which the financial year closely matches the calendar year but for which the school year is different from the calendar year, the enrolment data are weighted to match the calendar year. For countries in which the school year closely matches the calendar year but in which the financial year is different from the calendar year, the enrolment data remain unchanged but the GDP price deflators are used to match the financial data to the calendar year. For countries in which neither the school year nor the financial year matches the calendar year, the enrolment data are weighted to match the financial year and afterwards the above-mentioned GDP price deflators are used to adjust the financial year data to accord with the calendar year.

Full-time, part-time and full-time equivalent students (Tables 8, 9, 21)

Students are classified by their pattern of attendance, *i.e.*, full-time or part-time. The part-time/full-time classification is regarded as an *attribute of student participation* rather than as an attribute of the educational programmes or the provision of education in general. Four elements are used to decide whether a student is enrolled full-time or part-time: the units of measurement for course load; a normal full-time course load, which is used as the criterion for establishing full-time participation; the student's actual course load; and the period of time over which the course loads are measured. In general, students enrolled in *primary and secondary* level educational programmes are considered to participate *full-time* if they attend school for at least 75 per cent of the school day or week (as locally defined) and would normally be expected to be in the programme for the entire academic year. Otherwise, they are considered part-time. When determining full-time/part-time status, the work-based component in combined school and work-based programmes is included. At the *tertiary level*, an individual is considered *full-time* if he or she is taking a course load or educational programme considered to require at least 75 per cent of a full-time commitment of time and resources. Additionally, it is expected that the student will remain in the programme for the entire year.

The *full-time equivalent* (FTE) measure attempts to standardise a student's actual load against the normal load. For the reduction of head-count data to FTEs, where data and norms on individual participation are available, course load is measured as the product of the fraction of the normal course load for a full-time student and the fraction of the school/academic year. [FTE = (actual course load/normal course load) * (actual duration of study during reference period/normal duration of study during reference period)]. When actual course load information is not available, a full-time student is considered equal to one FTE.

Full-time, part-time and full-time equivalent teachers (Table 21)

The classification of educational personnel as "full-time" and "part-time" is based on a concept of statutory working time (as opposed to actual or total working time or actual teaching time). Part-time employment refers to individuals who have been employed to perform less than the amount of statutory working hours required of a full-time employee. A teacher who is employed for at least 90 per cent of the normal or statutory number of hours of work of a full-time teacher over the period of a complete school year is classified as a *full-time teacher* for the reporting of head-count data. A teacher who is employed for less than 90 per cent of the normal or statutory number of hours of work of a full-time teacher over the period of a complete school year is classified as a *part-time teacher*. *Full-time equivalents* are generally calculated in person years. The unit for the measurement of full-time equivalents is full-time employment, *i.e.* a full-time teacher equals one FTE. The full-time equivalence of part-time educational staff is then determined by calculating the ratio of hours worked over the statutory hours worked by a full-time employee during the school year.

Gini Index (Table 2)

The *Gini index* is used as a measure of income inequality that reflects the distribution of income in a population. The closer the coefficient is to 0, the more equal the distribution of income across the population, whereas the closer the coefficient is to 1, the greater the income inequality. *Gini index* is a measure of dispersion within a group of values, calculated as the average difference between every pair of values divided by two times the average of the sample. The larger the coefficient, the higher the degree of dispersion.

Graduation rates (Table 18, 19)

In order to calculate *gross graduation rates*, countries identified the ***typical ages*** at which graduation typically occurs. The graduates themselves, however, could be of any age. To estimate gross graduation rates, the number of all graduates is divided by the population at the typical graduation age (multiplied by 100). In many countries, defining a typical age of graduation is difficult because ages of graduates vary. Here the average cohort size for a wider age band was used as denominator.

Graduates are those who were enrolled in the final year of a level of education and completed it successfully during the reference year. However, there are exceptions (especially at the university tertiary level of education) where graduation can also be recognised by the awarding of a certificate without the requirement that the participants are enrolled. *Completion* is defined by each country: in some countries, completion occurs as a result of passing an examination or a series of examinations. In other countries, completion occurs after a requisite number of course hours have been accumulated (although completion of some or all of the course hours may also involve examinations). Success is also defined by each country: in some countries it is associated with the obtaining of a degree, certificate, or diploma after a final examination; while in other countries, it is defined by the completion of programmes without a final examination.

Gross Domestic Product (GDP) (Table 1)

Gross Domestic Product (GDP) refers to the producers' value of the gross outputs of resident producers, including distributive trades and transport, less the value of purchasers' intermediate consumption plus import duties.

Intended instruction time for students (Table 28, 29, 30, 35, 36)

Intended instruction time for students refers to the number of hours per year pupils are instructed according to the compulsory and the flexible part of the intended curriculum. The total number of intended instruction hours per year was calculated by multiplying the total number of classroom sessions per year by the duration time of one session.

The *intended curriculum* is the subject-matter content as defined by the government or the education system. The intended curriculum is embodied in textbooks, in curriculum guides, in the content of examinations, and in policies, regulations, and other official statements generated to direct the education system. The intended curriculum comprises the compulsory subjects as well as the flexible part of the curriculum (***subjects of the intended curriculum***).

Labour force (Table 31)

The labour force consists out of all individuals in the population who are either employed or unemployed, these terms being defined according to the guidelines of the International Labour Office (ILO). The unemployed are defined as individuals who are without work, actively seeking employment and currently available to start work. The employed are defined as those who during the survey reference week: i) work for pay (employees) or profit (self-employed and unpaid family workers) for at least one hour; or ii) have a job but are temporarily not at work (through injury, illness, holiday or vacation, strike or lock-out, educational or training leave, maternity or parental leave, etc.) and have a formal attachment to their job.

Net enrolment rate (Table 13, 20)

Net enrolment rates (also referred to as enrolment rates) are calculated by dividing the number of **students** of a particular age group enrolled in all levels of education by the number of persons in the population in that age-group (multiplied by 100). Figures are based on head counts, that is, they do not distinguish between full-time and part-time study.

Net enrolment rates for primary and secondary education are calculated for different age groups for different countries, dependent on the typical ages of participants at the corresponding level. This can influence the results. *e.g.* in countries with longer programme duration, the typical age for upper secondary education may include ages 17 and 18, while in other countries only age 16 is included. As a result, countries with longer duration may show lower rates due to the drop out of the 17 and 18 years old, although they have higher enrolment rates at all ages.

Entry rate (Tables 16, 17)

Gross entry rates are the ratio of all **new entrants**, regardless of their age, to the size of the population at the **typical age of entry** (multiplied by 100). Gross entry rates are more easily influenced by differences in the size of population by single year of age. However, data requirements for the calculation of gross rates are lower and therefore more countries can provide the necessary data. Since entry to lower secondary and upper secondary takes place at a narrower age band than entry to tertiary education, demographic changes are less important at those levels.

The *net entry rate of a specific age* used for tertiary education is obtained by dividing the number of new entrants to the university level of that given age by the total population in the corresponding age-group (multiplied by 100). The sum of net entry rates is calculated by adding the net entry rates for each single year of age. The result represents the proportion of persons of a synthetic age-cohort who enter the tertiary level of education, irrespective of changes in the population sizes and differences between countries in the typical entry age. The sums of net entry rates are more robust against demographic factors, such as changes in the cohort sizes of the ages of entrants. Since entry to tertiary education takes place at a wider age band are they a preferable measure than gross rates.

New entrant

New entrants to a level of education are students who are entering any programme leading to a recognised qualification at this level of education for the first time, irrespective of whether students enter the programme at the beginning or at an advanced stage of the programme. Individuals who are returning to study at a level following a period of absence from studying at that same level are not considered new entrants.

Pre-service training requirements for new teachers in public institutions (Table 34)

Pre-service training requirements refers to the formal requirements for new **teachers in public institutions** as requested by law or other regulations.

Pre-service requirements are classified by different components of the training, the level of educational attainment according to ISCED (Annex A5), the content and the duration of the programme.

Content refers to the different components of teacher training. Typically, teacher training programmes consist of three parts: i) subject specific studies (theoretical studies of the subject(s) to be taught); ii) pedagogical studies (theoretical studies of how to teach); and iii) assisted teaching practice (practical teaching under the supervision of a teacher trainer).

Duration refers to the typical duration of each of these programme components in years, assuming full-time attendance to the corresponding course.

Private expenditure (Private sources of funds) (Table 4)

Private expenditure refers to expenditure funded by private sources, *i.e.* households and other private entities. "*Households*" means students and their families. "*Other private entities*" include private business firms and non-profit organisations, including religious organisations, charitable organisations, and business and labour associations. Private expenditure comprises school fees; fees for materials such as textbooks and teaching equipment; fees for transport to school (if organised by the school), meals (if provided by the school) and boarding; and expenditure by employers on initial vocational education. Note that private educational institutions are considered service providers, not funding sources.

Public expenditure (Public sources) (Table 4, 6, 10)

Public expenditure includes expenditure by all public agencies at local, regional and central levels of government. No distinction is made between education authorities and other government agencies. Thus, central government expenditure includes not only the expenditure of the national education ministry, but also all expenditure on education by other central government ministries and authorities. Similarly, educational expenditure by regional and local governments includes not only the expenditure of the regional or local agencies with primary responsibility for operation of schools (*e.g.* provincial ministries of education; or local education authorities) but also the expenditure of other regional and local bodies that contribute to the financing of education.

Public and private educational institutions (Table 10, 14)

Educational institutions are classified as either public or private according to whether a public agency or a private entity has the ultimate power to make decisions concerning the institution's affairs.

An institution is classified as public if it is: i) controlled and managed directly by a public education authority or agency; or ii) controlled and managed either by a government agency directly or by a governing body (Council, Committee, etc.), most of whose members are either appointed by a public authority or elected by public franchise.

An institution is classified as *private* if it is controlled and managed by a non-governmental organisation (*e.g.* a Church, a Trade Union or a business enterprise), or if its Governing Board consists mostly of members not selected by a public agency.

In general, the question of who has the ultimate management control over an institution is decided with reference to the power to determine the general activity of the school and to appoint the officers managing the school. The extent to which an institution receives its funding from public or private sources does not determine the classification status of the institution.

A distinction is made between "government-dependent" and "independent" private institutions on the basis of the degree of a private institution's dependence on funding from government sources. A *government-dependent private institution* is one that receives more than 50 per cent of its core funding from government agencies. An independent private institution is one that receives less than 50 per cent of its core funding from government agencies. "Core funding" refers to the funds that support the basic educational services of the institution. It does not include funds provided specifically for research projects, payments for services purchased or contracted by private organisations, or fees and subsidies received for ancillary services, such as lodging and meals. Additionally, institutions should be classified as government-dependent if their teaching staff are paid by a government agency – either directly or through government.

Purchasing power parity (PPP) (Table 1)

Purchasing power parities (PPPs) are the currency exchange rates that equalise the purchasing power of different currencies. This means that a given sum of money, when converted into US dollar at the PPP rates (PPP dollars), will buy the same basket of goods and services in all countries. In other words, PPPs are the rates of currency conversion which eliminate the differences in price levels among countries. Thus, when expenditure on GDP for different countries is converted into a common currency by means of PPPs, it is, in effect, expressed at the same set of international prices so that comparisons between countries reflect only differences in the volume of goods and services purchased.

Repeater (Table 15)

Students enrolling in the same grade or year of study a second or further time are classified as *repeaters* except if the new programme is classified as "higher" than the previous one. "Higher" is thereby operationalised by the individual countries. Repeaters are distinguished from participants in second and further educational programmes (the latter must have completed the programme at the level of education successfully before they can enter as participants in a second or further educational programme).

School expectancy (Table 12)

The average duration of formal education that a 5-year-old child can expect to enrol in over its lifetime, referred to as "school expectancy" in this indicator, is calculated by adding the net enrolment rates for each single year of age from age 5 onwards, and dividing by 100. Should there be a tendency to lengthen (or shorten) studies during the ensuing years, the actual average duration of schooling for the cohort will be higher (or lower). Caution is required when data on school expectancy are compared. Neither the length of the school year nor the quality of education is necessarily the same in each country.

Figures are based on head counts, that is, they do not distinguish between full-time and part-time study. A standardised distinction between full-time and part-time participants is very difficult since many countries do not recognise the concept of part-time study, although in practice at least some of their students would be classified as part-time by other countries. Note that in some countries part-time education is not completely covered by the reported data.

Statutory salary costs per student (Tables 35, 36)

The statutory salary cost per student measures the theoretical cost per student of compensating the teaching force. It is calculated assuming that teachers are paid at the mid-career level (15 years' experience) and hold the minimum required qualifications (*teacher salaries, statutory*). For each level of education, the statutory salary cost is thus equivalent to this theoretical mid-career salary times the number of teachers working at that level of education (*full-time, part-time and full-time equivalent teachers*), divided by the number of students of that level (*full-time, part-time and full-time equivalent students*). Therefore, it can also be calculated by dividing the statutory salary of a given level of education by the corresponding student-teachers ratio (*student-teacher ratio*).

The statutory salary cost per student is a theoretical tool, and does not necessarily reflect the exact cost of teachers per student enrolled. In particular, it is strongly dependent on the skills and age composition of the teaching force (through its impact on salaries).

Student

A *student* is defined as any individual participating in educational services covered by the data collection. The *number of students enrolled* refers to the number of individuals (head count) who are enrolled within the reference period and not necessarily to the number of registrations. Each student enrolled is counted only once.

Student-teacher ratio (Table 21)

The *student-teacher ratio* is obtained by dividing the number of *full-time-equivalent students* at a given level of education by the number of *full-time-equivalent teachers* at that same level and for that same type of institution.

The concept of a ratio of students to teachers is different from that of *class size*. Although one country may have a lower ratio of students to teachers than another, this does not necessarily mean that classes are smaller in the first country or that students in the first country receive more teaching. The relationship between the ratio of students to teachers and both average class size and hours of instruction per student is complicated by many factors, including differences between countries in the length of the school year, the number of hours for which a student attends class each day, the length of a teacher's working day, the number of classes or students for which a teacher is responsible, the division of the teacher's time between teaching and other duties, the grouping of students within classes, and the practice of team teaching (see Box 2.4 in Chapter 2 for more details).

Subjects of the intended curriculum (Table 29, 30)

The *intended curriculum* is subdivided in compulsory and optional subjects. Compulsory subjects are to be taught by each school and to be attended by each student. Optional subjects form the flexible part of the curriculum. Compulsory subjects are subdivided into the following subjects:

• *Reading and writing in the mother tongue*: reading and writing in the mother tongue, reading and writing in a second "mother tongue", reading and writing in the tongue of the country as a second language (for non natives), language studies, public speaking, literature.

- *Mathematics*: mathematics, mathematics with statistics, geometry.

- *Science*: science, physics, physical science, chemistry, biology, human biology, environmental science, agriculture/horticulture/forestry.

- *Social studies*: social studies, community studies, contemporary studies, economics, environmental studies, geography, history, humanities, legal studies, studies of the own country, social sciences, ethical thinking, philosophy.

- *Modern foreign languages*: foreign languages.

- *Technology*: orientation in technology, including information technology, computer studies, construction/surveying, electronics, graphics and design, home economics, keyboard skills, word processing, workshop technology/design technology.

- *Arts*: arts, music, visual arts, practical art, drama, performance music, photography, drawing, creative handicraft, creative needlework.

- *Physical education*: physical education, gymnastics, dance, health.

- *Religion*: religion, history of religions, religion culture.

- *Vocational skills*: vocational skills (preparation for specific occupation), techniques, domestic science, accountancy, business studies, career education, clothing and textiles, polytechnic programmes, secretarial studies, tourism and hospitality.

Teacher (Tables 22-27, 31-34)

A *teacher* is defined as a person whose professional activity involves the transmission of knowledge, attitudes and skills that are stipulated in a formal curriculum to students enrolled in an educational programme. The teacher category includes only personnel who participate directly in instructing students.

This definition does not depend on the qualification held by the teacher or on the delivery mechanism. It is based on three concepts: activity, thus excluding those without active teaching duties – although teachers temporarily not at work (*e.g.* for reasons of illness or injury, maternity or parental leave, holiday or vacation) are included; *profession*, thus excluding people who work occasionally or in a voluntary capacity in educational institutions or as teacher aid (*educational personnel*); and *educational programme*, thus excluding people who provide services other than formal instruction to students (*e.g.* supervisors, activity organisers, etc.), whether the programme is established at the national or school level.

Headteachers without teaching responsibilities are not defined as teachers, but classified separately (*educational personnel*). Headteachers who do have teaching responsibilities are defined as (part-time) teachers, even if they only teach for 10 per cent of their time.

Former teachers, people who work occasionally or in a voluntary capacity in schools, people who provide services other than formal instruction, *e.g.*, supervisors or activity organisers, are also excluded.

Teacher salaries, statutory (Tables 25, 26, 27)

Statutory teacher salaries reported in Tables 25-27 refer to the average scheduled gross salary per year for a full-time teacher with the minimum training necessary to be fully qualified at the beginning of his or her teaching career. Reported salaries are defined as the sum of wages (total sum of money paid by the employer for the labour supplied minus the employer's contribution to social security and pension funding). Bonuses which constitute a regular part of the salary (such as a 13th month, holidays or regional bonuses) are included in the figures. *Additional bonuses* (for example, remuneration for teachers in educational priority areas, for participating in school improvement projects or special activities, or for exceptional performance) are excluded from the reported gross salaries. Tables 25a-27a show salaries including the maximum additional bonuses in order to show the incentives for teacher (those are also used in the country profiles).

Salaries at 15 years' experience refer to the scheduled annual salary of a full-time classroom teacher with the minimum training necessary to be fully qualified and with 15 years' experience. The maximum salaries reported refer to the scheduled maximum annual salary (top of the salary scale) of a full-time classroom teacher with the minimum training to be fully qualified for his or her job.

Salary data are reported in accordance with formal policies for public institutions.

Teaching time, statutory (Tables 33, 35, 36)

Statutory teaching time (sometime also referred to as instructional time) is defined as the total number of hours per year for which a full-time classroom teacher is responsible for teaching a group or class of students, according to the formal policy in the specific country. Periods of time formally allowed for breaks between lessons or groups of lessons are excluded.

Teaching hours per year are calculated on the basis of teaching hours per day multiplied by the number of teaching days per year, or on the basis of teaching hours per week multiplied by the number of weeks per year that the school is open for teaching. The number of hours per year that are accounted for by days when the school is closed for festivities and celebrations are excluded.

When no formal data were available, the number of teaching hours was estimated from survey data.

Total public expenditure (Tables 1, 6)

Total public expenditure as used for the calculation of the education indicators, corresponds to the non-repayable current and capital expenditure of all levels of government. Current expenditure includes final consumption expenditure (*e.g.* compensation of employees, consumption intermediate goods and services, consumption of fixed capital, and military expenditure), property income paid, subsidies, and other current transfers paid (*e.g.* social security, social assistance, pensions and other welfare benefits). Capital expenditure is spending to acquire and/or improve fixed capital assets, land, intangible assets, government stocks, and non-military, non-financial assets, and spending to finance net capital transfers.

Typical ages (Tables 16-19)

Typical ages refer to the ages that normally correspond to the age at entry and ending of a cycle of education. These ages relate to the theoretical duration of a cycle assuming full-time attendance and no repetition of a year. The assumption is made that, at least in the ordinary education system, a student can proceed through the educational programme in a standard number of years, which is referred to as the theoretical duration of the programme. The *typical starting age* is the age at the *beginning* of the first school/academic year of the relevant level and programme. The *typical ending* age is the age at the *beginning* of the *last* school/academic year of the relevant level and programme. The *typical graduation age* is the age at the *end* of the *last* school/academic year of the relevant level and programme when the qualification is obtained.

Vocational and technical education (Table 18)

The WEI/UOE programme uses three categories to describe the orientation of educational programmes:

General programmes

General programmes refer to education which is not designed explicitly to prepare participants for a specific class of occupations or trades or for entry into further vocational/technical education programmes. Less than 25 per cent of the programme content is vocational or technical.

Pre-vocational programmes

Pre-vocational programmes refer to education mainly designed as an introduction to the world of work and as preparation for further vocational or technical education. Does not lead to a labour-market relevant qualification. Content is at least 25 per cent vocational or technical.

Vocational programmes

Vocational programmes refer to education which prepares participants for direct entry, without further training, into specific occupations. Successful completion of such programmes leads to a labour-market relevant vocational qualification

■ ANNEX A3 – CROSS-REFERENCE BETWEEN DATA TABLES (ANNEX A4) AND NOTES

	See notes on:
Table 1	Gross Domestic Product (GDP), Purchasing power parity (PPP), Total public expenditure
Table 2	Gini Index
Table 4	Expenditure on educational institutions, Private expenditure (Private sources of funds), Public expenditure (Public sources)
Table 5	Expenditure on educational institutions, Gross Domestic Product (GDP)
Table 6	Public expenditure (Public sources), Total public expenditure
Table 7	Current and capital expenditure, Expenditure on educational institutions
Table 8	Expenditure on educational institutions, Student, Full-time, part-time and full-time equivalent students, Purchasing power parity (PPP), Educational institution
Table 9	Expenditure on educational institutions, Student, Gross Domestic Product (GDP), Educational institution
Table 10	Expenditure on educational institutions, Educational institution, Public and private educational institutions, Public expenditure (Public sources)
Table 11	Current and capital expenditure, Expenditure on educational institutions, Teacher
Table 12	School expectancy, Public and private educational institutions
Table 13	Public and private educational institutions, Net enrolment rate
Table 14	Public and private educational institutions, Student
Table 15	Student, Repeater
Table 16	Entry rate, New entrant, Typical ages
Table 17	Entry rate, New entrant , Typical ages
Table 18	Graduation rates, Typical ages, Vocational and technical education
Table 19	Graduation rates, Typical ages
Table 20	Net enrolment rate, Typical ages
Table 21	Student, Teacher, Full-time, part-time and full-time equivalent students, Full-time, part-time and full-time equivalent teachers, Student-teacher ratio

■ ANNEX A4 – DATA TABLES

SYMBOLS FOR MISSING DATA

Four symbols are employed in the tables and graphs
to denote missing data:

a	Data not applicable because the category does not apply.
m	Data not available.
n	Magnitude is either negligible or zero.
x	Data included in another category/column of the table.

Table 1
GDP per capita, in equivalent US dollars converted using PPPs and other basic reference statistics (1998)

	GDP per capita (in equivalent US dollars converted using PPPs)	Gross Domestic Product (in equivalent millions US dollars converted using PPPs)	GDP growth rate (%)	Total public expenditure as % of GDP	Official market exchange rate (local currency unit to US dollar, 1998 average)	Purchasing Power Parity exchange rate (PPP) to US$	Total population (in thousands)
WEI participants							
Argentina	11 524	431 137	3.9	m	1.0	0.69	36 125
Brazil	6 524	1 117 767	0.2	39.2	1.2	0.78	165 870
Chile	8 612	129 918	3.4	22.2	460.3	270.40	14 822
China	3 345	4 142 559 690	7.8	m	8.3	m	1 238 600
Egypt	3 263	200 344 702	5.6	m	3.4	m	61 401
India	2 217	2 033 806	6.1	m	41.3	8.88	979 670
Indonesia	2 626	538 688	−13.2	21.1	10 014.0	1 750.26	203 680
Jordan	3 714	17 431	2.2	m	0.7	0.31	4 563
Malaysia	8 057	180 906	−7.5	34.1	3.9	1.57	22 180
Paraguay	4 249	22 634	−0.4	22.1	2 755.7	1 048.09	5 219
Peru	4 534	108 200	0.3	12.9	2.9	1.70	24 801
Philippines	3 580	274 248	−0.5	17.9	40.9	8.83	75 174
Russian Federation	6 271	921 313 713	−4.6	m	9.7	m	146 910
Sri Lanka	2 972	5 580	4.7	m	64.6	m	18 778
Thailand	5 757	336 910	−9.4	17.3	41.4	13.76	61 201
Tunisia	5 732	54 199	5.0	m	1.1	0.46	9 335
Uruguay	8 418	28 291	4.5	22.4	10.5	7.71	3 289
Zimbabwe	2 701	31 124	2.5	m	23.7	4.36	11 689
WEI mean	**5 360**	**–**	**3.8**	**23.2**	**–**	**–**	**–**
OECD countries							
Australia	24 226	453 760	5.1	34.4	1.6	1.31	18 751
Austria	23 583	190 507	3.3	51.6	12.4	13.72	8 078
Belgium	23 804	242 877	2.9	50.9	36.3	37.39	10 204
Canada	25 203	762 303	3.0	44.4	1.5	1.16	30 301
Czech Republic	12 939	133 208	−2.3	46.2	32.3	13.50	10 295
Denmark	25 584	135 674	2.9	55.9	6.7	8.58	5 301
Finland	21 780	112 233	4.7	50.5	5.3	6.14	5 153
France[1]	21 676	1 263 682	3.2	52.9	5.9	6.69	58 847
Germany	22 904	1 878 803	2.7	47.5	1.8	2.01	82 047
Greece	14 327	150 667	3.5	50.7	295.5	238.09	10 515
Hungary	10 445	105 956	5.1	36.9	214.4	95.20	10 114
Iceland	25 260	6 921	5.0	39.8	71.0	83.43	274
Ireland	22 699	84 101	10.4	33.2	0.7	0.72	3 705
Italy	22 160	1 276 146	1.4	48.8	1 736.2	1 620.27	57 589
Japan	24 102	3 048 505	−2.8	42.7	130.9	163.52	126 410
Korea	14 384	667 832	−5.8	24.7	1 401.4	665.39	46 430
Luxembourg	37 348	16 022	5.7	43.6	36.3	41.55	427
Mexico	7 879	752 658	4.8	18.8	9.1	5.11	95 846
Netherlands	24 678	387 452	3.8	46.2	2.0	2.00	15 698
New Zealand	17 785	67 440	−0.8	m	1.9	1.47	3 792
Norway	26 147	115 883	2.0	48.0	7.5	9.57	4 432
Poland	8 183	316 392	4.8	44.5	3.5	1.75	38 666
Portugal	15 592	155 435	3.9	42.0	180.1	128.63	9 968
Spain	17 027	670 388	3.8	40.7	149.4	130.59	39 371
Sweden	21 845	193 350	2.9	58.2	7.9	9.85	8 852
Switzerland	27 338	194 372	2.1	37.7	1.4	1.96	7 106
Turkey	6 544	424 011	2.8	m	260 720.0	123 168.96	63 451
United Kingdom	22 050	1 306 171	2.1	39.7	0.6	0.65	59 055
United States	32 262	8 728 800	3.9	m	1.0	1.00	270 300
OECD mean	**20 681**	**–**	**3.8**	**43.5**	**–**	**–**	**–**

1. Excluding DOM (Départements d'Outre-Mer).
Sources: OECD/UNESCO WEI, World Bank, *2001 World Development Indicators.*

Table 2   Income disparity: Gini indices[1]

	Year	Gini index
WEI participants		
Brazil	1998	60.0
Chile	1991	56.5
China	1998	40.3
Indonesia	1996	36.5
Malaysia	1996	48.5
Paraguay	1998	59.1
Peru	1995	46.2
Philippines	1995	45.0
Russia	1994	37.4
Thailand	1996	42.1
WEI mean		*47.2*
OECD countries		
Belgium	1992	25.0
Denmark	1992	24.7
Finland	1991	25.6
Germany	1994	30.0
Greece	1993	32.7
Portugal	1995	35.6
Spain	1990	38.5
Sweden	1992	25.0

1. For explanation of Gini index, see Annex A2.
Source: United Nations University (*WIDER*), World Income Inequality Database.

Table 3   Relative size and expected changes of the school-age population (1999)
Size of the population at the age of primary/lower secondary, upper secondary and tertiary education
as a percentage of the total population and population projections

	Percentage of the population (1999)			Change in the size of the population (2000 = 100)					
				Ages 5-14		Ages 15-19		Ages 20-29	
	Ages 5-14	Ages 15-19	Ages 20-29	1995	2010[1]	1995	2010[1]	1995	2010[1]
WEI participants									
Argentina	19	9	16	98	104	102	104	86	108
Brazil	21	11	18	104	97	96	92	92	109
Chile	19	8	16	94	98	95	113	102	110
China	18	7	17	99	85	98	101	114	99
Egypt	23	12	17	99	100	84	103	89	136
India	m	m	m	96	99	88	110	94	120
Indonesia	21	11	19	101	99	99	99	93	104
Jordan	m	m	m	89	126	90	128	89	124
Malaysia	22	10	18	91	102	87	119	91	121
Paraguay	26	11	16	91	114	81	121	89	140
Peru	23	11	18	98	100	96	105	89	114
Philippines	25	12	16	94	108	94	114	89	122
Russian Federation	14	8	14	120	75	91	67	94	112
Sri Lanka	23	11	19	112	97	92	80	95	109
Thailand	16	9	19	107	90	109	87	100	93
Tunisia	24	11	18	m	m	m	m	m	m
Uruguay	16	8	15	97	103	108	108	92	98
Zimbabwe	27	13	18	95	97	84	112	90	131
WEI mean	*21*	*10*	*17*	*99*	*100*	*94*	*104*	*94*	*115*
OECD countries									
Australia	14	7	15	98	98	96	104	101	103
Austria	12	6	14	98	87	93	99	113	97
Belgium	12	6	13	100	87	103	100	108	94
Canada	14	7	14	97	91	96	106	101	106
Czech Republic	12	7	16	108	73	126	85	89	79
Denmark	12	5	14	90	99	117	124	111	83
Finland	13	6	12	100	89	99	99	104	102
France	13	7	14	102	94	100	95	105	95
Germany	11	6	12	102	84	93	95	122	104
Greece	11	7	15	113	88	112	77	101	81
Hungary	12	7	16	104	79	129	92	91	78
Iceland	16	8	15	97	98	99	106	100	101
Ireland	15	9	16	114	101	104	77	87	97
Italy	10	5	15	102	89	116	95	115	74
Japan	10	6	15	112	101	115	80	101	76
Korea	14	8	18	106	100	104	90	104	84
Luxembourg	12	6	13	90	103	95	113	101	95
Mexico	23	11	19	98	100	102	105	92	101
Netherlands	12	6	14	95	88	101	109	117	92
New Zealand	15	7	14	96	100	99	109	101	105
Norway	13	6	14	92	98	102	117	111	94
Poland	15	9	15	117	78	96	74	88	104
Portugal	11	7	16	108	91	120	86	98	74
Slovak Republic	15	8	16	110	76	107	82	89	94
Spain	10	7	17	114	89	126	78	102	69
Sweden	13	6	13	91	78	101	122	109	101
Switzerland	12	6	13	93	91	94	109	113	100
Turkey	21	11	18	104	108	100	92	86	97
United Kingdom	13	6	13	99	89	97	103	111	102
United States	15	7	14	96	94	92	109	103	113
OECD mean	*13*	*7*	*15*	*102*	*91*	*104*	*98*	*102*	*93*

1. Projections
Source: OECD/UNESCO WEI.

Table 4

Expenditure on educational institutions as a percentage of GDP (1998)

Direct and indirect expenditure on educational institutions from public and private sources for all levels of education,
by source of funds and level of education

	All levels of education			Primary, secondary and post-secondary non-tertiary education			Tertiary education		
	Public[1]	Private[2]	Total	Public[1]	Private[2]	Total	Public[1]	Private[2]	Total
WEI participants									
Argentina[3]	4.0	0.8	4.8	2.7	0.3	3.1	0.8	0.3	1.1
Brazil[3, 4]	4.6	m	m	3.1	m	m	1.1	m	m
Chile	3.5	2.6	6.2	2.7	1.2	3.9	0.6	1.3	1.8
India[3]	m	m	m	2.0	m	m	m	m	m
Indonesia[3, 5]	1.4	0.6	2.0	1.1	0.2	1.4	0.3	0.3	0.6
Jordan[5]	m	m	m	4.1	n	4.1	m	m	m
Malaysia[3]	4.5	m	m	3.0	m	m	1.3	m	m
Paraguay[3]	4.4	m	m	3.5	m	m	0.9	m	m
Peru	2.9	2.1	5.0	2.0	1.3	3.3	0.6	0.7	1.3
Philippines[3, 4]	3.5	2.7	6.2	2.9	1.9	4.9	0.5	0.6	1.2
Sri Lanka[3]	2.8	m	m	x	m	m	x	m	m
Thailand[3]	4.3	3.4	7.6	2.4	1.4	3.8	0.8	1.7	2.6
Tunisia[3, 5]	6.8	m	m	5.4	m	m	1.5	m	m
Uruguay[6]	2.8	m	m	2.0	0.1	2.1	0.6	m	m
Zimbabwe	11.6	m	m	9.3	m	m	2.3	m	m
WEI mean	*4.4*	*–*	*–*	*3.3*	*–*	*–*	*0.9*	*–*	*–*
OECD countries									
Australia	4.3	1.1	5.5	3.2	0.6	3.8	1.1	0.5	1.6
Austria[3]	6.0	0.4	6.4	4.0	0.2	4.2	1.4	0.0	1.5
Belgium	5.0	m	4.9	3.5	x	3.5	0.9	m	0.9
Belgium (Fl.)	4.7	n	4.7	3.4	n	3.4	0.8	n	0.8
Canada	5.5	0.7	6.2	3.7	0.3	4.1	1.5	0.3	1.9
Czech Republic	4.1	0.6	4.7	2.7	0.4	3.1	0.8	0.1	0.9
Denmark	6.8	0.4	7.2	4.3	0.1	4.3	1.5	0.0	1.5
Finland	5.7	x	5.7	3.7	x	3.7	1.7	x	1.7
France	5.9	0.4	6.2	4.1	0.2	4.4	1.0	0.1	1.1
Germany	4.4	1.2	5.5	2.8	0.9	3.7	1.0	0.1	1.0
Greece[3]	3.4	1.3	4.8	2.3	1.1	3.5	1.0	0.2	1.2
Hungary	4.5	0.6	5.0	2.9	0.2	3.1	0.8	0.2	1.0
Iceland	6.5	0.3	6.9	4.2	m	m	1.7	0.0	1.8
Ireland	4.3	0.4	4.7	3.2	0.1	3.3	1.1	0.3	1.4
Italy	4.8	0.2	5.0	3.4	0.0	3.5	0.7	0.2	0.8
Japan	3.5	1.2	4.7	2.8	0.3	3.0	0.4	0.6	1.0
Korea[3]	4.1	3.0	7.0	3.1	0.8	4.0	0.4	2.1	2.5
Mexico	4.1	0.6	4.7	3.0	0.5	3.5	0.8	0.1	0.9
Netherlands	4.5	0.1	4.6	3.0	0.1	3.1	1.1	0.0	1.2
New Zealand[3]	6.0	m	m	4.6	m	m	1.1	m	m
Norway[3]	6.8	0.1	6.9	4.4	0.0	4.4	1.4	0.1	1.5
Poland[3]	5.3	m	m	3.5	m	m	1.2	m	m
Portugal	5.6	0.1	5.7	4.2	n	4.2	1.0	0.1	1.0
Spain	4.4	0.9	5.3	3.3	0.4	3.7	0.8	0.3	1.1
Sweden	6.6	0.2	6.8	4.5	0.0	4.5	1.5	0.2	1.7
Switzerland	5.4	0.5	5.9	4.0	0.5	4.5	1.1	n	1.1
Turkey	2.9	0.5	3.5	1.8	0.5	2.3	0.8	0.0	0.8
United Kingdom	4.6	0.3	4.9	3.4	m	m	0.8	0.3	1.1
United States[3, 6]	4.8	1.6	6.4	3.4	0.3	3.7	1.1	1.2	2.3
OECD mean	*5.0*	*0.7*	*5.7*	*3.5*	*0.4*	*3.7*	*1.1*	*0.3*	*1.3*

1. Including public subsidies to households attributable for educational institutions.

2. Net of public subsidies attributable for educational institutions.

3. Public subsides to households not included in public expenditure, but in private expenditure.

4. Year of reference 1997.

5. Year of reference 1999.

6. Direct expenditure on educational institutions from international sources exceed 1.5% of all public expenditure (1998).

Source: OECD/UNESCO WEI.

Table 5

Expenditure on educational institutions as a percentage of GDP (1998)

Direct and indirect expenditure from public and private sources on educational institutions, by level of education

	Pre-primary education	Primary and secondary education				Tertiary education			All levels of education combined (including undistributed and advanced research programmes)
		All	Primary & lower secondary	Upper secondary	Post-secondary non-tertiary	All	Tertiary-type B (ISCED 5B)	Tertiary-type A (ISCED 5A & 6)	
WEI participants									
Argentina	0.5	3.1	2.4	0.7	n	1.1	0.4	0.7	4.8
Chile	0.4	3.9	2.7	1.2	n	1.8	0.2	1.7	6.2
Indonesia[1]	n	1.4	1.0	0.4	n	0.6	x	x	2.0
Jordan[1]	n	4.1	3.5	0.6	a	m	m	m	m
Peru	0.4	3.3	2.8	0.5	a	1.3	0.3	1.0	5.0
Philippines[2]	0.1	4.9	4.3	0.4	0.1	1.2	n	1.2	6.2
Thailand	0.6	3.8	2.9	0.9	n	2.6	0.6	2.0	7.6
Uruguay	0.3	2.1	1.6	0.5	n	0.6	x	0.6	3.0
WEI mean	*0.3*	*3.3*	*2.7*	*0.6*	*n*	*1.3*	*–*	*–*	*5.0*
OECD countries									
Australia	0.1	3.8	2.8	1.0	0.1	1.6	0.2	1.4	5.5
Austria	0.5	4.2	2.8	1.4	n	1.5	0.3	1.2	6.4
Belgium	0.5	3.5	x	x	x	0.9	m	m	4.9
Canada	0.2	4.1	x	x	0.2	1.9	0.5	1.3	6.2
Czech Republic	0.5	3.1	2.0	1.1	0.1	0.9	0.1	0.8	4.7
Denmark	1.1	4.3	2.9	1.4	n	1.5	x	x	7.2
Finland	0.4	3.7	2.4	1.2	x	1.7	0.2	1.5	5.7
France	0.7	4.4	2.8	1.5	n	1.1	0.3	0.9	6.2
Germany	0.6	3.7	2.1	1.3	0.3	1.0	0.1	1.0	5.5
Greece	x	3.5	x	x	x	1.2	x	x	4.8
Hungary	0.8	3.1	1.9	1.1	0.1	1.0	a	1.0	5.0
Ireland	n	3.3	2.4	0.7	0.1	1.4	x	x	4.7
Italy	0.4	3.5	2.1	1.3	0.1	0.8	n	0.8	5.0
Japan	0.2	3.0	2.1	0.9	x	1.0	0.1	0.9	4.7
Korea	0.1	4.0	2.7	1.3	n	2.5	0.7	1.8	7.0
Mexico	0.4	3.5	2.7	0.8	a	0.9	x	0.9	4.7
Netherlands	0.4	3.1	2.2	0.8	n	1.2	n	1.2	4.6
Norway	0.6	4.4	3.0	1.5	x	1.5	x	1.5	6.9
Portugal	0.2	4.2	2.8	1.2	n	1.0	x	x	5.7
Spain	0.4	3.7	1.3	2.4	x	1.1	x	x	5.3
Sweden	0.6	4.5	3.0	1.5	n	1.7	x	x	6.8
Switzerland	0.2	4.5	2.8	1.6	0.1	1.1	0.1	1.0	5.9
Turkey	m	2.3	1.6	0.7	m	0.8	x	x	3.5
United Kingdom	m	m	m	m	m	1.1	x	x	4.9
United States[3]	0.4	3.7	x	x	x	2.3	x	x	6.4
OECD mean	*0.4*	*3.7*	*2.4*	*1.2*	*0.1*	*1.3*	*0.3*	*1.1*	*5.5*

1. Year of reference 1999.

2. Year of reference 1997.

3. Post-secondary non-tertiary data included in tertiary education.

Source: OECD/UNESCO WEI.

Table 6

Public expenditure on education as a percentage of total public expenditure (1998)
Direct public expenditure on educational institutions plus public subsidies to private sector
(including subsidies for living costs) as a percentage of total public expenditure, by level of education

	Primary, secondary and post-secondary non-tertiary education	Tertiary education	All levels of education combined
WEI participants			
Brazil[1]	7.9	2.9	12.0
Chile	12.1	2.7	16.1
Indonesia[2]	5.7	1.2	6.9
Malaysia	8.9	4.4	14.0
Paraguay	15.8	4.4	20.2
Peru	15.6	4.5	22.3
Philippines[1]	16.2	2.9	19.7
Thailand	14.6	6.6	27.2
Uruguay	8.5	2.6	12.2
WEI mean	*11.7*	*3.6*	*16.7*
OECD countries			
Australia	10.2	3.6	13.9
Austria	7.8	3.2	12.2
Belgium	6.9	2.2	10.2
Canada	8.2	3.9	12.6
Czech Republic	6.3	1.8	9.3
Denmark	8.8	3.9	14.8
Finland	7.6	4.0	12.4
France	7.9	2.0	11.3
Germany	6.3	2.3	9.8
Greece	4.6	2.1	6.9
Hungary	7.8	2.4	12.4
Iceland	10.8	5.6	17.8
Ireland	9.9	3.5	13.5
Italy	7.1	1.6	10.0
Japan[2]	6.6	1.0	8.4
Korea	12.7	1.8	16.5
Mexico	16.2	4.5	22.4
Netherlands	6.8	3.0	10.6
Norway	9.7	4.2	16.1
Poland	7.8	2.7	12.2
Portugal	10.2	2.4	13.5
Spain	8.1	2.2	11.1
Sweden	9.1	3.6	13.7
Switzerland	10.8	3.0	14.6
United Kingdom	8.3	2.6	11.9
OECD mean	*8.7*	*2.9*	*12.7*

1. Year of reference 1997.
2. Year of reference 1999.

Source: OECD/UNESCO WEI.

Table 7

Educational expenditure by resource category (1998)

Distribution of total and current expenditure on educational institutions, by resource category and level of education

	Primary, secondary and post-secondary non-tertiary education						Tertiary education					
	Percentage of total expenditure		Percentage of current expenditure			Other current	Percentage of total expenditure		Percentage of current expenditure			Other current
	Current	Capital	Compensation of teachers	Compensation of other staff	Compensation of all staff		Current	Capital	Compensation of teachers	Compensation of other staff	Compensation of all staff	
WEI participants												
Argentina[1]	95	5	51	44	95	5	96	4	49	35	84	16
Brazil[1,2]	95	5	x	x	83	17	97	3	x	x	85	15
Chile[1]	91	9	x	x	61	39	m	m	m	m	m	m
India[3,4]	97	3	79	8	88	12	m	m	m	m	m	m
Indonesia[1,5]	96	4	66	4	71	29	m	m	33	14	47	53
Malaysia[1]	88	12	70	13	84	16	63	37	42	12	55	45
Paraguay[1]	93	7	72	21	93	7	83	17	7	3	10	1
Peru[1]	90	10	x	x	72	28	88	12	x	x	51	49
Philippines[1,2]	89	11	x	x	62	38	90	10	x	x	69	31
Sri Lanka[1]	m	m	m	m	m	m	73	27	36	24	60	25
Tunisia[1,5]	90	10	x	x	94	6	74	26	x	x	63	37
Uruguay[1]	92	8	70	14	84	16	93	7	64	20	84	16
WEI mean	*93*	*7*	*68*	*15*	*81*	*19*	*84*	*16*	*39*	*16*	*61*	*29*
OECD countries												
Australia	93	7	61	16	77	23	91	9	29	37	65	35
Austria	93	7	72	8	80	20	92	8	57	15	71	29
Belgium[3]	98	2	76	8	84	16	96	4	x	x	76	24
Canada	97	3	62	15	77	23	94	6	36	33	69	31
Czech Republic	92	8	44	16	61	39	88	12	30	21	51	49
Denmark	96	4	53	26	80	20	87	13	52	25	78	22
Finland	91	9	57	13	70	30	91	9	38	25	64	36
France[3]	92	8	x	x	79	21	89	11	x	x	70	30
Germany[3]	92	8	x	x	89	11	89	11	x	x	76	24
Greece	85	15	88	x	88	12	70	30	x	x	62	38
Hungary[1]	92	8	x	x	75	25	88	12	x	x	64	36
Ireland[1]	94	6	81	5	86	14	92	8	48	25	73	27
Italy[1]	96	4	69	14	83	17	82	18	50	26	76	24
Japan	88	12	x	x	87	13	83	17	x	x	65	35
Korea	83	17	72	9	81	19	68	32	38	15	53	47
Mexico[1]	95	5	79	12	91	9	92	8	66	18	84	16
Netherlands	95	5	x	x	76	24	94	6	x	x	76	24
Norway[1]	86	14	x	x	82	18	88	12	x	x	65	35
Poland[1]	91	9	x	x	76	24	85	15	x	x	66	34
Portugal	95	5	x	x	94	6	84	16	x	x	70	30
Spain	94	6	75	10	84	16	78	22	58	20	79	21
Sweden	m	m	46	11	57	43	m	m	x	x	56	44
Switzerland[1]	89	11	72	14	85	15	88	12	56	22	77	23
Turkey[1,4]	84	16	95	1	96	4	77	23	53	36	89	11
United Kingdom[3]	96	4	50	20	70	30	99	1	32	25	57	43
United States[1,4]	89	11	56	26	83	17	91	9	40	35	76	24
OECD mean	*92*	*8*	*67*	*13*	*80*	*20*	*87*	*13*	*46*	*25*	*70*	*30*

1. Public institutions only.
2. Year of reference 1997.
3. Public and government-dependent private institutions only.
4. Post-secondary non-tertiary education included at the tertiary level.
5. Year of reference 1999.

Source: OECD/UNESCO WEI.

Table 8

Expenditure per student (1998)

Expenditure per student in US dollars converted using PPPs on public and private institutions,
by level of education, based on full-time equivalents

	Pre-primary education	Primary education	Lower secondary education	Upper secondary education	All secondary education	Post-secondary non-tertiary education	Tertiary education		
							All	Tertiary-type B	Tertiary-type A & advanced research programmes
	1	2	3	4	5	6	7	8	9
WEI participants									
Argentina[1]	1 662	1 389	1 667	2 229	1 860	a	2 965	4 425	2 572
Brazil[1, 2]	1 065	837	995	1 154	1 076	a	14 618	x (9)	14 618
Chile	1 318	1 500	1 624	1 764	1 713	a	5 897	3 121	6 565
Indonesia[1, 3]	425	116	433	647	497	a	6 840	x (7)	x (7)
Malaysia[1]	385	919	x (5)	x (5)	1 469	5 999	m	m	m
Paraguay[1]	x (2)	572	x (4)	948	948	a	m	2 511	m
Peru	463	480	671	671	671	a	2 088	1 035	3 039
Philippines[1, 2]	433	689	640	1 089	726	3 614	2 799	a	2 799
Thailand	802	1 048	1 091	1 289	1 177	m	6 360	4 971	6 951
Tunisia[1, 3]	239	891	x (5)	x (5)	1 633	a	5 136	5 753	x
Uruguay[1]	1 096	971	1 068	1 480	1 246	a	2 081	x (9)	x (7)
Zimbabwe	m	768	x (5)	x (5)	1 179	x (5)	10 670	5 355	13 521
WEI mean	*789*	*848*	*1 024*	*1 252*	*1 183*	*–*	*5 945*	*3 882*	*7 152*
OECD countries									
Australia	m	3 981	5 184	6 830	5 830	7 218	11 539	8 341	12 279
Austria[1]	5 029	6 065	7 669	8 783	8 163	7 245	11 279	x (7)	x (7)
Belgium[4]	2 726	3 743	x (5)	x (5)	5 970	x (5)	6 508	x (7)	x (7)
Belgium (Fl.)[4]	2 601	3 799	x (5)	x (5)	6 238	x (5)	6 597	x (7)	x (7)
Canada	4 535	m	m	m	m	5 735	14 579	13 795	14 899
Czech Republic	2 231	1 645	2 879	3 575	3 182	1 334	5 584	3 191	6 326
Denmark	5 664	6 713	6 617	7 705	7 200	6 826	9 562	x (7)	x (7)
Finland	3 665	4 641	4 616	5 515	5 111	x (5)	7 327	5 776	7 582
France	3 609	3 752	6 133	7 191	6 605	m	7 226	7 636	7 113
Germany	4 648	3 531	4 641	9 519	6 209	10 924	9 481	5 422	10 139
Greece[2]	x (2)	2 368	x (5)	x (5)	3 287	2 773	4 157	3 232	4 521
Hungary	2 160	2 028	1 906	2 383	2 140	2 304	5 073	a	5 080
Iceland[1]	m	m	m	m	m	m	m	m	m
Ireland	2 555	2 745	x (5)	x (5)	3 934	4 361	8 522	x (7)	x (7)
Italy[1]	4 730	5 653	6 627	6 340	6 458	x (5)	6 295	6 283	6 295
Japan	3 123	5 075	5 515	6 257	5 890	x (5)	9 871	7 270	10 374
Korea	1 287	2 838	3 374	3 692	3 544	a	6 356	4 185	7 820
Luxembourg	m	m	m	m	m	m	m	m	m
Mexico	865	863	1 268	2 253	1 586	a	3 800	x (7)	3 800
Netherlands	3 630	3 795	5 459	5 120	5 304	x (5.7)	10 757	7 592	10 796
New Zealand	m	m	m	m	m	m	m	m	m
Norway[1]	7 924	5 761	7 116	7 839	7 343	x (5)	10 918	x (9)	10 918
Poland	2 747	1 496	x (2)	1 438	1 438	m	4 262	x (9)	4 262
Portugal	1 717	3 121	4 219	5 137	4 636	a	m	m	m
Spain	2 586	3 267	x (5)	x (5)	4 274	x (5)	5 038	4 767	5 056
Sweden	3 210	5 579	5 567	5 701	5 648	m	13 224	x (7)	x (7)
Switzerland[1]	2 593	6 470	7 618	11 219	9 348	7 621	16 563	10 273	17 310
Turkey[1]	m	m	m	m	m	m	m	m	m
United Kingdom[4]	4 910	3 329	x (5)	x (5)	5 230	x (5)	9 699	x (7)	x (7)
United States	6 441	6 043	x (5)	x (5)	7 764	x (7)	19 802	x (7)	x (7)
OECD mean	*3 585*	*3 940*	*5 083*	*5 916*	*5 294*	*5 634*	*9 063*	*–*	*–*

Note: Column of reference is given in brackets after "x". x (2) means that the data are included in column 2.

1. Public institutions only.
2. Year of reference 1997.
3. Year of reference 1999.
4. Public and government-dependent private institutions only.

Source: OECD/UNESCO WEI.

Table 9
Ratio of expenditure per student to GDP per capita (1998)
Expenditure per student relative to GDP per capita on public and private institutions, by level of education, based on full-time equivalents (multiplied by 100)

	Pre-primary education	Primary education	Lower secondary education	Upper secondary education	All secondary education	Post-secondary non-tertiary education	Tertiary education		
							All	Tertiary-type B	Tertiary-type A & advanced research programmes
	1	2	3	4	5	6	7	8	9
WEI participants									
Argentina[1]	14	12	14	19	16	a	25	37	22
Brazil[1,2]	16	12	15	17	16	a	214	x (9)	214
Chile	15	17	19	20	20	a	67	36	75
India[1]	2	10	13	15	14	m	m	m	m
Indonesia[1,3]	16	4	16	24	19	a	259	x (7)	x (7)
Malaysia[1]	5	11	x (5)	x (5)	18	74	m	m	m
Paraguay[1]	x (2)	13	x (4)	22	22	a	m	58	m
Peru	10	11	15	15	15	a	46	23	67
Philippines[1,2]	12	18	17	29	19	97	75	a	75
Thailand	15	19	20	23	21	m	116	90	126
Tunisia[1,3]	4	16	x (5)	x (5)	28	a	90	100	x (8)
Uruguay[1]	13	11	12	17	14	a	24	x (7)	x (7)
Zimbabwe	m	29	x (5)	x (5)	44	x (5)	401	201	508
WEI mean	*11*	*14*	*16*	*20*	*20*	*–*	*132*	*78*	*155*
OECD countries									
Australia	m	16	21	28	24	30	48	34	51
Austria[1]	21	26	33	37	35	31	48	x (7)	x (7)
Belgium[4]	11	16	x (5)	x (5)	28	x (5)	28	x (7)	x (7)
Canada	18	m	m	m	m	23	58	55	59
Czech Republic	17	13	22	28	25	10	43	25	49
Denmark	22	26	26	30	28	27	37	x (7)	x (7)
Finland	17	21	21	25	23	x (5)	34	27	35
France	17	18	29	34	31	x (5)	34	36	34
Germany	20	15	20	42	27	48	41	24	44
Greece[2]	x (2)	17	x (5)	x (5)	23	19	29	23	32
Hungary[1]	21	20	18	23	20	24	53	a	53
Ireland	11	12	x (5)	x (5)	17	19	38	x (7)	38
Italy[1]	21	26	30	29	29	x (5)	28	28	28
Japan	13	21	23	26	24	x (5, 6)	41	30	43
Korea	9	20	23	26	25	a	44	29	54
Mexico	11	11	16	29	20	a	48	x (7)	x (7)
Netherlands	15	15	22	21	21	x (5, 6)	44	31	44
Norway[1]	30	22	27	29	28	x (5)	42	x (9)	42
Poland	34	18	x (2)	18	18	x (5)	52	x (9)	52
Portugal[1]	17	21	28	30	29	a	m	m	m
Spain	15	19	x (5)	x (5)	27	x (5)	30	28	30
Sweden	15	26	25	26	26	m	61	x (7)	x (7)
Switzerland[1]	9	24	28	41	34	28	61	38	63
United Kingdom[4]	23	16	x (5)	x (5)	25	x (5)	46	x (7)	x (7)
United States	20	19	x (5)	x (5)	24	x (6)	61	x (7)	x (7)
OECD mean	*18*	*19*	*24*	*29*	*26*	*26*	*44*	*31*	*45*

Note: Column of reference is given in brackets after "x". x (2) means that the data are included in column 2.

1. Public institutions only.
2. Year of reference 1997.
3. Year of reference 1999.
4. Public and government-dependent private institutions only.

Source: OECD/UNESCO WEI.

Table 10

Public spending on public and private educational institutions (1998)

Proportion of public direct expenditure on public and private educational institutions

	Primary, secondary and post-secondary non-tertiary education				Tertiary education			
	Public institutions	Government-dependent private institutions	Independent private institutions	All private institutions	Public institutions	Government-dependent private institutions	Independent private institutions	All private institutions
WEI participants								
Argentina	86.9	13.1	x	13.1	97.6	2.4	x	2.4
Brazil[1]	99.7	a	0.3	0.3	99.1	n	0.9	0.9
Chile	65.6	33.9	0.5	34.4	56.3	39.6	4.1	43.7
India	69.6	30.4	x	30.4	m	m	m	m
Indonesia[2]	99.9	a	0.1	0.1	100	a	m	m
Jordan[2]	100	a	a	a	m	m	m	m
Peru	98.4	1.6	n	1.6	99.9	0.0	n	0.1
Thailand	96.4	3.6	a	3.6	100	0.0	a	0.0
Tunisia[2]	100	n	n	n	100	n	n	n
Uruguay	100	a	a	a	100	a	a	a
Zimbabwe	100	n	n	n	100	n	n	n
WEI mean	*92.4*	*7.5*	*0.1*	*7.6*	*94.8*	*4.8*	*0.7*	*5.9*
OECD mean	*89.5*	*10.3*	*0.3*	*10.8*	*89.3*	*8.1*	*2.9*	*10.7*

1. Year of reference 1997.
2. Year of reference 1999.
Source: OECD/UNESCO WEI.

Table 11

Change in expenditure on educational institutions due to in/decreases in the expected number of teachers at primary and secondary levels of education, 1998-2010 (1998 = 0)

(assuming changes in the number of teachers lead to equal increases in all current and capital expenditure)

	Scenario	
	Current conditions	100% enrolment rate in primary and 87% in secondary
WEI participants		
Argentina	0.2	0.2
Brazil[1,2]	−0.2	−0.1
Chile	0.1	0.2
Indonesia[3]	0.0	0.5
Malaysia[1]	0.3	0.7
Paraguay[1]	0.7	1.4
Peru	n	n
Philippines[2]	0.6	0.8
Thailand	−0.5	−0.4
Tunisia[1,3]	−0.5	0.2
Uruguay	0.1	0.1
WEI mean	*0.1*	*0.3*

1. Calculations made from student-teacher ratios in public institutions only.
2. Year of reference 1997.
3. Year of reference 1999.
Source: OECD/UNESCO WEI.

Table 12

School expectancy (1999)

Expected years of schooling under current conditions in public and private institutions, excluding education for children under five years of age,
by level of education (based on head counts)

	All levels of education combined			Primary and lower secondary education	Upper secondary education	Post-secondary non-tertiary education	Tertiary education
	M + W	Men	Women	M + W			
WEI participants							
Argentina[1]	14.2	13.8	14.5	10.4	1.8	a	2.6
Brazil[1]	14.9	14.7	15.0	10.6	2.3	a	0.8
Chile[1]	14.3	14.4	14.1	8.2	3.4	a	1.6
China	10.1	m	m	8.6	1.1	0.1	0.3
Egypt	11.0	m	m	7.8	1.8	m	1.3
Indonesia[2]	9.7	9.9	9.4	7.8	1.1	a	0.5
Jordan	11.6	11.6	11.6	8.9	1.5	a	1.0
Malaysia[1]	12.5	12.3	12.8	8.6	1.7	0.1	1.0
Paraguay[1]	11.0	11.0	11.0	9.1	1.2	a	m
Peru[1]	13.9	14.1	13.7	10.7	1.9	n	1.4
Philippines[1]	11.8	11.6	12.1	9.5	0.6	0.1	1.3
Russian Federation	12.2	13.6	14.1	2.5	1.3	n	2.5
Thailand[3]	13.1	13.1	13.0	9.9	2.4	n	1.7
Tunisia	13.4	13.6	13.3	9.9	2.4	a	0.8
Uruguay[1]	15.2	14.0	16.4	9.9	2.2	a	1.9
Zimbabwe	9.9	10.5	9.3	8.6	1.2	a	0.1
WEI mean	*12.4*	*12.7*	*12.8*	*8.8*	*1.7*	*0.1*	*1.3*
OECD countries							
Australia	19.9	19.5	19.9	11.7	4.4	0.5	3.0
Austria	16.0	16.1	15.9	8.2	3.8	0.5	2.2
Belgium	18.5	18.2	18.9	9.0	5.3	0.5	2.7
Canada	16.5	16.3	16.8	8.8	3.3	0.8	2.8
Czech Republic	15.1	15.0	15.2	9.2	2.7	0.4	1.4
Denmark	17.7	17.2	18.2	9.8	3.4	0.1	2.5
Finland	18.3	17.7	19.0	9.0	4.2	x	3.9
France	16.5	16.3	16.7	9.5	3.3	n	2.6
Germany	17.2	17.3	17.1	10.1	2.9	0.5	2.0
Greece	15.6	15.4	15.8	9.1	2.8	0.4	2.5
Hungary	16.0	15.8	16.2	8.2	3.7	0.6	1.8
Iceland	17.7	17.1	18.3	9.9	4.7	0.1	2.0
Ireland	16.0	15.6	16.4	10.7	2.3	0.6	2.4
Italy	15.8	15.5	16.0	8.2	4.2	n	2.3
Japan	m	m	m	9.1	3.0	m	m
Korea	15.8	16.7	14.8	8.9	2.9	a	3.5
Luxembourg	m	m	m	9.2	3.5	0.1	m
Mexico	12.4	12.5	12.4	9.4	1.3	a	0.9
Netherlands	17.1	17.4	16.9	10.4	3.3	0.1	2.3
New Zealand	17.2	16.5	17.8	10.1	3.8	0.3	3.0
Norway	17.9	17.4	18.5	9.9	4.1	0.1	3.1
Poland	16.0	15.6	16.4	8.0	4.0	0.3	2.3
Portugal	16.8	16.5	17.1	10.9	2.9	a	2.3
Spain	17.3	17.0	17.7	10.5	2.6	0.4	2.8
Sweden	20.3	18.6	22.2	9.8	5.7	0.1	2.9
Switzerland	16.3	16.7	15.9	9.6	3.3	0.2	1.7
Turkey	10.6	11.3	9.5	7.3	1.9	a	1.2
United Kingdom	18.9	18.1	19.7	8.9	7.3	x	2.6
United States	17.2	17.7	16.6	9.7	2.7	0.4	3.6
OECD mean	*16.7*	*16.5*	*16.9*	*9.4*	*3.6*	*0.2*	*2.5*

1. Year of reference 1998.
2. Year of reference 2000.
3. Thailand: Full-time participation only. Participation by adults in part-time education accounts for around five more years of school expectancy.

Source: OECD/UNESCO WEI.

Table 13

Transition characteristics at ages 11 through 20 (1999)

Net enrolment rates in public and private institutions, by level of education and age (based on head counts)

	Age 11	Age 12	Age 13	Age 14	Age 15	Age 16		Age 17		Age 18		Age 19		Age 20	
	Primary & Secondary[1]	Primary & Secondary[1]	Primary & Secondary[1]	Primary & Secondary[1]	Primary & Secondary[1]	Primary & Secondary[1]	Tertiary	Primary & Secondary[1]	Tertiary	Primary & Secondary[1]	Tertiary	Primary & Secondary[1]	Tertiary	Primary & Secondary[1]	Tertiary
WEI participants															
Argentina[2]	106	105	95	91	80	71	n	61	3	32	18	17	21	m	22
Brazil[2]	97	97	96	93	85	84	n	71	n	60	3	43	6	30	7
Chile[1]	95	93	90	89	86	87	n	78	m	53	m	20	m	8	m
Egypt	93	86	73	65	67	53	n	m	m	m	m	m	m	m	m
Indonesia[3]	79	94	70	59	45	38	a	39	a	26	12	9	15	2	14
Jordan	87	85	87	79	79	72	m	56	m	16	m	4	m	m	m
Malaysia[2]	95	100	92	90	76	73	n	10	m	13	23	3	21	1	20
Paraguay[2]	91	90	78	70	59	50	n	42	n	27	1	10	2	5	3
Peru[1]	105	99	95	86	82	70	1	m	8	m	15	m	18	m	19
Philippines[2]	95	61	82	78	80	72	24	31	37	13	27	7	12	1	24
Russian Federation	90	95	97	89	74	56	m	22	m	1	m	m	m	m	m
Thailand	99	100	93	86	77	63	n	49	m	33	34	5	29	1	16
Tunisia	102	94	91	84	71	60	m	51	m	42	m	32	m	19	m
Uruguay[2]	109	129	99	81	72	67	a	55	4	34	15	20	14	14	12
Zimbabwe	93	93	121	39	51	53	m	40	m	22	m	13	m	m	m
WEI mean	*96*	*94*	*91*	*79*	*72*	*65*	*2*	*46*	*7*	*29*	*17*	*15*	*15*	*9*	*15*
OECD countries															
Australia	99	99	98	99	97	92	n	79	5	39	29	25	34	20	32
Austria	99	99	99	99	95	92	a	87	n	61	6	26	14	9	20
Belgium	98	99	99	99	100	98	n	95	1	50	35	28	46	16	47
Belgium (Fl.)	96	96	96	95	97	95	n	93	n	42	37	21	45	10	46
Canada	98	99	98	97	98	94	n	81	3	39	15	17	30	13	33
Czech Republic	100	100	100	100	100	100	n	88	n	50	10	17	18	5	20
Denmark	100	100	100	98	97	93	n	82	n	76	n	55	3	30	10
Finland	99	99	99	99	100	94	n	96	n	84	1	27	19	16	31
France	99	99	99	99	98	96	n	90	2	56	25	31	38	13	42
Germany	99	99	100	100	99	97	n	92	1	82	3	59	8	33	15
Greece	99	99	96	97	93	92	a	65	a	20	48	22	69	5	57
Hungary	101	101	99	99	96	93	a	88	a	59	11	29	21	17	24
Iceland	99	99	99	100	98	90	a	77	a	67	n	63	1	36	11
Ireland	101	99	100	99	102	93	n	77	5	42	32	13	36	7	35
Italy	99	101	99	94	88	79	a	73	a	64	5	20	27	7	28
Japan	101	103	102	101	99	95	a	94	m	2	m	1	m	m	m
Korea	99	94	100	98	97	98	n	93	3	12	44	2	59	n	53
Luxembourg	98	90	99	95	92	87	a	81	a	66	m	42	m	25	m
Mexico	96	90	82	73	55	43	a	32	3	17	10	22	13	4	13
Netherlands	98	99	100	99	102	108	a	91	4	64	16	29	26	25	31
New Zealand	100	99	98	98	96	90	n	72	3	31	23	16	32	10	33
Norway	99	99	99	99	100	94	n	93	n	87	n	42	14	19	28
Poland	97	97	97	97	96	93	a	90	x	74	1	35	25	21	30
Portugal	110	115	111	112	95	84	a	81	4	50	16	29	26	13	29
Spain	106	105	105	104	96	87	a	79	n	42	24	26	32	19	37
Sweden	101	101	101	101	97	97	n	97	n	95	n	33	13	25	22
Switzerland	100	100	99	99	97	91	n	85	n	79	1	57	6	27	13
Turkey	89	74	63	51	47	40	n	22	3	8	10	6	15	n	15
United Kingdom	99	99	98	98	103	84	n	71	2	29	24	16	33	13	34
United States	104	113	102	96	107	88	n	81	1	27	35	8	41	4	34
OECD mean	*100*	*99*	*98*	*97*	*95*	*89*	*n*	*81*	*1*	*51*	*17*	*27*	*27*	*16*	*29*

1. Including post-secondary non-tertiary.
2. Year of reference 1998.
3. Year of reference 2000.

Source: OECD/UNESCO WEI.

Table 14

Distribution of students in primary, secondary and tertiary education, by type of institution (1999)

	Primary and secondary education				Tertiary education			
	Public institutions	Government-dependent private institutions	Independent private institutions	All private institutions	Public institutions	Government-dependent private institutions	Independent private institutions	All private institutions
WEI participants								
Argentina[1]	78	19	4	22	79	7	14	21
Brazil[1]	89	a	11	11	39	a	61	61
Chile[1]	56	35	9	44	29	20	51	71
Egypt	94	a	6	6	m	a	m	m
Indonesia[2]	83	a	17	17	15	a	85	85
Jordan	76	a	24	24	m	m	m	m
Malaysia[1]	97	x	3	3	61	a	39	39
Paraguay[1]	81	9	9	19	m	m	m	m
Peru[1]	86	3	11	14	53	a	47	47
Philippines[1]	86	a	14	14	26	a	74	74
Russian Federation	100	a	n	n	95	a	5	5
Thailand	89	9	2	11	79	a	21	21
Tunisia	96	a	4	4	m	a	m	m
Uruguay[1]	86	a	14	14	89	a	11	11
Zimbabwe	16	84	a	84	m	m	a	m
WEI mean	*81*	*11*	*8*	*19*	*57*	*2*	*37*	*43*
OECD countries								
Australia	74	25	a	25	m	m	m	m
Austria	93	7	n	7	93	7	n	7
Belgium (Fl.)	34	66	m	66	x	x	m	x
Canada	95	2	3	5	100	n	n	n
Czech Republic	96	4	a	4	95	5	a	5
Denmark	89	11	a	11	100	n	a	n
Finland	96	4	a	4	89	11	a	11
France	79	17	4	21	86	3	11	14
Germany	95	x	x	5	94	x	x	6
Iceland	97	3	n	3	94	6	n	6
Ireland	99	a	1	1	94	a	6	6
Italy	94	1	6	6	88	a	12	12
Japan	89	a	10	10	21	a	79	79
Korea	78	21	1	22	20	a	80	80
Luxembourg	88	6	6	12	43	57	a	57
Mexico	90	a	10	10	72	a	28	28
Netherlands	23	76	n	77	32	68	a	68
New Zealand	94	1	5	6	96	4	n	4
Norway	96	x	x	4	89	x	x	11
Poland	98	2	n	2	76	n	24	24
Portugal	89	a	11	11	67	a	33	33
Spain	70	24	6	30	88	1	11	12
Sweden	98	2	a	2	94	5	1	6
Switzerland	94	2	3	6	81	12	6	19
Turkey	98	a	2	2	m	a	m	m
United Kingdom	65	31	4	35	a	100	n	100
United States	89	a	11	11	71	a	29	29
OECD mean	*86*	*12*	*4*	*14*	*74*	*12*	*15*	*26*

1. Year of reference 1998.
2. Year of reference 2000.
Source: OECD/UNESCO WEI.

Table 15

Percentage of students repeating current grade (1999)

	Primary education	Lower secondary education	Upper secondary education
WEI participants			
Argentina[1]	5.3	7.6	5.3
Brazil[1]	25.1	15.0	18.1
Chile[1]	3.2	3.8	5.1
China	0.8	0.1	m
Egypt	6.0	9.7	3.5
Jordan	0.7	1.4	1.2
Malaysia[1]	a	a	0.3
Paraguay[1]	8.6	1.9	1.4
Peru[1]	9.8	7.0	2.7
Philippines[1]	1.9	2.2	0.8
Russian Federation	1.2	1.0	0.5
Sri Lanka[1]	5.1	3.3	m
Thailand	3.5	a	a
Tunisia	18.3	20.9	23.9
Uruguay[1]	8.4	18.9	5.7
Zimbabwe	a	a	a
WEI mean	*6.1*	*5.8*	*4.9*

1. Year of reference 1998.

Source: OECD/UNESCO WEI.

Table 16

Gross entry rates to secondary education (1999)

	Lower secondary education			Upper secondary education		
	M + W	Men	Women	M + W	Men	Women
WEI participants						
Argentina[1]	96	94	99	62	57	68
Chile[1]	83	83	84	83	82	84
China	80	83	77	43	44	41
Indonesia[2]	61	61	61	37	38	36
Malaysia[1]	96	96	95	80	73	88
Paraguay	69	70	69	42	41	43
Peru[1]	91	93	88	67	68	67
Philippines[1]	90	89	92	59	53	64
Thailand	123	127	118	90	90	90
Tunisia	118	110	127	53	55	50
Uruguay[1]	109	111	107	78	72	84
WEI mean	*92*	*92*	*92*	*61*	*59*	*63*

1. Year of reference 1998.
2. Year of reference 2000.

Source: OECD/UNESCO WEI.

Table 17

Entry rates to tertiary education (1999)

Sum of net entry rates for single years of age in tertiary-type A and tertiary-type B education in public and private institutions, by gender

	Tertiary-type B (Net entry rates)			Tertiary-type A (Net entry rates)		
	M + W	Men	Women	M + W	Men	Women
WEI participants						
Argentina[1]	26	16	37	51	45	57
Chile[1, 2]	15	15	14	37	39	35
China[2]	7	m	m	6	x	x
Indonesia[3]	6	6	7	11	13	9
Malaysia[1]	10	11	9	13	11	15
Paraguay[1]	1	1	1	m	m	m
Peru[1, 2]	18	15	21	15	x	x
Philippines[1]	a	a	a	31	27	35
Thailand[2]	20	20	21	35	32	38
Tunisia[2]	4	4	3	19	17	20
Uruguay[1, 2]	17	8	26	26	20	32
WEI mean	*12*	*11*	*15*	*24*	*25*	*30*
OECD countries						
Australia	m	m	m	45	37	53
Belgium (Fl.)	26	21	31	30	29	30
Czech Republic[2]	13	10	16	23	24	22
Denmark	34	24	46	34	32	36
Finland	a	a	a	67	58	77
France	21	21	20	35	29	42
Germany[4]	13	10	17	28	28	29
Hungary	n	n	1	58	53	64
Iceland	10	10	9	55	36	75
Italy	1	1	1	40	35	46
Japan[2]	33	22	44	37	46	28
Korea[2]	46	48	44	43	48	37
Mexico	1	1	1	24	26	22
Netherlands	1	1	1	54	51	57
New Zealand	37	27	46	71	59	82
Norway	7	7	7	57	44	71
Poland[2]	1	x	x	59	x	x
Slovak Republic[4]	3	1	4	35	35	35
Spain	11	11	11	46	39	53
Sweden	5	5	5	65	54	77
Switzerland	15	16	13	29	32	26
United Kingdom	28	28	29	45	43	48
United States	14	13	15	45	42	48
OECD mean	*15*	*13*	*17*	*45*	*40*	*48*

1. Year of reference 1998.
2. Entry rate for type A and B programmes calculated as gross entry rate.
3. Year of reference 2000.
4. Entry rate for type B programmes calculated as gross entry rate.

Source: OECD/UNESCO WEI.

Table 18

Upper secondary graduation rates and enrolment patterns (1999)

Ratio of upper secondary graduates to total population at typical age of graduation (multiplied by 100)
in public and private institutions, by programme orientation and gender
Enrolment patterns in public and private institutions, by programme orientation

| | Graduation rates | | | | | | | Distribution of enrolment by type of programme | | |
| | Total (unduplicated) | | | General programmes | | Pre-vocational/ Vocational programmes | | | | |
	M + W	Men	Women	M + W	Women	M + W	Women	General	Pre-vocational	Vocational
WEI participants[1]										
Argentina[2]	40	38	43	19	26	21	17	57		43
Brazil[3]	44	39	50	26	29	21	23	70	a	30
Chile[2]	56	52	61	31	36	25	26	58	a	42
China	37	39	36	17	15	20	21	43	x	57
Egypt	m	m	m	m	m	m	m	34	a	67
India	47	m	m	m	m	m	m	94	a	58
Indonesia[4]	32	32	31	19	19	13	12	61	a	39
Jordan	73	69	77	55	63	17	14	74	a	26
Malaysia[5]	62	49	76	60	74	2	1	89	n	12
Paraguay[2]	31	28	34	27	30	4	4	84	a	16
Peru[2]	57	57	57	44	45	13	12	76	24	a
Philippines[2]	57	52	63	57	63	a	a	100	a	a
Russian Federation	m	m	m	m	m	m	m	100	n	n
Thailand	65	54	76	49	59	16	16	72	a	28
Tunisia	34	m	m	30	32	4	m	93	n	70
Uruguay[2]	m	m	m	m	m	m	m	81	a	19
WEI mean	*49*	*46*	*55*	*36*	*41*	*13*	*13*	*74*	*17*	*24*
OECD countries										
Austria	m	m	m	m	m	m	m	22	73	71
Belgium	m	m	m	m	m	m	m	34	a	66
Belgium (Fl.)[6]	83	82	85	33	38	63	64	m	m	m
Canada								92	82	a
Czech Republic[7]	52	44	59	13	15	43	49	20	5	80
Denmark	90	82	98	54	66	59	63	47	a	53
Finland	89	84	94	53	64	67	71	47	a	53
France	85	84	86	33	39	67	61	43	n	57
Germany[2]	92	90	94	33	36	59	58	35	a	65
Greece	67	58	76	59	62	20	16	74	a	26
Hungary	92	91	93	24	30	71	65	34	55	11
Iceland	82	79	84	54	65	43	32	67	1	32
Ireland[6]	86	79	94	78	85	15	16	79	21	a
Italy[2]	73	69	79	28	37	65	63	35	12	6
Japan	95	92	97	69	73	27	26	74	0	26
Korea	91	91	91	56	53	36	38	62	a	38
Luxembourg[1]	60	57	63	26	30	34	33	36	n	64
Mexico[1]	31	29	33	28	29	4	4	86	a	14
Netherlands[1]	92	88	95	35	39	56	56	33	a	67
New Zealand[1]	m	m	m	a	a	a	a	m	m	m
Norway[1]	m	m	m	67	82	66	48	46	a	54
Poland[1]	m	m	m	30	41	69	59	34	a	66
Portugal	m	m	m	m	m	m	m	75	a	25
Slovak Republic	93	92	92	m	m	m	m	20	a	80
Spain	68	62	74	47	53	29	31	69	n	31
Sweden	74	71	78	41	45	33	31	50	a	47
Switzerland[1]	83	86	81	m	m	m	m	35	a	65
Turkey[1]	m	m	m	20	19	19	16	51	a	49
United Kingdom	m	m	m	m	m	m	m	33	x	67
United States	78	79	77	m	m	m	m	m	m	m
OECD mean	*79*	*76*	*82*	*40*	*46*	*43*	*41*	*49*	*36*	*47*

1. Graduation rate may include some double-counting.
2. Year of reference 1998.
3. Year of reference 1997 for graduation rates and 1998 for enrolment patterns.
4. Year of reference 2000.
5. Year of reference 1999 for graduation rates and 1998 for enrolment patterns.
6. Short ISCED 3C programmes excluded.
7. Low figure due to extension of lower secondary education by one year in 1996.

Source: OECD/UNESCO WEI.

Table 19

Gross graduation rates in tertiary education (1999)

Ratio of graduates to total population at typical age of graduation (multiplied by 100)
in public and private institutions, by destination, type and duration of programme

	Tertiary-type B programmes	Tertiary-type A programmes				Advanced research programmes
	All first degree programmes	Medium first-degree programmes (3 to less than 5 years)	Long first-degree programmes (5 to 6 years)	Very long first-degree programmes (more than 6 years)	Second-degree programmes	Ph. D or equivalent
WEI participants						
Argentina[1]	10.0	x	7.5	x	x	0.1
Brazil[2]	x	8.9	x	x	x	0.6
Chile[1]	10.8	7.8	8.7	0.2	n	0.8
China	m	m	a	a	a	m
Indonesia[3]	9.1	3.2	1.5	1.8	a	0.2
Malaysia	5.3	6.9	0.1	x	x	0.8
Paraguay[1]	2.5	m	m	m	m	m
Peru[1]	3.2	n	7.8	x	a	x
Philippines[1]	a	20.0	x	x	x	0.4
Russian Federation	m	m	26.1	m	m	m
Sri Lanka[1]	m	1.6	0.3	n	n	0.6
Thailand	20.0	13.1	x	n	m	2.0
Tunisia	1.9	7.3	a	a	1.2	m
Uruguay[1]	3.8	1.7	2.1	2.5	x	1.1
WEI mean	*6.1*	*6.4*	*4.2*	*0.6*	*0.2*	*0.7*
OECD countries						
Australia	m	47.7	a	a	9.1	1.2
Austria	m	1.0	13.3	n	0.1	1.7
Belgium (Fl.)	26.2	11.0	5.8	1.1	5.4	0.7
Canada	16.7	27.6	1.4	1.1	5.3	0.9
Czech Republic	5.8	2.2	8.6	a	1.7	0.5
Denmark	25.2	6.5	n	a	9.5	m
Finland	22.1	17.1	19.1	a	n	1.9
France	17.9	33.9	5.6	0.8	6.7	1.2
Germany	11.8	6.3	12.4	a	n	2.0
Hungary	m	24.4	x	a	m	m
Iceland	8.5	26.0	2.8	a	1.7	n
Ireland	21.0	24.8	1.2	x	13.1	0.8
Italy	0.6	1.2	15.5	a	3.3	0.4
Japan	29.9	29.0	x	a	2.6	0.6
Korea	31.2	26.5	0.6	a	3.0	0.6
Netherlands	1.0	35.0	1.4	a	1.4	1.2
New Zealand	10.5	31.0	7.4	0.6	17.3	0.8
Norway	6.4	32.6	2.7	2.9	4.8	1.0
Poland	0.8	15.9	14.0	a	18.2	m
Slovak Republic	2.5	5.3	14.4	n	n	0.5
Spain	5.8	14.4	20.6	n	m	m
Sweden	2.9	26.6	1.3	a	0.6	2.5
Switzerland	19.0	7.8	11.8	0.9	5.1	2.6
Turkey	4.2	9.5	n	a	0.8	0.2
United Kingdom	13.4	38.8	1.2	n	15.2	1.5
United States	8.6	33.2	a	n	14.3	1.3
OECD mean	*10.4*	*22.4*	*6.3*	*0.3*	*7.2*	*1.0*

1. Year of reference 1998.
2. Year of reference 1997.
3. Year of reference 2000.

Source: OECD/UNESCO WEI.

Table 20

Net enrolment rates for primary and secondary education (1999)

Ratio of students enrolled of typical primary and secondary school age to total population at corresponding age

	Age group	Enrolment rate[1]	Of which:		
			In primary education	In lower secondary education	In upper secondary education
Primary school-age population					
Argentina[2]	6-11	107.2	106.7	0.4	n
Brazil[2]	7-12	96.2	92.0	0.5	n
Chile[2]	6-11	97.3	88.5	0.1	n
Egypt	6-10	98.0	95.1	2.7	n
Indonesia[3]	7-12	88.6	85.2	3.5	n
Malaysia[2]	6-11	107.5	95.6	n	n
Paraguay[2]	6-11	93.8	92.2	n	n
Peru[2]	6-11	105.3	103.2	2.1	n
Philippines[2]	6-11	99.4	99.4	n	n
Thailand	6-11	102.2	86.7	0.2	n
Tunisia	6-11	93.5	92.7	0.6	n
Uruguay[2]	6-11	101.7	92.3	1.3	n
Zimbabwe	6-12	89.8	89.1	0.7	n
WEI mean		*98.5*	*93.7*	*0.9*	*n*
Secondary school-age population					
Argentina[2]	12-17	84.2	10.2	49.3	24.2
Brazil[2]	13-17	85.9	42.9	25.4	17.4
Chile[2]	12-17	87.4	17.5	30.8	39.2
Egypt	11-16	72.6	5.3	41.8	25.5
Indonesia[3]	13-18	48.1	4.9	25.3	15.9
Malaysia[2]	12-18	69.1	0.1	41.7	23.9
Paraguay[2]	12-17	65.6	23.4	30.5	11.7
Peru[2]	12-16	86.6	25.1	45.2	16.3
Philippines[2]	12-15	75.6	26.2	46.4	2.9
Thailand	12-17	77.1	14.9	41.0	21.1
Tunisia	12-18	71.2	16.5	36.8	17.7
Uruguay[2]	12-17	84.5	18.4	44.3	21.1
Zimbabwe	13-18	55.5	18.0	20.5	17.1
WEI mean		*74.1*	*17.1*	*38.8*	*19.6*

Note: Students at the typical age of primary and secondary school age can be enrolled at different levels of education, *e.g.* due to repetition. The net enrolment rate takes all levels into account.

1. Net enrolment rates higher than 100% are due to inconsistencies between the enrolment and the population data.
2. Year of reference 1998.
3. Year of reference 2000.

Source: OECD/UNESCO WEI.

Table 21

Student-teacher ratio (1999)

For public and private institutions, by level of education (based on full-time equivalents)

	Pre-primary education	Primary education	Lower secondary education	Upper secondary education	All secondary education	Tertiary-type B	Tertiary-type A and advanced research programmes	All tertiary education
WEI participants								
Argentina[1]	18.1	20.7	15.5	12.4	14.3	19.7	29.0	m
Brazil[1]	21.2	28.9	33.7	38.6	36.2	x	x	13.3
Chile[1]	m	33.4	33.4	26.9	29.1	m	m	m
China[1]	27.4	20.3	16.9	m	m	14.2	14.7	m
Egypt	m	23.4	22.0	12.6	16.9	m	m	m
Indonesia[2]	19.0	23.1	19.8	17.2	18.7	x	x	12.5
Jordan[1, 3]	21.4	m	m	17.3	m	m	m	m
Malaysia[1, 3]	27.1	21.6	x	x	19.3	m	m	m
Paraguay[1]	24.6	19.7	x	x	9.9	10.3	m	m
Peru[1]	29.3	25.2	17.2	17.2	17.2	14.3	13.6	13.8
Philippines[1]	11.3	34.4	x	x	32.9	a	17.2	17.2
Russian Federation[2]	m	17.6	14.1	x	11.5	12.3	10.1	11.0
Thailand	24.6	20.7	23.5	21.6	22.7	30.9	27.5	28.5
Tunisia[1, 3]	10.9	23.9	25.8	21.3	23.8	x	x	26.5
Uruguay[1]	31.0	20.6	11.7	24.8	15.1	x	x	7.4
Zimbabwe	m	41.0	x	x	27.3	x	x	32.3
WEI mean	*24.5*	*25.0*	*21.2*	*21.4*	*21.1*	*16.9*	*18.7*	*18.1*
OECD countries								
Australia[4]	m	17.3	13.7	10.8	12.7	m	11.8	m
Austria	17.5	14.5	9.6	10.0	9.8	m	16.5	15.0
Belgium (Fl.)	17.7	13.9	x	x	8.8	x	x	18.1
Canada	15.1	18.7	18.7	20.0	19.3	14.5	m	m
Czech Republic	19.5	23.4	16.2	13.1	14.7	15.3	14.8	14.9
Denmark	6.5	10.6	11.6	13.2	12.4	m	m	m
Finland	12.3	17.4	10.6	16.6	13.5	x	15.7	m
France	19.3	19.6	12.9	12.7	12.8	21.4	15.8	16.9
Germany	23.7	21.0	16.4	12.4	15.2	13.9	12.0	12.3
Greece	15.9	13.5	10.6	10.7	10.6	20.2	29.3	26.0
Hungary	11.8	10.9	10.9	10.3	10.6	x	x	12.1
Iceland	5.7	13.3	x	13.5	m	7.0	8.2	8.0
Ireland	14.7	21.6	x	x	14.6	15.9	18.2	17.3
Italy	13.2	11.3	10.3	10.2	10.3	10.6	25.6	24.8
Japan	19.0	21.2	17.1	14.1	15.4	9.1	13.0	11.5
Korea	23.9	32.2	21.9	22.5	22.2	m	m	m
Luxembourg[3]	16.7	12.5	x	x	9.9	m	m	m
Mexico	24.4	27.2	35.5	26.9	32.2	x	x	14.8
Netherlands	x	16.6	x	x	17.7	m	m	12.0
New Zealand	6.6	20.5	19.8	12.8	16.1	11.3	16.0	14.8
Norway	5.1	12.6	10.1	9.9	m	x	x	13.4
Slovak Republic	10.4	19.6	13.5	13.8	13.6	x	x	10.3
Spain	17.1	15.4	x	x	12.9	10.2	17.3	16.4
Sweden	m	13.3	13.3	15.5	14.5	x	9.3	9.5
Switzerland[3]	17.8	16.1	12.1	12.6	12.3	m	m	m
Turkey	15.3	30.0	a	16.1	16.1	45.4	19.5	21.5
United Kingdom[5]	16.5	22.5	17.4	12.4	14.7	x	x	18.5
United States	19.3	16.3	16.8	14.5	15.6	9.8	15.4	14.0
OECD mean	*15.4*	*18.0*	*15.2*	*14.1*	*14.6*	*15.7*	*16.2*	*15.3*

1. Year of reference 1998.
2. Year of reference 2000.
3. Public institutions only.
4. Includes only general programmes at the lower and upper secondary levels of education.
5. Includes only general programmes at the upper secondary level of education.

Source: OECD/UNESCO WEI.

Table 22

Age distribution of teachers (1999)

Percentage of teachers in public and private institutions, by level of education and age group (based on head counts)

	Primary education					Lower secondary education					Upper secondary education				
	< 30	30-39	40-49	50-59	> 60	< 30	30-39	40-49	50-59	> 60	< 30	30-39	40-49	50-59	> 60
WEI participants															
Argentina[1]	30	31	28	10	1	24	35	27	12	2	24	35	27	12	2
Brazil[1]	35	36	22	5	1	28	34	29	9	1	29	33	29	9	1
Chile[1]	9	24	37	26	5	9	24	37	26	5	10	31	35	18	5
China[1]	33	27	27	13	0	48	28	15	8	n	41	34	14	12	n
Indonesia[2]	52	35	10	4	n	21	53	18	7	1	19	51	20	8	1
Jordan[1, 3]	x	x	x	x	x	43	40	14	3	x	39	43	14	5	x
Malaysia[1, 3]	23	49	18	10	0	15	51	25	9	n	x	x	x	x	x
Philippines[3]	10	25	21	37	7	13	38	31	16	3	13	38	31	16	3
Tunisia[1, 3]	x	x	x	x	x	32	43	21	5	n	28	42	24	6	n
WEI mean	*27*	*32*	*23*	*15*	*2*	*26*	*38*	*24*	*10*	*1*	*25*	*38*	*24*	*11*	*2*
OECD countries															
Austria	16	31	38	14	1	9	31	43	16	1	7	28	40	23	1
Belgium (Fl.)	20	31	28	20	n	x	x	x	x	x	14	23	36	26	2
Canada	12	24	39	24	1	12	24	39	24	1	12	24	39	24	1
Czech Republic	15	27	25	29	5	15	27	25	28	5	9	26	31	28	6
Finland	14	32	28	25	1	9	27	31	31	1	6	25	34	30	5
France	13	29	38	21	n	14	23	31	32	1	11	26	31	30	1
Germany	7	15	38	37	4	4	10	41	41	4	3	22	40	31	4
Iceland	16	30	32	17	6	x	x	x	x	x	7	24	34	24	11
Ireland	13	28	34	19	6	11	26	35	23	5	x	x	x	x	x
Italy	5	27	40	25	4	n	9	46	41	3	n	18	45	34	3
Korea	22	31	30	15	2	14	49	23	11	3	11	44	31	13	2
Luxembourg[3]	27	21	29	22	n	9	26	32	30	3	x	x	x	x	x
Netherlands	14	21	40	23	1	x	x	x	x	x	7	19	40	32	2
New Zealand	19	21	36	20	3	17	21	36	22	3	13	21	38	24	4
Norway	x	x	x	x	x	16	22	30	27	5	7	19	34	32	7
Slovak Republic	24	23	28	23	3	14	20	37	27	3	16	28	33	19	4
Sweden	12	15	33	35	6	14	19	25	35	7	7	17	28	40	8
Switzerland[3]	21	25	34	18	2	12	26	35	24	3	5	27	35	27	6
United Kingdom[4]	21	20	37	22	1	17	22	39	21	1	18	22	39	21	1
OECD mean	*16*	*25*	*34*	*23*	*3*	*12*	*24*	*34*	*27*	*3*	*9*	*24*	*36*	*27*	*4*

1. Year of reference 1998.
2. Year of reference 2000.
3. Public institutions only.
4. Includes only general programmes in upper secondary education.

Source: OECD/UNESCO WEI.

Table 23

Gender distribution of teachers (1999)

Percentage of women among teaching staff in public and private institutions, by level of education (based on head counts)

	Pre-primary education	Primary education	Lower secondary education	Upper secondary education	Post-secondary non-tertiary education	Tertiary-type B programmes	Tertiary-type A and advanced research programmes	All levels of education
WEI participants								
Argentina[1]	96	89	71	65	a	67	45	75
Brazil[1]	98	94	86	73	a	x	42	85
Chile[1]	98	74	74	53	a	m	m	70
China[1]	94	49	40	36	m	m	36	48
Indonesia[2]	m	54	44	38	a	x	27	47
Jordan[1, 3]	99	x	62	46	a	m	m	62
Malaysia[1, 3]	m	63	61	x	15	34	40	60
Peru[1]	96	60	41	x	a	28	m	55
Philippines[1]	92	87	76	76	x	a	m	84
Russian Federation[2]	x	98	m	82	49	74	49	77
Tunisia[1, 3]	95	50	41	41	a	28	44	47
WEI mean	96	72	60	57	–	46	40	65
OECD countries								
Australia	m	m	m	m	m	m	45	m
Austria	99	89	64	49	50	43	26	62
Belgium (Fl.)	99	73	x	55	x	41	13	63
Canada	68	67	67	67	45	x	m	64
Czech Republic	100	85	81	56	50	54	50	72
Denmark	92	63	63	30	30	m	m	67
Finland	96	71	71	57	x	x	45	66
France	78	78	63	51	m	42	31	61
Germany	97	82	57	39	37	45	26	57
Hungary	100	85	86	59	x	x	38	76
Iceland	98	77	x	44	x	34	45	73
Ireland	92	85	56	x	x	33	33	61
Italy	99	95	73	59	m	30	28	75
Korea	100	67	56	28	a	29	24	46
Luxembourg[3]	98	60	38	x	m	m	m	54
Mexico	94	66	49	41	a	x	x	62
Netherlands	x	71	x	40	x	m	m	m
New Zealand	98	82	62	53	50	52	40	66
Norway	m	x	72	44	x	x	36	59
Slovak Republic	100	93	77	66	x	x	37	76
Spain	93	68	x	52	x	50	34	58
Sweden	97	80	62	50	45	x	37	66
Switzerland[3]	99	72	45	32	m	m	25	51
United Kingdom	90	76	55	56	a	x	32	61
United States	95	86	60	51	41	49	37	66
OECD mean	95	77	63	49	43	42	34	64

1. Year of reference 1998.
2. Year of reference 2000.
3. Public institutions only.

Source: OECD/UNESCO WEI.

Table 24

Percentage of women teaching staff by age group (1999)

Percentage of women among teaching staff in public and private institutions, by level of education and age group
(based on head counts)

	Primary education					Lower secondary education					Upper secondary education				
	< 30	30-39	40-49	50-60	> 60	< 30	30-39	40-49	50-60	> 60	< 30	30-39	40-49	50-60	> 60
WEI participants															
Argentina[1]	87	87	93	92	86	69	70	75	72	58	63	65	70	66	51
Brazil[1]	90	96	97	95	82	82	89	87	85	74	67	78	74	71	56
Chile[1]	79	76	74	73	59	79	76	74	73	59	55	54	51	55	42
China[1]	60	50	43	29	10	47	39	35	22	11	45	34	31	20	11
Indonesia[2]	54	54	54	54	n	44	44	44	44	44	39	38	38	37	36
Jordan[1,3]	x	x	x	x	x	65	68	47	28	x	56	51	15	1.8	x
Malaysia[1,3]	70	65	57	46	29	72	64	53	42	21	x	x	x	x	x
Philippines[1]	88	89	90	86	84	75	75	79	77	75	75	75	79	77	75
Tunisia[1,3]	x	x	x	x	x	56	48	40	30	n	50	39	36	31	11
WEI mean	*76*	*74*	*72*	*68*	*50*	*65*	*64*	*59*	*52*	*43*	*56*	*54*	*49*	*45*	*41*
OECD countries															
Austria	93	90	89	83	41	76	71	62	49	43	68	57	48	34	24
Belgium (Fl.)	84	76	72	59	52	x	x	x	x	x	66	61	55	45	18
Canada	78	71	70	57	57	78	71	69	57	57	78	70	69	56	56
Czech Republic	83	87	86	84	73	81	83	83	82	68	62	62	59	50	31
Finland	79	70	71	69	63	70	68	71	73	78	64	61	54	56	57
France	89	78	75	76	73	67	62	63	61	61	54	52	51	48	46
Germany	95	93	85	73	57	73	63	60	52	41	59	51	41	28	21
Iceland	75	79	79	74	63	x	x	x	x	x	50	52	43	38	34
Ireland	90	87	81	83	88	70	65	56	42	44	x	x	x	x	x
Italy	97	97	95	92	86	82	78	75	71	59	35	67	60	52	41
Korea	83	80	58	38	19	83	65	44	17	5	64	33	18	8	3
Luxembourg[3]	70	59	56	53	60	51	44	39	30	17	x	x	x	x	x
Netherlands	87	81	67	60	64	x	x	x	x	x	61	50	40	31	25
New Zealand	86	83	82	78	82	71	62	61	57	55	63	54	53	52	54
Norway	x	x	x	x	x	73	76	73	68	67	59	53	45	36	30
Slovak Republic	92	95	96	89	80	76	83	82	69	40	72	75	68	52	24
Sweden	82	76	80	81	84	66	62	61	62	60	55	51	48	51	47
Switzerland[3]	84	73	69	67	55	65	51	41	38	25	44	37	31	27	20
United Kingdom[4]	83	72	75	73	73	67	55	52	50	47	68	57	54	51	49
OECD mean	*85*	*80*	*77*	*72*	*65*	*72*	*66*	*62*	*55*	*48*	*60*	*55*	*49*	*42*	*34*

1. Year of reference 1998.
2. Year of reference 2000.
3. Public institutions only.
4. Includes only general programmes in upper secondary education.

Source: OECD/UNESCO WEI.

Table 25
Teachers' salaries in primary education (1999)
Annual statutory teachers' salaries in public institutions in primary education, in equivalent US dollars converted using PPPs

	Starting salary /minimum training	Salary after 15 years' experience /minimum training	Salary at top of scale /minimum training	Ratio of starting salary to GDP per capita	Ratio of salary after 15 years' experience (min. train.) to GDP per capita	Ratio of salary after 15 years' experience to starting salary	Years from starting to top salary	Salary after 15 years' experience (typical train.) per teaching hour
WEI participants								
Argentina[1]	8 906	12 377	14 697	0.8	1.1	1.4	21–24	2
Brazil[1]	4 818	7 191	10 877	0.7	1.1	1.5	25	9
Chile[1]	9 067	10 476	14 043	1.1	1.2	1.2	30	19
Indonesia[1]	1 160	1 836	3 499	0.6	0.7	1.6	33	1
Jordan[2]	8 096	10 652	27 347	2.2	2.9	1.3	41	14
Malaysia[1]	6 635	11 017	15 756	0.8	1.4	1.7	29	15
Peru[1]	4 282	4 282	4 282	0.9	0.9	1.0	a	8
Philippines[1]	9 638	10 640	11 457	2.7	3.0	1.1	22	12
Thailand[1]	5 781	14 208	27 098	1.0	2.5	2.5	37	19
Tunisia[1]	11 706	12 877	13 449	2.0	2.2	1.1	35	22
Uruguay[1]	5 241	6 281	7 582	0.6	0.7	1.2	32	20
WEI mean	*6 848*	*9 258*	*13 644*	*1.2*	*1.6*	*1.4*	*31*	*13*
OECD countries								
Australia	25 661	36 971	37 502	1.0	1.5	1.4	9	44
Austria	21 804	26 389	44 159	0.9	1.1	1.2	34	39
Belgium (Fl.)	22 901	30 801	36 594	0.9	1.3	1.3	27	37
Belgium (Fr.)	22 043	29 878	35 685	0.9	1.2	1.4	27	35
Czech Republic	6 806	9 032	12 103	0.5	0.7	1.3	32	12
Denmark	28 140	32 684	32 684	1.1	1.2	1.2	8	51
England	19 999	33 540	33 540	0.9	1.5	1.7	9	m
Finland	18 110	24 799	25 615	0.8	1.1	1.4	20	38
France	19 761	26 599	39 271	0.9	1.2	1.3	34	30
Germany	29 697	36 046	38 996	1.3	1.5	1.2	28	46
Greece	19 327	23 619	28 027	1.3	1.6	1.2	33	30
Hungary	5 763	8 252	11 105	0.5	0.7	1.4	40	14
Iceland	19 939	21 891	25 377	0.7	0.8	1.1	18	34
Ireland	21 940	35 561	40 141	0.8	1.4	1.6	23	39
Italy	19 188	23 137	28 038	0.9	1.0	1.2	35	31
Korea	23 759	39 411	62 281	1.5	2.5	1.7	37	60
Mexico	10 465	13 294	22 345	1.2	1.5	1.3	11	17
Netherlands	25 896	30 881	37 381	1.0	1.2	1.2	25	33
Norway	22 194	25 854	27 453	0.8	0.9	1.2	28	36
New Zealand	16 678	32 573	32 573	0.9	1.8	2.0	8	33
Portugal	18 751	27 465	50 061	1.1	1.6	1.5	26	31
Scotland	19 765	32 858	32 858	0.9	1.5	1.7	11	35
Spain	24 464	28 614	37 317	1.3	1.6	1.2	42	36
Sweden	18 581	24 364	m	0.8	1.1	1.3	m	m
Switzerland	33 209	43 627	51 813	1.2	1.6	1.3	25	49
Turkey	9 116	10 327	11 541	1.2	1.4	1.1	27	14
United States	25 707	34 705	43 094	0.8	1.0	1.4	30	36
OECD mean	*20 358*	*27 597*	*33 752*	*1.0*	*1.3*	*1.4*	*25*	*34*

1. Year of reference 1998.
2. Year of reference 2000.
Source: OECD/UNESCO WEI.

Table 25a
Teachers' salaries in primary education *including all additional bonuses* (1999)
Annual statutory teachers' salaries in public institutions in *primary* education, in equivalent US dollars converted using PPPs

	Starting salary /minimum training	Salary after 15 years' experience /minimum training	Salary at top of scale /minimum training	Ratio of starting salary to GDP per capita	Ratio of salary after 15 years' experience (min. train.) to GDP per capita	Percentage additional bonus of years' experience (see Table 25)
WEI participants						
Argentina[1]	9 857	13 327	15 647	0.9	1.2	7.7
Brazil[1]	4 818	7 191	10 877	0.7	1.1	n
Chile[1]	14 459	15 868	19 435	1.7	1.8	51.5
Indonesia[1]	1 624	2 938	5 598	0.6	1.1	60.0
Jordan[2]	8 096	10 652	27 347	2.2	2.9	n
Malaysia[1]	7 056	11 803	17 001	0.9	1.5	7.1
Peru[1]	4 752	4 752	4 752	1.0	1.0	11.0
Philippines[1]	12 620	13 715	14 609	3.5	3.8	28.9
Thailand[1]	5 781	14 208	27 098	1.0	2.5	n
Tunisia[1]	11 706	12 877	13 449	2.0	2.2	m
Uruguay[1]	9 842	11 675	14 724	1.2	1.4	85.9
WEI mean	*8 237*	*10 819*	*15 504*	*1.4*	*1.9*	*16.9*

1. Year of reference 1998.
2. Year of reference 2000.
3. Including additional bonuses.
Source: OECD/UNESCO WEI.

Table 26

Teachers' salaries in lower secondary education (1999)

Annual statutory teachers' salaries in public institutions in lower secondary education, in equivalent US dollars converted using PPPs

	Starting salary /minimum training	Salary after 15 years' experience /minimum training	Salary at top of scale /minimum training	Ratio of starting salary to GDP per capita	Ratio of salary after 15 years' experience (min. train.) to GDP per capita	Ratio of salary after 15 years' experience to starting salary	Years from starting to top salary	Salary after 15 years' experience (typical train.) per teaching hour
WEI participants								
Argentina[1]	14 426	20 903	25 396	1.3	1.8	1.4	21–24	3
Brazil[1]	11 970	11 180	13 954	1.8	1.7	0.9	25	14
Chile[1]	9 067	10 476	14 043	1.1	1.2	1.2	30	19
Indonesia[1]	1 160	1 836	3 499	0.4	0.7	1.6	32	2
Jordan[2]	8 096	10 652	27 347	2.2	2.9	1.3	41	14
Malaysia[1]	12 698	20 076	27 772	1.6	2.5	1.6	22	28
Peru[1]	4 235	4 235	4 235	0.9	0.9	1.0	a	9
Philippines[1]	9 638	10 640	11 457	2.7	3.0	1.1	22	12
Thailand[1]	5 781	14 208	27 098	1.0	2.5	2.5	37	22
Tunisia[1]	15 062	16 467	17 169	2.6	2.9	1.1	30	36
Uruguay[1]	5 241	6 281	7 582	0.6	0.7	1.2	32	21
WEI mean	*8 852*	*11 541*	*16 323*	*1.5*	*1.9*	*1.4*	*29*	*16*
OECD countries								
Australia	26 658	37 138	37 577	1.1	1.5	1.4	8	47
Austria	22 421	27 503	46 735	0.9	1.1	1.2	34	42
Belgium (Fl.)	23 428	32 819	40 017	1.0	1.3	1.4	27	46
Belgium (Fr.)	22 561	31 903	39 115	0.9	1.3	1.4	27	44
Czech Republic	6 806	9 032	12 103	0.5	0.7	1.3	32	13
Denmark	28 140	32 684	32 684	1.1	1.2	1.2	8	51
England	19 999	33 540	33 540	0.9	1.5	1.7	9	m
Finland	20 394	28 225	29 530	0.9	1.2	1.4	20	43
France	21 918	28 757	41 537	1.0	1.3	1.3	34	45
Germany	33 196	38 596	43 945	1.4	1.6	1.2	28	53
Greece	19 650	23 943	28 987	1.3	1.6	1.2	33	38
Hungary	5 763	8 252	11 105	0.5	0.7	1.4	40	15
Iceland	19 939	21 891	25 377	0.7	0.8	1.1	18	34
Ireland	23 033	35 944	40 523	0.9	1.4	1.6	22	49
Italy	20 822	25 397	31 062	0.9	1.1	1.2	35	41
Korea	23 613	39 265	62 135	1.5	2.5	1.7	37	77
Mexico	13 357	15 592	27 643	1.5	1.8	1.2	11	19
Netherlands	26 874	33 056	41 066	1.1	1.3	1.2	24	38
Norway	22 194	25 854	27 453	0.8	0.9	1.2	28	41
New Zealand	16 678	32 573	32 573	0.9	1.8	2.0	8	35
Portugal	18 751	27 465	50 061	1.1	1.6	1.5	26	41
Scotland	19 765	32 858	32 858	0.9	1.5	1.7	11	37
Spain	26 669	31 178	40 082	1.5	1.7	1.2	42	56
Sweden	18 704	24 487	m	0.8	1.1	1.3	m	m
Switzerland	39 162	52 247	60 615	1.4	1.9	1.3	23	61
Turkey	8 144	9 355	10 568	1.1	1.2	1.1	m	16
United States	25 155	33 418	44 397	0.7	1.0	1.3	30	35
OECD mean	*21 252*	*28 629*	*35 511*	*1.0*	*1.4*	*1.4*	*25*	*41*

1. Year of reference 1998.
2. Year of reference 2000.
Source: OECD/UNESCO WEI.

Table 26a

Teachers' salaries in lower secondary education *including all additional bonuses* (1999)

Annual statutory teachers' salaries in public institutions in *lower secondary* education, in equivalent US dollars converted using PPPs

	Starting salary /minimum training	Salary after 15 years' experience /minimum training	Salary at top of scale /minimum training	Ratio of starting salary to GDP per capita	Ratio of salary after 15 years' experience (min. train.) to GDP per capita	Percentage additional bonus of starting salaries (see Table 26)
WEI participants						
Argentina[1]	15 789	22 266	26 759	1.4	1.9	9.4
Brazil[1]	11 970	11 180	13 954	1.8	1.7	n
Chile[1]	14 459	15 868	19 435	1.7	1.8	59.5
Indonesia[1]	1 624	2 938	5 598	0.6	1.1	40.0
Jordan[2]	8 096	10 652	27 347	2.2	2.9	n
Malaysia[1]	13 575	21 568	29 822	1.7	2.7	6.9
Peru[1]	4 701	4 701	4 701	1.0	1.0	11.0
Philippines[1]	12 620	13 715	14 609	3.5	3.8	30.9
Thailand[1]	5 781	14 208	27 098	1.0	2.5	n
Tunisia[1]	15 062	16 467	17 169	2.6	2.9	m
Uruguay[1]	9 842	11 675	14 724	1.2	1.4	87.8
WEI mean	*10 320*	*13 203*	*18 292*	*1.7*	*2.2*	*24.6*

1. Year of reference 1998.
2. Year of reference 2000.
3. Including additional bonuses.
Source: OECD/UNESCO WEI

Table 27

Teachers' salaries in upper secondary education (1999)

Annual statutory teachers' salaries in public institutions in upper secondary education, in equivalent US dollars converted using PPPs

	Starting salary /minimum training	Salary after 15 years' experience /minimum training	Salary at top of scale /minimum training	Ratio of starting salary to GDP per capita	Ratio of salary after 15 years' experience (min. train.) to GDP per capita	Ratio of salary after 15 years' experience to starting salary	Years from starting to top salary	Salary after 15 years' experience (typical train.) per teaching hour
WEI participants								
Argentina[1]	14 426	20 903	25 396	1.3	1.8	1.4	21–24	3
Brazil[1]	12 598	16 103	18 556	1.9	2.5	1.3	25	20
Chile[1]	9 067	10 637	14 020	1.1	1.2	1.2	30	19
Indonesia[1]	1 207	2 211	3 499	0.5	0.8	1.8	32	2
Jordan[2]	8 096	10 652	27 347	2.2	2.9	1.3	41	14
Malaysia[1]	12 698	20 076	27 772	1.6	2.5	1.6	22	28
Peru[1]	4 235	4 235	4 235	0.9	0.9	1.0	a	9
Philippines[1]	9 638	10 640	11 457	2.7	3.0	1.1	22	12
Thailand[1]	5 781	14 208	27 098	1.0	2.5	2.5	37	22
Tunisia (general)[1]	18 235	19 770	20 577	3.2	3.4	1.1	30	42
Tunisia (vocational)[1]	16 545	18 105	18 886	2.9	3.2	1.1	30	m
Uruguay[1]	5 703	6 744	8 044	0.7	0.8	1.2	32	22
WEI mean	*9 852*	*12 857*	*17 241*	*1.7*	*2.1*	*1.4*	*29*	*17*
OECD countries (general programmes)								
Australia	26 658	37 138	37 577	1.1	1.5	1.4	8	48
Austria	24 027	30 376	53 443	1.0	1.2	1.3	34	49
Belgium (Fl.)	29 075	41 977	50 461	1.2	1.7	1.4	25	62
Belgium (Fr.)	28 151	41 079	49 581	1.1	1.7	1.5	25	61
Czech Republic	8 052	10 695	14 316	0.6	0.8	1.3	32	16
Denmark	29 986	40 019	42 672	1.1	1.5	1.3	7	80
England	19 999	33 540	33 540	0.9	1.5	1.7	9	m
Finland	21 047	29 530	31 325	0.9	1.3	1.4	20	47
France	21 918	28 757	41 537	1.0	1.3	1.3	34	49
Germany	35 546	41 745	49 445	1.5	1.8	1.2	28	61
Greece	19 650	23 943	28 987	1.3	1.6	1.2	33	38
Hungary	6 908	10 355	13 217	0.6	0.9	1.5	40	19
Iceland	20 775	25 795	30 954	0.8	1.0	1.2	18	56
Ireland	23 033	35 944	40 523	0.9	1.4	1.6	22	49
Italy	20 822	26 175	32 602	0.9	1.2	1.3	35	43
Korea	23 613	39 265	62 135	1.5	2.5	1.7	37	80
Netherlands	27 133	46 148	54 720	1.1	1.8	1.7	24	53
Norway	22 194	25 854	27 453	0.8	0.9	1.2	28	51
New Zealand	16 678	32 573	32 573	0.9	1.8	2.0	8	37
Portugal	18 751	27 465	50 061	1.1	1.6	1.5	26	46
Scotland	19 765	32 858	32 858	0.9	1.5	1.7	11	36
Spain	29 058	33 988	43 100	1.6	1.8	1.2	39	62
Sweden	20 549	26 210	m	0.9	1.1	1.3	m	m
Switzerland	46 866	62 052	70 548	1.7	2.2	1.3	23	92
Turkey	8 144	9 355	10 568	1.1	1.2	1.1	27	19
United States	25 405	36 219	44 394	0.8	1.1	1.4	30	38
OECD mean	*22 839*	*31 887*	*39 144*	*1.0*	*1.5*	*1.4*	*25*	*50*

1. Year of reference 1998.
2. Year of reference 2000.
Source: OECD/UNESCO WEI.

Table 27a

Teachers' salaries in upper secondary education *including all additional bonuses* (1999)

Annual statutory teachers' salaries in public institutions in *upper secondary* education, in equivalent US dollars converted using PPPs

	Starting salary /minimum training	Salary after 15 years' experience /minimum training	Salary at top of scale /minimum training	Ratio of starting salary to GDP per capita	Ratio of salary after 15 years' experience (min. train.) to GDP per capita	Percentage additional bonus of starting salaries (see Table 27)
WEI participants						
Argentina[1]	15 789	22 266	26 759	1.4	1.9	9.4
Brazil[1]	12 598	16 103	18 556	1.9	2.5	n
Chile[1]	14 644	16 214	19 597	1.7	1.9	61.5
Indonesia[1]	1 689	3 537	5 598	0.6	1.3	40.0
Jordan[2]	8 096	10 652	27 347	2.2	2.9	n
Malaysia[1]	13 575	21 568	29 822	1.7	2.7	6.9
Peru[1]	4 701	4 701	4 701	1.0	1.0	11.0
Philippines[1]	12 620	13 715	14 609	3.5	3.8	30.9
Thailand[1]	5 781	14 208	27 098	1.0	2.5	n
Tunisia (general)[1]	18 235	19 770	20 577	3.2	3.4	m
Tunisia (vocational)[1]	16 545	18 105	18 886	2.9	3.2	n
Uruguay[1]	10 305	12 489	15 585	1.2	1.5	80.7
WEI mean	*11 215*	*14 444*	*19 095*	*1.9*	*2.4*	*23.1*

1. Year of reference 1998.
2. Year of reference 2000.
3. Including additional bonuses.
Source: OECD/UNESCO WEI

Table 28
Intended instruction time (1999)
Total intended instruction time per year for students 9 to 14 years of age (in hours)

	Ages						Total 9-11	Total 12-14
	9	10	11	12	13	14		
WEI participants								
Argentina[1]	729	729	729	816	936	936	2 187	2 688
Brazil[1]	800	800	800	800	800	800	2 400	2 400
Chile[1]	1 140	900	900	990	990	1 020	2 940	3 000
Egypt[1]	918	1 053	1 053	972	1 026	1 026	3 024	3 024
Indonesia[1]	1 114	1 172	1 231	1 231	1 231	1 231	3 516	3 692
Jordan[2]	777	916	944	944	974	974	2 636	2 892
Malaysia[1]	964	1 005	1 005	1 189	1 189	1 189	2 973	3 567
Paraguay[1]	660	660	660	912	912	912	1 980	2 736
Peru[1]	774	774	774	903	903	903	2 322	2 709
Philippines[1]	1 067	1 067	1 067	1 467	1 467	1 467	3 200	4 400
Russian Federation[1]	756	675	837	864	1 143	945	2 268	2 952
Thailand[1]	1 080	1 200	1 200	1 167	1 167	1 167	3 480	3 500
Tunisia[1]	960	960	960	840	900	900	2 880	2 640
Uruguay[1]	455	455	455	1 295	1 295	1 517	1 365	4 107
Zimbabwe[1]	753	753	753	753	1 289	1 289	2 259	3 331
WEI mean	*863*	*875*	*891*	*1 009*	*1 081*	*1 085*	*2 629*	*3 176*
OECD countries								
Australia	m	m	m	a	1 013	1 017	m	m
Austria	m	m	m	1 002	1 156	1 249	m	3 407
Belgium (Fl.)	m	m	m	a	960	960	m	m
Belgium (Fr.)	m	m	m	1 048	1 048	m	m	m
Czech Republic	m	m	m	798	827	887	m	2 512
Denmark	m	m	m	840	900	930	m	2 670
England	m	m	m	940	940	940	m	2 820
Finland	m	m	m	684	855	855	m	2 394
France	m	m	m	841	979	979	m	2 799
Germany	m	m	m	864	921	921	m	2 706
Greece	m	m	m	1 036	1 036	1 036	m	3 108
Hungary	m	m	m	780	902	902	m	2 584
Iceland	m	m	m	793	817	817	m	2 427
Ireland	m	m	m	935	935	935	m	2 806
Italy	m	m	m	1 105	1 105	1 105	m	3 315
Japan	m	m	m	875	875	875	m	2 625
Korea	m	m	m	867	867	867	m	2 601
Mexico	m	m	m	1 167	1 167	1 167	m	3 500
Netherlands	m	m	m	1 067	1 067	1 067	m	3 200
New Zealand	m	m	m	903	988	988	m	2 879
Norway	m	m	m	770	855	855	m	2 480
Portugal	m	m	m	930	930	930	m	2 790
Scotland	m	m	m	1 000	1 000	1 000	m	3 000
Spain	m	m	m	794	870	870	m	2 534
Sweden	m	m	m	741	741	741	m	2 222
Turkey	m	m	m	864	864	864	m	2 592
United States	m	m	m	m	m	980	m	m
OECD mean	*m*	*m*	*m*	*902*	*947*	*951*	*m*	*2 781*

1. Year of reference 1998.
2. Year of reference 2000.
Source: OECD/UNESCO WEI.

Table 29
Distribution of instruction time by subject, ages 9-11 (1999)
Intended instruction time as a percentage of total intended instruction time for students 9 to 11 years of age, by subject,
and division of instruction time into compulsory and non-compulsory parts of the curriculum

	Reading and writing/ mother tongue	Mathematics	Science	Social studies	Modern foreign languages	Technology	Arts	Physical education	Religion	Vocational skills	Other	Total compulsory part	Flexible part
WEI participants													
Argentina[1]	19	19	15	15	7	4	7	7	a	a	n	93	7
Chile[1]	x	x	x	x	x	x	x	x	x	x	x	88	12
Egypt[1]	34	16	5	4	5	2	4	5	8	2	15	100	m
Indonesia[1]	22	22	13	11	a	a	5	5	5	13	5	100	a
Jordan[2]	24	16	13	8	12	a	3	6	9	5	3	100	a
Malaysia[1]	21	14	10	8	14	n	4	4	12	4	n	93	7
Paraguay[1]	29	15	9	11	x	7	11	7	x	x	11	100	a
Peru[1]	x	x	x	x	x	x	x	x	x	x	x	70	30
Philippines[1]	13	13	13	13	13	n	8	4	a	13	13	100	a
Russian Federation[1]	35	17	7	7	x	7	7	7	a	m	0	87	0
Thailand[1]	14	10	x	x	x	x	x	x	x	23	39	86	14
Tunisia[1]	27	13	5	7	a	2	3	3	4	a	36	100	a
Uruguay[1]	28	29	13	19	a	a	9	3	a	a	a	100	a
Zimbabwe[1]	17	17	14	11	17	n	5	5	8	3	3	100	n
WEI mean	*22*	*15*	*10*	*9*	*7*	*2*	*6*	*5*	*4*	*6*	*10*	*94*	*5*

1. Year of reference 1998.
2. Year of reference 2000.
Source: OECD/UNESCO WEI.

Table 30

Distribution of instruction time by subject, ages 12-14 (1999)

Intended instruction time as a percentage of total intended instruction time for students 12 to 14 years of age, by subject, and division of instruction time into compulsory and non-compulsory parts of the curriculum

	Reading and writing/ mother tongue	Mathematics	Science	Social studies	Modern foreign languages	Technology	Arts	Physical education	Religion	Vocational skills	Other	Total compulsory part	Flexible part
WEI participants													
Argentina[1]	13	13	13	15	8	8	8	8	a	a	5	93	7
Chile[1]	x	x	x	x	x	x	x	x	x	x	x	100	n
India[1]	25	14	11	8	14	a	6	6	6	3	8	100	n
Indonesia[1]	16	16	14	13	6	a	5	5	5	15	5	100	n
Jordan[2]	20	13	15	9	16	4	3	4	9	6	3	100	a
Malaysia[1]	14	11	11	14	11	5	5	5	9	5	n	90	10
Paraguay[1]	21	13	15	14	x	13	11	5	x	x	8	100	a
Peru[1]	14	14	12	23	6	a	6	6	6	7	0	93	7
Philippines[1]	9	9	9	9	9	18	6	3	a	n	9	82	18
Russian Federation[1]	24	14	15	14	x	6	4	5	a	m	0	81	18
Thailand[1]	11	6	9	11	x	x	3	9	x	6	14	69	31
Tunisia[1]	17	14	5	15	5	5	7	10	5	a	17	100	a
Uruguay[1]	13	13	19	18	8	a	5	5	a	a	a	81	19
Zimbabwe[1]	14	14	11	9	14	9	7	4	7	10	2	100	n
WEI mean	*16*	*13*	*12*	*13*	*7*	*5*	*6*	*6*	*4*	*4*	*7*	*92*	*8*
OECD countries													
Australia	12	12	11	11	6	9	8	9	n	n	1	80	20
Austria	11	14	13	11	9	5	11	10	5	2	9	100	n
Belgium (Fl.)	14	13	5	9	14	6	6	6	6	n	n	80	20
Belgium (Fr.)	15	13	6	12	12	3	3	9	6	n	4	82	18
Czech Republic	14	14	13	18	11	n	9	7	n	4	5	94	6
Denmark	20	13	12	11	10	n	9	7	3	n	3	90	10
England	12	12	12	14	16	13	5	8	5	n	2	100	n
Finland	20	12	10	10	9	4	8	8	4	n	16	100	n
France	17	14	12	12	11	7	7	11	n	n	1	93	7
Germany	14	13	10	12	16	4	10	10	5	1	2	96	4
Greece	12	11	10	10	15	5	6	8	6	1	16	100	n
Hungary	12	12	12	10	9	2	7	6	n	4	4	78	22
Iceland	15	12	8	7	15	n	14	9	3	6	n	88	12
Ireland	24	12	10	19	10	n	n	5	7	n	2	88	12
Italy	23	10	10	14	11	9	13	7	3	n	n	100	n
Japan	14	12	11	12	13	8	11	10	n	n	8	100	n
Korea	14	12	12	11	12	5	10	9	n	4	6	93	7
Mexico	14	14	19	18	9	9	6	6	n	3	3	100	n
Netherlands	10	10	8	11	14	5	7	9	n	n	3	78	22
New Zealand	17	16	14	14	n	8	4	11	n	n	n	84	16
Norway	16	13	9	11	16	n	8	10	7	n	10	100	n
Portugal	13	13	15	17	10	n	10	10	3	n	10	100	n
Scotland	12	12	9	9	7	9	9	6	7	n	n	80	20
Spain	18	13	10	10	11	5	12	8	x	n	n	88	12
Sweden	22	14	12	13	12	x	3	8	x	n	10	94	6
Turkey	14	11	8	11	11	8	5	2	5	5	n	83	17
United States	17	16	14	12	7	3	7	12	1	5	7	100	n
OECD mean	*15*	*13*	*11*	*12*	*11*	*5*	*8*	*8*	*3*	*1*	*5*	*92*	*8*

1. Year of reference 1998.
2. Year of reference 2000.

Source: OECD/UNESCO WEI.

Table 31

Educational personnel as a percentage of the labour force aged 25 to 64 (1999)

	All levels of education			Primary and secondary education			Tertiary education		
	Classroom teachers, academic staff & other teachers	Other educational personnel	Total educational personnel	Classroom teachers, academic staff & other teachers	Other educational personnel	Total educational personnel	Classroom teachers, academic staff & other teachers	Other educational personnel	Total educational personnel
WEI participants									
Argentina[1]	5.9	x	5.9	4.4	x	4.4	1.0	x	1.0
Brazil[1]	3.9	m	m	3.1	m	m	0.3	m	m
Chile[1]	2.4	0.4	2.8	2.1	0.4	2.5	m	m	m
Indonesia[2]	3.0	0.5	3.5	2.6	0.4	3.0	0.3	0.1	0.4
Malaysia[1]	4.2	1.9	6.1	3.5	1.2	4.7	0.2	0.0	0.2
Paraguay[1]	3.5	1.4	4.9	3.1	1.4	4.5	0.1	n	0.1
Peru[1]	4.9	1.7	6.6	3.8	1.1	4.9	0.6	0.3	1.0
Philippines[1]	2.9	0.3	3.2	2.3	0.3	2.5	0.4	m	m
Thailand	3.0	0.3	3.3	2.1	m	2.1	0.2	m	m
Tunisia[1]	6.6	3.1	9.7	6.0	2.5	8.5	0.3	0.3	0.6
Uruguay[1]	4.2	m	m	2.8	m	m	1.1	m	m
Zimbabwe	3.1	m	m	3.1	m	m	0.1	m	m
WEI mean	*4.0*	*1.2*	*5.1*	*3.2*	*1.0*	*4.1*	*0.4*	*0.1*	*0.6*
OECD countries									
Australia[3]	3.7	m	m	3.1	m	m	0.6	m	m
Austria	4.7	m	m	3.2	m	m	0.8	m	m
Belgium (Fl.)	m	m	m	m	m	m	m	m	m
Canada	3.5	0.6	4.1	2.2	0.5	2.7	1.0	n	1.1
Czech Republic[4]	3.7	3.3	7.0	2.7	2.1	4.8	0.5	0.4	0.9
Denmark	m	m	m	3.5	m	m	m	m	m
Finland	4.3	4.2	8.5	3.0	1.7	4.7	0.8	0.9	1.7
France	4.5	2.8	7.3	3.3	2.2	5.5	0.6	0.3	0.8
Germany	3.9	m	m	2.4	m	m	0.9	m	m
Hungary	6.2	2.8	9.0	4.6	1.8	6.4	0.7	m	m
Iceland	7.8	3.5	11.4	4.3	2.4	6.7	1.2	0.4	1.6
Ireland	4.7	0.6	5.3	3.8	0.1	3.9	0.8	0.5	1.3
Italy	4.7	1.7	6.4	3.6	1.5	5.1	0.4	n	0.4
Japan	3.0	1.1	4.2	1.9	0.7	2.6	0.9	0.4	1.3
Korea	2.7	0.8	3.5	1.8	0.5	2.2	0.8	0.3	1.1
Luxembourg	3.7	m	m	3.3	m	m	m	m	m
Mexico	4.9	3.9	8.8	3.6	2.8	6.5	0.7	0.7	1.4
Netherlands	m	m	m	3.4	m	m	m	m	m
New Zealand	4.7	1.6	6.3	3.4	0.5	3.9	0.8	1.0	1.7
Norway	5.2	m	m	4.4	m	m	0.7	m	m
Spain	5.2	m	m	3.8	m	m	0.9	m	m
Sweden	4.2	m	m	3.4	m	m	0.8	m	m
Switzerland	3.9	m	m	2.8	m	m	0.8	m	m
Turkey	3.4	m	m	2.9	m	m	0.4	m	m
United Kingdom	3.8	m	m	3.1	m	m	0.4	m	m
United States[4]	4.2	3.9	8.1	2.8	2.4	5.2	0.9	1.3	2.2
OECD mean	*4.4*	*2.4*	*6.9*	*3.2*	*1.5*	*4.6*	*0.7*	*0.5*	*1.3*

1. Year of reference 1998.
2. Year of reference 2000.
3. The figures for teaching staff are expressed in full-time equivalents.
4. The figures in the column «Other educational personnel» are expressed in full-time equivalents.

Source: OECD/UNESCO WEI.

Table 32

Distribution of teachers by teachers qualification (1999)

	Below upper secondary education		Upper secondary education uncomplete tertiary education		ISCED 5B		ISCED 5A & 6	
	no teacher training	with teacher training	no teacher training	with teacher training	no teacher training	with teacher training	no teacher training	with teacher training
Primary education								
Argentina[1]	1.2	x	33.9	x	39.1	x	25.8	x
Brazil[1]	11.9	x	66.5	x	n	n	21.6	x
Chile[1]	n	n	5.8	n	n	n	0.5	93.7
China[1]	5.4	x	81.8	x	12.3	x	0.5	x
Egypt	0.2	x	76.8	x	x	x	23.0	x
Indonesia[2]	2.6	n	2.3	53.8	32.1	2.7	n	6.4
Jordan[1]	0.1	x	0.4	x	48.6	x	50.9	x
Malaysia[1]	n	n	3.4	n	n	96.6	n	n
Peru[1]	n	n	2.6	12.7	12.7	83.4	n	n
Philippines[1]	n	n	n	n	n	n	n	100
Thailand	x	x	17.7	n	n	n	82.3	n
Tunisia[1]	n	6.4	n	79.2	n	14.5	n	n
Zimbabwe	n	n	5.6	n	n	90.6	n	3.7
WEI mean	*1.6*	*0.5*	*22.8*	*11.2*	*10.3*	*22.1*	*15.8*	*15.7*
Lower secondary education								
Argentina[1]	1.2	x	33.9	x	39.1	x	25.8	x
Brazil[1]	1.0	x	23.2	x	n	n	75.8	x
Chile[1]	n	n	5.8	n	n	n	0.5	93.7
China[1]	n	x	47.3	x	20.7	x	32.0	x
Egypt	0.1	x	11.0	x	x	x	89.0	x
Indonesia[2]	n	n	n	n	40.0	21.3	3.0	35.7
Jordan[1]	0.1	x	0.4	x	48.6	x	50.9	x
Malaysia[1]	n	n	3.6	n	n	37.7	n	58.7
Peru[1]	n	n	9.2	8.1	2.7	80.1	n	n
Philippines[1]	n	n	n	n	n	n	n	100
Thailand	x	x	9.4	n	n	n	90.6	n
Tunisia[1]	n	1.4	n	14.6	n	28.8	n	55.2
Zimbabwe	n	n	1.2	n	n	71.8	n	27.0
WEI mean	*0.2*	*0.1*	*11.1*	*1.7*	*11.6*	*18.4*	*28.3*	*28.5*
Upper secondary education								
Argentina[1]	1.2	x	33.9	x	39.1	x	25.8	x
Brazil[1]	0.2	x	10.5	x	n	n	89.3	x
Chile[1]	n	n	7.7	n	n	n	7.2	85.2
China[1]	n	x	4.6	x	40.2	x	55.3	x
Egypt	n	x	23.7	x	x	x	76.3	x
Indonesia[2]	n	n	n	n	10.5	21.6	6.8	61.1
Jordan[1]	1.6	x	2.7	x	15.3	x	80.4	x
Malaysia[1]	n	n	3.6	n	n	37.7	n	58.7
Peru[1]	n	n	9.2	8.1	2.7	80.1	n	n
Philippines[1]	n	n	n	n	n	n	n	100
Thailand	x	x	9.9	n	n	n	90.1	n
Tunisia[1]	n	2.4	n	1.3	n	11.0	n	85.3
Zimbabwe	n	n	1.2	n	n	71.8	n	27.0
WEI mean	*0.2*	*0.2*	*8.2*	*0.7*	*8.3*	*17.1*	*33.2*	*32.1*

1. Year of reference 1998.
2. Year of reference 2000.

Source: OECD/UNESCO WEI.

Table 33

Statutory number of teaching hours per year (1999)

Net contact time in hours per year in public institutions, by level of education

	Primary education	Lower secondary education	Upper secondary education, general programmes	Upper secondary education, vocational programmes
WEI participants				
Argentina[1]	810	900	900	1 044
Brazil[1]	800	800	800	800
Chile[1]	860	860	860	860
Indonesia[1]	1 260	738	738	738
Jordan[2]	745	745	745	688
Malaysia[1]	762	778	778	813
Paraguay[1]	696	774	870	922
Peru[1]	774	619	619	a
Philippines[1]	1 176	1 176	1 176	a
Russian Federation[1]	686	686	686	a
Sri Lanka[1]	1 260	1 260	1 260	m
Thailand[1]	760	652	652	615
Tunisia[1]	735	548	548	a
Uruguay[1]	732	712	712	712
Zimbabwe[1]	975	936	936	936
WEI mean	*869*	*812*	*819*	*581*
OECD countries				
Australia	996	955	941	m
Austria	684	658	623	623
Belgium (Fl.)	840	720	675	833
Belgium (Fr.)	854	733	671	1 008
Czech Republic	739	709	680	680
Denmark	644	644	500	a
Finland	656	656	627	m
France	892	634	589	653
Germany	783	733	685	695
Greece	780	629	629	629
Hungary	583	555	555	555
Iceland	636	636	464	464
Ireland	915	735	735	a
Italy	748	612	612	612
Korea	658	507	492	502
Mexico	800	832	m	m
Netherlands	930	868	868	843
New Zealand	985	930	874	a
Norway	713	633	505	589
Portugal	900	666	594	594
Scotland	950	893	893	a
Spain	788	561	548	548
Switzerland	884	859	674	727
Turkey	720	576	504	960
United States	958	964	943	943
OECD mean	*801*	*716*	*662*	*692*

1. Year of reference 1998.
2. Year of reference 2000.

Source: OECD/UNESCO WEI.

Table 34 Pre-service training requirements for new teachers in public institutions by level of education (2000)

Level of education	Option	Teacher qualification level after training	Qualification to enter teacher training	Specific studies	Duration of pre-service teacher training (years)				Provider of training programme
					Pedagogical studies	Teaching practice	Total duration of pre-service training	Total duration of tertiary training	
Pre-primary									
Argentina	1	5B	3A	x	x	x	2.5	2.5	Institutos de Formación Docente (Teaching Career Institutes)
Brazil	1	3A	2A	x	x	x	4.0	n	Secondary education institutions
	2	5A	3A	x	x	x	4.0	4.0	Universities
	3	5B	3A	x	x	x	3.0	3.0	Tertiary institutions (university and non-university)
Chile	1	5A	3 (A or B)	0.5	3.0	1.0	4.5	4.5	Universities or professional institutes
Indonesia	1	5B	2A	2	0.5	0.5	3.0	3.0	Teacher training school for kindergarten
	2	5B	3A	1	0.5	0.5	2.0	2.0	Teacher training institute
	3	5A	3A	2.5	1	0.5	4.0	4.0	Teacher training institute
Malaysia	1	5B	3A, 3C	1.0	1.0	1.0	3.0	3.0	Teachers Training College, Special teachers training institute or Islamic Teachers Training college
Paraguay	1	3 (A or B)	2A	x	x	x	3.0	n	Secondary education institutions
	2	5B	3 (A or B)	1.0	1.0	1.0	3.0	3.0	Teachers Training Institute o Centros Regionales
	3	5A	3 (A or B)	x	2.5	0.5	4.0	4.0	Universities
Peru	1	5A, 5B, 6	3	1.8	2.6	0.6	5.0	5.0	Universities, Teachers Training Institutes
Philippines[1]	1	5A	3A	2.0	1.5	0.5	4.0	4.0	Universities offering teacher training
Russian Federation	1	5B	m	x	x	x	at least 2	at least 2	
Thailand	1	5A	3A	2.5	1.0	0.5	4.0	4.0	Universities, higher education institutions
	2	5B	5A	a	1.0	a	1.0	1.0	Universities, higher education institutions
	3	5B	3A	a	1.0	a	1.0	1.0	Universities, higher education institutions
Uruguay	1	5B	3A, 3B	x	x	x	3.0	3.0	Admsinstración de Educación Pública. Dirección de Formación Docente
Primary									
Argentina	1	5B	3A	x	x	x	2.5	2.5	Institutos de Formación Docente (Teaching Career Institutes)
Brazil	1	3A	2A	x	x	x	4.0	n	Secondary education institutions
	2	5A	3A	x	x	x	4.0	4.0	Universities
	3	5B	3A	x	x	x	3.0	3.0	Tertiary institutions (university and non-university)
Chile	1	5A	3A, 3B	1.0	2.0	1.0	4.0	4.0	Universities or professional institutes
Indonesia	1	5B	2A	2	0.5	0.5	3.0	3.0	Teacher training school for kindergarten
Malaysia	1	5B	3A, 3C	1.0	1.0	1.0	3.0	3.0	Teachers Training College, Special teachers training institute or Islamic Teachers Training college
Paraguay	1	3 (A or B)	2A	x	x	x	3.0	n	Secondary education institutions
	2	5B	3 (A or B)	1.0	1.0	1.0	3.0	3.0	Teachers Training Institute o Centros Regionales
	3	5B	3 (A or B)	x	x	x	4.0 – 5.0	4.0 – 5.0	Universities
Peru	1	5A, 5B, 6	3	4.0	x: specific studies	1.1	5.0	5.0	Universities, Teachers Training Institutes
Philippines[1]	1	5A	3A	2.0	1.5	0.5	4.0	4.0	Universities offering teacher training
Russian Federation	1	5A	5B	x	x	x	at least 2	at least 2	
Thailand	1	5A	3A	2.5	1.0	0.5	4.0	4.0	Universities, higher education institutions
Uruguay	1	5B	3A, 3B	x	x	x	3.0	3.0	Admsinstración de Educación Pública. Dirección de Formación Docente
Lower secondary									
Argentina	1	5B	3A	x	x	x	2.5	2.5	Institutos de Formación Docente (Teaching Career Institutes)
	2	5B	3A	x	x	x	4.0	4.0	Institutos de Formación Docente (Teaching Career Institutes)
Brazil	1	5A	3A	x	x	x	4.0	4.0	Universities
Chile	1	5A	3A, 3B	1.0	2.0	1.0	4.0	4.0	Universities or professional institutes
Indonesia	1	5B	2A	2	0.5	0.5	3.0	3.0	Teacher training institute
	2	5A/B	3A	2	0.5	0.5	3.0	3.0	Teacher training institute
	3	5A	3A	2.5	1	0.5	4.0	4.0	Teacher training institute
Malaysia	1	5A	3A	1.0	1.0	1.0	3.0	3.0	Universities
	2	5A	5A	3.0	0.7	0.3	4.0	4.0	Universities and/or Teachers Training Colleges
Paraguay	1	5B	3 (A or B)	1.5	1.5	1.0	4.0	4.0	Teachers Training Institute o Centros Regionales
	2	5A	3 (A or B)	x	x	x	4.5 – 6.0	4.5 – 6.0	Universities
Peru	1	5A, 5B, 6	3	1.8	2.6	0.6	5.0	5.0	Universities, Teachers Training Institutes
Philippines[1]	1	5A	3A	2.0	1.5	0.5	4.0	4.0	Universities offering teacher training
Russian Federation	1	5A	5B	x	x	x	5.0	5.0	
Thailand	1	5A	3A	2.5	1.0	0.5	4.0	4.0	Universities, higher education institutions
	2	5B	5A	a	1.0	a	1.0	1.0	Universities, higher education institutions
	3	5B	3A	a	1.0	a	1.0	1.0	Universities, higher education institutions
Uruguay	1	5B	3A, 3B	x	x	x	4.0	5.0	Admsinstración de Educación Pública. Dirección de Formación Docente
Upper secondary (general)									
Argentina	1	5B	3A	x	x	x	4.0	4.0	Institutos de Formación Docente (Teaching Career Institutes)
	1	5A	3A	x	x	x	5–6	5–6	University
Brazil[2]	1	5A	3A	x	x	x	4.0	4.0	Universities
Chile[2]	1	5A	3A, 3B	2.5	1.5	1.0	5.0	5.0	Universities or professional institutes
Indonesia[2]	1	5B	3A	2	0.5	0.5	3.0	3.0	Teacher training institute
	2	5A/B	3A	2	0.5	0.5	3.0	3.0	Teacher training institute
	3	5A	3A	2.5	1	0.5	4.0	4.0	Teacher training institute
Malaysia	1	5A	3A	1.0	1.0	1.0	3.0	3.0	Universities
	2	5A	5A	3.0	0.7	0.3	4.0	4.0	Universities and/or Teachers Training Colleges
Paraguay	1	5B	3 (A or B)	1.0	1.0	1.0	3.0	3.0	Teachers Training Institute o Centros Regionales
	2		3 (A or B)	x	x	x	4.5 – 6.0	4.5 – 6.0	Universities
Peru[2]	1	5A, 5B, 6	3	1.8	2.6	0.6	5.0	5.0	Universities, Teachers Training Institutes
Philippines[1]	1	5A	3A	2.0	1.5	0.5	4.0	4.0	Universities offering teacher training
Russian Federation	1	5A	5B	x	x	x	5.0	5.0	
Thailand[2]	1	5B	5A	a	1.0	0.5	1.5	1.5	Universities, higher education institutions
	2	5B	5B	a	2.0	a	2.0	2.0	Universities, higher education institutions
	3	5A	3A	a	1.0	a	1.0	1.0	Universities, higher education institutions
	4	5B	3A	a	1.0	a	1.0	1.0	Universities, higher education institutions
Uruguay[2]	1	5B	3A, 3B	x	x	x	4.0	4.0	Admsinstración de Educación Pública. Dirección de Formación Docente

1. Year of reference 1998.
2. Data also refer to ISCED 3 vocational programmes.

Source: OECD/UNESCO WEI.

Table 35

Contributions of various factors to change in statutory teachers' salary costs at 15 years' experience
(US$ converted using PPPs) per student enrolled relative to the country average

| | Country average statutory salary cost per student enrolled | Incremental or decremental effect of specified factor (in US dollars per student converted using PPPs) | | | | | Statutory salary costs per student enrolled |
| | | Statutory salary (after 15 years' experience) | Students' hours of instruction | Teachers' teaching hours | Class size | Two or more of the other factors jointly considered | |
	1	2	3	4	5	6	1 + 2 + 3 + 4 + 5
Primary education							
Argentina	352	126	−70	24	81	−10	504
Brazil	352	−75	−43	29	−30	8	242
Chile	352	53	27	2	−78	−15	342
Indonesia	352	−282	107	−111	95	−82	81
Malaysia	352	73	31	47	−11	16	510
Peru	352	−187	−53	53	−24	9	151
Philippines	352	59	61	−93	−49	−24	306
Thailand	352	197	97	48	−42	49	703
Tunisia	352	145	19	62	−46	4	538
Uruguay	352	−110	−176	64	396	−222	304
Lower secondary education							
Argentina	479	382	−85	−63	365	5	1 083
Brazil	479	−19	−127	−11	−10	11	323
Chile	479	−48	−44	−44	−20	17	342
Indonesia	479	−404	62	28	14	−86	93
Malaysia	479	348	44	2	68	95	1 037
Peru	479	−305	−82	98	117	−91	217
Philippines	479	−41	166	−161	−153	−24	267
Thailand	479	106	34	95	−94	−16	605
Tunisia	479	199	−92	204	−88	−64	638
Uruguay	479	−220	123	47	136	−106	458

Source: OECD/UNESCO WEI.

How to read the table?

Expenditure per student on teachers' salaries can be estimated from teachers' salaries, students' hours of instruction, teachers' hours of teaching, and class size, calculated on the basis of student-teacher ratios.

This chart shows how the different factors influence expenditure in each country. It illustrates the effect on salary costs of each individual factor in turn, by showing the national value for that factor and assuming that all other factors are at the WEI average level.

How to read each column?

Column 1 shows expenditure on teachers' salaries per student, if all four factors are at WEI average level. In other words, this column shows WEI average expenditure per student.

Column 2 shows the effect on teachers' salary costs per student if students' hours of instruction, teaching time and class size are at the WEI average, but teachers' salaries are at the national level. Since higher teachers' salaries lead to an increase in costs per student, a positive value indicates that salaries are above the WEI average.

Column 3 shows the effect on teachers' salary costs per student if the other three factors are at the WEI average, but the number of hours of instruction is at the national level. Since more hours of instruction per student lead to an increase in costs per student, a positive value indicates that hours of instruction are above the WEI average.

Column 4 shows the effect on teachers' salary costs per student if the other three factors are at the WEI average, but the number of teaching hours is at the national level. In this case, if teachers teach more hours, costs per student decrease. A positive value therefore indicates that teaching hours are below the WEI average.

Column 5 shows the effect on teachers' salary costs per student if the other three factors are at the WEI average, but class size is at the national level. Again, since costs increase if fewer students are in a class, a positive value indicates that class sizes are above the WEI average.

Column 6 shows the residual value due to the interaction of all four factors.

Column 7 shows the teachers' salary costs per student for each country. This is the sum of columns 1 to 6.

Table 36

Factors contributing to change in statutory teachers' salary cost at 15 years' experience in public institutions[1]

	Statutory salary (after 15 years' experience)	Students' hours of instruction	Teachers' teaching hours	Student /teaching staff ratio	Class size	Country statutory salary cost per teaching hour	Statutory salary costs per student enrolled
	A	B	C	D	E = (B*D)/C	F = A/C	G = A/D
Primary education							
Argentina	12 377	729	810	24.6	22.1	16	504
Brazil	7 191	800	800	29.7	29.7	9	242
Chile	10 476	980	860	30.7	34.9	18	342
Egypt	m	913	965	23.5	22.3	m	m
Indonesia	1 836	1 187	1 260	22.8	21.4	2	81
Malaysia	11 017	991	762	21.6	28.1	15	510
Paraguay	m	690	696	19.9	19.7	m	m
Peru	4 282	774	774	28.4	28.4	6	151
Philippines	10 640	1 067	1 176	34.8	31.6	12	306
Russian Federation	m	756	686	17.6	19.4	m	m
Thailand	14 208	1 160	760	20.2	30.9	19	703
Tunisia	12 877	960	735	23.9	31.3	18	538
Uruguay	6 281	455	732	20.6	12.8	16	304
Zimbabwe	m	753	975	37.9	29.3	m	m
Lower secondary education							
Argentina	20 903	896	900	19.3	19.2	25	1 083
Brazil	11 180	800	800	34.6	34.6	14	323
Chile	10 476	990	860	30.7	35.3	18	342
Egypt	m	1 034	724	21.8	31.2	m	m
Indonesia	1 836	1 231	738	19.7	32.9	4	93
Malaysia	20 076	1 189	778	19.4	29.6	28	1 037
Paraguay	m	860	774	10.5	11.7	m	m
Peru	4 235	903	619	19.5	28.5	8	217
Philippines	10 640	1 467	1 176	39.8	49.7	12	267
Russian Federation	m	892.8	686	14.1	18.3	m	m
Thailand	14 208	1 167	652	23.5	42.1	22	605
Tunisia	16 467	880	548	25.8	41.4	30	638
Uruguay	6 281	1 369	712	13.7	26.3	16	458

1. For years of reference, see Tables 25, 26, 28 and 33.
Source: OECD/UNESCO WEI.

Table 37

Estimated change in the demand for teachers due to changes in the population of primary school-age under different enrolment scenarios (1998 with current conditions = 100)

	Age group	Change in the number of teachers due to **changing population** size (given current enrolment rates and student-teacher ratios)			Change in the number of teachers due to **changing population** size and under the assumption **universal participation** can be reached (given current student-teacher ratios)		
		1998	2005	2010	1998	2005	2010
Primary education							
Argentina	6-11	100	104	106	100	104	106
Brazil	7-12	100	94	94	104	98	98
Chile	6-11	100	100	98	103	103	100
Egypt	6-10	100	99	99	102	101	101
Indonesia	7-12	100	100	99	113	112	111
Malaysia	6-11	100	109	103	100	109	103
Paraguay	6-11	100	109	117	107	116	124
Peru	6-11	100	101	100	100	101	100
Philippines	6-11	100	108	110	101	108	111
Thailand	6-11	100	88	88	100	88	88
Tunisia	6-11	100	91	93	107	98	99
Uruguay	6-11	100	104	104	100	104	104
Zimbabwe	6-12	100	97	96	111	109	107
Secondary education							
Argentina	12-17	100	102	104	103	105	107
Brazil	13-17	100	95	91	101	96	92
Chile	12-17	100	111	111	100	111	111
Egypt	11-16	100	101	101	119	120	120
Indonesia	13-18	100	100	100	180	180	179
Malaysia	12-18	100	111	122	125	139	153
Paraguay	12-17	100	116	123	132	153	163
Peru	12-16	100	103	104	100	103	104
Philippines	12-15	100	108	115	115	124	132
Thailand	12-17	100	92	83	112	104	93
Tunisia	12-18	100	96	89	122	117	108
Uruguay	12-17	100	105	107	102	107	110
Zimbabwe	13-18	100	115	113	156	179	176

Source: OECD/UNESCO WEI.

■ ANNEX A5a –
INTERNATIONAL STANDARD CLASSIFICATION OF EDUCATION (ISCED)

■ ANNEX A5b –
ALLOCATION OF NATIONAL EDUCATION PROGRAMMES ACCORDING TO ISCED

- Argentina
- Brazil
- Chile
- China
- Egypt
- India
- Indonesia
- Jordan
- Malaysia
- Paraguay
- Peru
- Philippines
- Russian Federation
- Sri Lanka
- Thailand
- Tunisia
- Uruguay
- Zimbabwe

■ ANNEX A5*a*
INTERNATIONAL STANDARD CLASSIFICATION OF EDUCATION (ISCED)

0 PRE-PRIMARY LEVEL OF EDUCATION	Main criteria	Auxiliary criteria
Initial stage of organised instruction, designed primarily to introduce very young children to a school-type environment.	Should be centre or school-based, be designed to meet the educational and developmental needs of children at least 3 years of age, and have staff that are adequately trained (*i.e.*, qualified) to provide an educational programme for the children.	Pedagogical qualifications for the teaching staff; implementation of a curriculum with educational elements.

1 PRIMARY LEVEL OF EDUCATION	Main criteria	Auxiliary criteria
Normally designed to give students a sound basic education in reading, writing and mathematics.	Beginning of systematic studies characteristic of primary education, *e.g.* reading, writing and mathematics. Entry into the nationally designated primary institutions or programmes. The commencement of reading activities alone is not a sufficient criteria for classification of an educational programmes at ISCED 1.	In countries where the age of compulsory attendance (or at least the age at which virtually all students begin their education) comes after the beginning of systematic study in the subjects noted, the first year of compulsory attendance should be used to determine the boundary between ISCED 0 and ISCED 1.

2 LOWER SECONDARY LEVEL OF EDUCATION	Main criteria	Auxiliary criteria
The lower secondary level of education generally continues the basic programmes of the primary level, although teaching is typically more subject-focused, often employing more specialised teachers who conduct classes in their field of specialisation.	Programmes at the start of level 2 should correspond to the point where programmes are beginning to be organised in a more subject-oriented pattern, using more specialised teachers conducting classes in their field of specialisation. If this organisational transition point does not correspond to a natural split in the boundaries between national educational programmes, then programmes should be split at the point where national programmes begin to reflect this organisational change.	If there is no clear break-point for this organisational change, however, then countries should artificially split national programmes into ISCED 1 and 2 at the end of 6 years of primary education. In countries with no system break between lower secondary and upper secondary education, and where lower secondary education lasts for more than 3 years, only the first 3 years following primary education should be counted as lower secondary education.

3 UPPER SECONDARY LEVEL OF EDUCATION	Main criteria	Modular programmes
The final stage of secondary education in most OECD countries. Instruction is often more organised along subject-matter lines than at ISCED level 2 and teachers typically need to have a higher level, or more subject-specific, qualification that at ISCED 2.	National boundaries between lower secondary and upper secondary education should be the dominant factor for splitting levels 2 and 3. Admission into educational programmes usually require the completion of ISCED 2 for admission, or a combination of basic education and life experience that demonstrates the ability to handle ISCED 3 subject matter.	An educational qualification is earned in a modular programme by combining blocks of courses, or modules, into a programme meeting specific curricular requirements. A single module, however, may not have a specific educational or labour market destination or a particular programme orientation. Modular programmes should be classified at level 3 only, without reference to the educational or labour market destination of the programme.

4 POST-SECONDARY NON-TERTIARY	Main criteria	Types of programmes which can fit into level 4
These programmes straddle the boundary between upper secondary and post-secondary education from an international point of view, even though they might clearly be considered as upper secondary or post-secondary programmes in a national context. They are often not significantly more advanced than programmes at ISCED 3 but they serve to broaden the knowledge of participants who have already completed a programme at level 3. The students are typically older than those in ISCED 3 programmes. ISCED 4 programmes typically have a full-time equivalent duration of between 6 months and 2 years.	Students entering ISCED 4 programmes will typically have completed ISCED 3. As described above, successful completion of any programme at level 3A or 3B counts as a level 3 completion. For 3C programmes, a cumulative theoretical duration of 3 years is specified in ISCED-97 as the minimum programme length in order meet the requirements for a level 3 completion.	The first type are short vocational programmes where either the content is not considered "tertiary" in many OECD countries or the programme didn't meet the duration requirement for ISCED 5B – at least 2 years FTE since the start of level 5. These programmes are often designed for students who have completed level 3, although a formal ISCED level 3 qualification may not be required for entry. The second type of programmes are nationally considered as upper secondary programmes, even though entrants to these programmes will have typically already completed another upper secondary programme (*i.e.*, second-cycle programmes).

5 FIRST STAGE OF TERTIARY EDUCATION	Classification criteria for level and sub-categories (5A and 5B)	
ISCED 5 programmes have an educational content more advanced than those offered at levels 3 and 4.	Entry to these programmes normally requires the successful completion of ISCED level 3A or 3B or a similar qualification at ISCED level 4A or 4B. Programmes at level 5 must have a cumulative theoretical duration of at least 2 years from the beginning of the first programme.	
5A ISCED 5A programmes that are largely theoretically based and are intended to provide sufficient qualifications for gaining entry into advanced research programmes and professions with high skills requirements.	1. have a minimum cumulative theoretical duration (at tertiary level) of three years (FTE); 2. typically require that the faculty have advanced research credentials; 3. may involve completion of a research project or thesis; 4. provide the level of education required for entry into a profession with high skills requirements or an advanced research programme.	
5B ISCED 5B programmes that are generally more practical/technical/occupationally specific than ISCED 5A programmes.	1. it is more practically oriented and occupationally specific than programmes at ISCED 5A and does not prepare students for direct access to advanced research programmes; 2. it has a minimum of two years' full-time equivalent duration; 3. the programme content is typically designed to prepare students to enter a particular occupation.	

6 SECOND STAGE OF TERTIARY EDUCATION (LEADING TO AN ADVANCED RESEARCH QUALIFICATION)

This level is reserved for tertiary programmes that lead to the award of an advanced research qualification. The programmes are devoted to advanced study and original research.	1. requires the submission of a thesis or dissertation of publishable quality that is the product of original research and represents a significant contribution to knowledge; 2. is not solely based on course-work; 3. prepares recipients for faculty posts in institutions offering ISCED 5A programmes, as well as research posts in government and industry.

Destination for which the programmes have been designed to prepare students	Programme orientation
2A Programmes designed to prepare students for direct access to level 3 in a sequence which would ultimately lead to tertiary education, that is, entrance to ISCED 3A or 3B.	1 Education which is not designed explicitly to prepare participants for a specific class of occupations or trades or for entry into further vocational/technical education programmes. Less than 25% of the programme content is vocational or technical.
2B Programmes designed to prepare students for direct access to programmes at level 3C.	2 Education mainly designed as an introduction to the world of work and as preparation for further vocational or technical education. Does not lead to a labour-market relevant qualification. Content is at least 25% vocational or technical.
2C Programmes primarily designed for direct access to the labour market at the end of this level (sometimes referred to as "terminal" programmes).	3 Education which prepares participants for direct entry, without further training, into specific occupations. Successful completion of such programmes leads to a labour-market relevant vocational qualification.

Destination for which the programmes have been designed to prepare students	Programme orientation
3A Programmes at level 3 designed to provide direct access to ISCED 5A.	1 Education which is not designed explicitly to prepare participants for a specific class of occupations or trades or for entry into further vocational/technical education programmes. Less than 25% of the programme content is vocational or technical.
3B Programmes at level 3 designed to provide direct access to ISCED 5B.	2 Education mainly designed as an introduction to the world of work and as preparation for further vocational or technical education. Does not lead to a labour-market relevant qualification. Content is at least 25% vocational or technical.
3C Programmes at level 3 not designed to lead directly to ISCED 5A or 5B. Therefore, these programmes lead directly to labour market, ISCED 4 programmes or other ISCED 3 programmes.	3 Education which prepares participants for direct entry, without further training, into specific occupations. Successful completion of such programmes leads to a labour-market relevant vocational qualification.

Destination for which the programmes have been designed to prepare students	Programme orientation
4A Programmes at level 4, designed to provide direct access to ISCED 5A.	1 Education which is not designed explicitly to prepare participants for a specific class of occupations or trades or for entry into further vocational/technical education programmes. Less than 25% of the programme content is vocational or technical.
4B Programmes at level 4, designed to provide direct access to ISCED 5A.	2 Education mainly designed as an introduction to the world of work and as preparation for further vocational or technical education. Does not lead to a labour-market relevant qualification. Content is at least 25% vocational or technical.
4C Programmes at level 4 not designed to lead directly to ISCED 5A or 5B. These programmes lead directly to labour market or other ISCED 4 programmes.	3 Education which prepares participants for direct entry, without further training, into specific occupations. Successful completion of such programmes leads to a labour-market relevant vocational qualification.

Cumulative theoretical duration at tertiary level	Position in the national degree and qualification structure
5A Duration categories: Medium: 3 to less than 5 years; Long: 5 to 6 years; Very long: More than 6 years.	5A Categories: Intermediate; First; Second; Third and further.
5B Duration categories: Short: 2 to less than 3 years; 3 to less than 5 years; Long: 5 to 6 years; Very long: More than 6 years.	5B Categories: Intermediate; First; Second; Third and further.

LEGEND

PROGRAMME ORIENTATION

Type 1   *Education which is not designed explicitly to prepare participants for a specific class of occupations or trades or for entry into further vocational/ technical education programmes. Less than 25% of the programme content is vocational or technical.*

Type 2   *Education mainly designed as an introduction to the world of work and as preparation for further vocational or technical education. Does not lead to a labour-market relevant qualification. Content is at least 25% vocational or technical.*

Type 3   *Education which prepares participants for direct entry, without further training, into specific occupations. Successful completion of such programmes leads to a labour-market relevant vocational qualification*

CUMULATIVE DURATION AT ISCED5

Short	*2 to less than 3 years*
Medium	*3 to less than 5 years*
Long	*5 to 6 Years*

POSITION IN THE NATIONAL DEGREE AND QUALIFICATIONS STRUCTURE

Inter.	*Intermediate*
1st	*First*
2nd	*Second*
3rd	*Third*

ANNEX A5*b*
ALLOCATION OF NATIONAL EDUCATION PROGRAMMES TO ISCED97 USED IN THE WEI DATA COLLECTION

ARGENTINA

ISCED97 Level for the WEI Data Collection	National title of programme	Entrance requirements	Qualifications awarded	Typical starting age	Typical completion age	Theoretical duration	Theoretical cumulative duration – primary/secondary levels	Theoretical cumulative duration – tertiary level	Notes	ISCED97 Flows
0	Pre-primary	None		3	5	2	...	...		
0	Pre-primary (compulsory)	None		5	6	1	...	...	Obligatory for 5-year olds, and 4-year olds in some provinces	**0**
1	Primary (Educacion General Basica, 1st and 2nd cycles)	Approval pre-primary		6	12	6	6	...	Typically half day	**1**
2A	Lower Secondary, (Educacion General Basica, 3rd cycle)	Approval of Educacion General Basica, 2nd cycle	Lower Secondary Diploma	12	15	3	9	...	Separate schools for severe mentally retarded and handicapped.	**2A**
3A	Upper Secondary (Polimodal)	Lower Secondary diploma	Secondary diploma	15	18	3	12		General and technical education. It is possible to earn a technical qualification through combined work and study	**3A**
5B	Non-University Tertiary Programmes	Upper Secondary diploma	Primary Teacher, Secondary Professor, Technician diploma	18	21-22	3-4	...	3-4	Occupational training for medical auxiliaries, laboratory technicians, radio operators, mechanics, meteorologists, librarians, social workers, etc. Training for primary and secondary school teachers.	**5B**
5A (1st, Long)	Tertiary-University	Upper Secondary diploma	Licenciatura/ professional qualification.	18	23-24	5-6	...	5-6	Professional qualifications are sometimes awarded at the same time as the licenciatura (*e.g.* secondary-school teacher's certificate). Courses in medicine last 6 years, courses in the fine arts last 7 years.	**5A**
5A (2nd)	Master's, Post-graduate Courses	Tertiary University diploma (*e.g.*, Licenciatura, Accountant, Lawyer)	Master's degree, Specialization diploma	(a)	(a)	(a)	(a)	(a)	(a) ISCED 5A, 2nd degree programmes are just starting and do not have a uniform curricular organisation and entrance requirements. For these reasons it is difficult to indicate their typical starting and ending ages, duration, and so on.	
6	Doctorate programmes	Tertiary University diploma (e.g., Licenciatura, Accountant, Lawyer) or Master's degree	Doctorado	(b)	(b)	(b)	(b)	(b)	Requires submission of a thesis. (b) ISCED 6 programmes are just starting and do not have a uniform curricular organisation and entrance requirements. For these reasons it is difficult to indicate their typical starting and ending ages, duration, and so on.	**6**

BRAZIL

ISCED97 Level for the WEI Data Collection	National title of programme	Entrance requirements	Qualifications awarded	Typical starting age	Typical completion age	Theoretical duration	Theoretical cumulative duration – primary/secondary levels	Theoretical cumulative duration – tertiary level	Notes	ISCED97 Flows
0	Nursery schools			3	4	1	…	…		**0**
0	Preschool/ Kindergarten			4	7	3	…	…		
1	Primary-1st cycle Primary-2nd cycle (1st-2nd grades)			7	13	6	6	…		**1**
2A	Primary-2nd cycle (3rd-4th grades)		Primary Education Certificate	13	15	2	8			**2A**
3A	Secondary	Primary Education Certificate	Secondary Education Certificate	15	18 to 19	3 to 4	11 to 12	…		**3A**
5B	Pre-service Teachers Training (Licenciatura court)	Secondary Education Certificate	Teachers Certificate (Licenciatura court)	18 to 19	20 to 22	2 to 3		2 to 3		**5B**
5B	Non-University Programmes (Tecnologo)	Secondary Education Certificate	Teachers Certificate (Tecnologo)	18 to 19	20 to 22	2 to 3	…	2 to 3		
5A	Teachers Training Programmes with subject specialization (Licenciatura Plena)	Secondary Education Certificate	Teachers Diploma (Licenciatura Plena)	18 to 19	20 to 22	4	…	4	Awarded to students in philosophy, humanities or science who wish to become secondary-school teachers. Frequently obtained concurrently with the Bacharelado.	**5A**
5A	Bachelor's programmes – most subjects (Bacharelado)	Secondary Education Certificate	Bachelor's Diploma (Bacharelado)	18 to 19	22 to 23	4	…	4		
5A	Bachelor's programmes – some subjects (Bacharelado)	Secondary Education Certificate	Bachelor's Diploma – architecture, law, medicine (Bacharelado)	18 to 19	23 to 25	5 to 6	…	5 to 6		
6	Master's programmes (Mestrado)	University Tertiary Education Diploma	Master's Degree (Mestrado)	22 upwards	25 upwards	3	…	7 to 9	Requires an examination and the submission of a thesis	**6**
6	Doctorate programmes (Doutorado)	University Tertiary Education Diploma	Doctorate's Degree (Doutorado)	22 upwards	26 upwards	4	…	8 to 13		

CHILE

ISCED97 Level for the WEI Data Collection	National title of programme	Entrance requirements	Qualifications awarded	Typical starting age	Typical completion age	Theoretical duration	Theoretical cumulative duration – primary/secondary levels	Theoretical cumulative duration – tertiary level	Notes	ISCED97 Flows
0	Pre-primary			2	4	2	…	…		
0	Pre-primary: Prekinder and Kinder			4	6	2	…	…		
1	Basic education (1st-6th grades)			6	12	6	6	…	It is recommended that the last two years of Basic Education be reported at ISCED 2	
2A	Basic education (7th-8th grades)		Basic Education License	12	14	2	8	…		
3A	Middle education – General (9th-12th grades)		Middle Education License	14	18	4	12	…		
3B	Middle education – Vocational Programmes (9th-12th grades)		Middle Education License	14	18	4	12	…		
5B	Higher Education – Technical Programmes	1. Middle education license 2. Some institutions require passing a National Exam	Technical Diploma with specific specialization	18	22	4	…	4	Training for technicians	
5A (1st stage, long)	Higher Education – Bachelor – All professional programmes	1. Middle education license 2. Most institutions require passing a National Exam	Bachelor of other professional qualification	18	23	5	…	5	The first degree in most universities	
5A (2nd stage)	Higher Education – 2nd Title – All professional programmes	Bachelor or other professional qualification	Post-diploma	23	23	1	…	6		
6	Magister and doctoral programmes	Bachelor or other professional qualification	Magister or PhD	23	25	2	…	7		

CHINA

ISCED97 Level for the WEI Data Collection	National title of programme	Entrance requirements	Qualifications awarded	Typical starting age	Typical completion age	Theoretical duration	Theoretical cumulative duration – primary/secondary levels	Theoretical cumulative duration – tertiary level	Notes	ISCED97 Flows
0	Preschool			3	6	…	…	…	Mostly full time.	**0**
1	Primary			6 to 7	11 or 12	5 or 6	…	…		**1**
2A	Junior Secondary school			11 to 12	14 or 15	3 or 4	9	…		**2A**
3A	Senior Secondary school			15	18	3	12	…		**3A**
4C	Post-secondary non-tertiary programmes			…	…	…	…	…	Generally, occupationally specific training but at a lower level than the programmes reported in 5B.	**4C**
5B	Non-university level post-secondary	12 years of primary and secondary education and success in annual national undergraduate entrance examination	Diploma	18	20 to 21	2 to 3	…	…	Generally, occupationally specific training.	**5B**
5A (1st, Short)	University-level education (4 year programmes)	12 years of primary and secondary education and success in annual national undergraduate entrance examination	Bachelor's degree	18	22	4	…	4		**5A**
5A (1st, Long)	University-level education (5 year programmes)	12 years of primary and secondary education and success in annual national undergraduate entrance examination	Bachelor's degree	18	23	5	…	5	Engineering and medicine.	
5A (2nd)	Master's programmes	Bachelor's degree	Master's degree	22	24 to 25	2 to 3	…	6 to 7	Candidates are usually required to submit a research project and a thesis.	
6	Doctorate programmes	Master's degree	Doctor's degree (Ph.D.)	24 to 25	27 to 29	3 to 4	…	9 to 11		**6**

EGYPT

ISCED97 Level for the WEI Data Collection	National title of programme	Entrance requirements	Qualifications awarded	Typical starting age	Typical completion age	Theoretical duration	Theoretical cumulative duration – primary/secondary levels	Theoretical cumulative duration – tertiary level	Notes	ISCED97 Flows
0	Pre-primary			4	6	2	…	…		**0**
1	Primary			6	11	5	5	…		**1**
2A	Preparatory school		Basic Education Certificate	11	14	3	8	…		**2A**
2C	Vocational school	Having repeated two times in primary school	Certificate	13	16	3	8	…		**2C**
3A	General secondary school	High score on basic education certificate examination	Secondary School Leaving Certificate (Thanawiya Amma)	14	17	3	11	…	Must pass Secondary School Leaving Examination to graduate.	**3A**
3B/C	Technical school	Basic Education Certificate	Middle Diploma	14	17	3	11	…	Egypt has well over 500 technical schools, almost 50 percent of all secondary schools.	**3B/C**
4C	Industrial, commercial and technical institutes	Secondary School Leaving Certificate (Thanawiya Amma)	Above Middle Diploma	17	19	2	…	…	Some new institutions offer programmes of less than 2-years' duration.	**4C**
5B	Community Service Programmes – Non credit studies. Industrial, commercial and technical institutes or technical programme within university	Different requirement according to type of study	Certificate (in accountancy, secretarial work, insurance, computer sciences, electronics, etc.) or Technician degree	17	19 to 22	0.5 to 2	…	0.5 to 2	Egypt has 34 higher technical institutes, with about 8 per cent of higher education enrolment. Some universities also offer 2-year, occupationally-specific programmes.	**5B**
5A (short)	University (main stage)	High score on Secondary School Leaving Examination	Baccelaureos or license	17	21 to 23	4 to 6	…	4 to 6		**5A**
5A (2nd)	University (second stage)	Baccelaureos or license	Magister	21 to 23	23 to 25	2	…	6 to 8		
6	University (third stage)	Magister	Doctoral	23 to 25	25+	2+	…	8 and above		**6**

INDIA

ISCED97 Level for the WEI Data Collection	National title of programme	Entrance requirements	Qualifications awarded	Typical starting age	Typical completion age	Theoretical duration	Theoretical cumulative duration – primary/secondary levels	Theoretical cumulative duration – tertiary level	Notes	ISCED97 Flows
0	Pre-primary	Test, age (3-5)	Pre-primary	3	5 or 6	2 or 3	...		Nursery, kindergarten, (upper) pre-primary.	0
1	Primary	Age 6	Primary	6	12	6	6	...	In some provinces admission to class 1 is 5+ years, in others it is 6+years.	1
2A	Upper primary	Primary	Upper primary	12	15	3	9	...	In some provinces, the state school boards conduct public examinations at class VIII. Candidates have to pass a minimum of five subjects.	2A
2C	ITI (various lower level technical or vocational programmes)	Upper primary pass	ITI Certificate	15	16	1	9	...	The examinations are conducted by the State Technical Boards supervised by the National Council for Vocational Training.	2C
3A	High school	Upper primary pass	Matriculation certificate	15	16	1	10	...	Matriculation certificate awarded after ten years' schooling and a public examination organized by the secondary boards.	3A
3A	Senior secondary	Matriculation certificate	Senior secondary-school-leaving-certificate	16	18	2	12	...	Must pass five subjects at the public examination.	
5B	3 year technical programmes	Senior secondary school-leaving certificate	Bachelor's degree	17 or 18	20 or 21	3	...	3	Nursing and paramedical studies.	5B
5B	4 year technical programmes	Senior secondary school-leaving certificate	Bachelor's degree	17 or 18	21 or 22	4	...	4	Agriculture, horticulture and engineering.	
5B	5 year professional programmes	Senior secondary school-leaving certificate	Bachelor's degree	17 or 18	22 or 23	5	...	5	Architecture.	
5A (1st, Short)	First degree programmes	Higher senior-secondary pre-university certificate	Bachelor's degree	17 or 18	20 or 21	3	...	3		5A
5A (2nd)	BEd programmes	Bachelor's degree	Bachelor of Education	20 or 21	21 or 22	1	...	4		
5A (2nd)	LL.B programmes	Bachelor's degree	LL.B. (law)	20 or 21	23 or 24	3	...	6		
5A (2nd)	Master's programmes	Bachelor's degree	Master's degree	20 or 21	22 or 23	2	...	5		
6	MPhil programmes	Master's degree	Master of Philosophy (MPhil)	22 or 23	23 or 24	1	...	6		6
6	Doctorate programmes	Master's/ Master of Philosophy	Doctor of Philosophy (Ph.D.)	...	...	3 to 4	...	9 to 10	Requires submission of a thesis containing original research work.	
6 (2nd)	Doctor of Letters programmes	Doctor of Philosophy (Ph.D.)	Doctor of Literature (DLitt)/ Doctor of Science (D.Sc.)	...	...	2 to 3	...	10 to 12	Awarded by some universities.	

INDONESIA

ISCED97 Level for the WEI Data Collection	National title of programme	Entrance requirements	Qualifications awarded	Typical starting age	Typical completion age	Theoretical duration	Theoretical cumulative duration – primary/secondary levels	Theoretical cumulative duration – tertiary level	Notes	ISCED97 Flows
0	Pre-primary (playgroup)			3	5	1 to 2	...	...		**0**
0	Kindergarten			5	6	1 to 2	...	...		
1	Primary			7	12	6	6	...		**1**
2A, Type 1	Junior secondary, General	Primary school graduates	Junior Secondary graduates	13	15	3	9	...		**2A**
3A, Type 1	Senior secondary, General	Junior Secondary graduates	Secondary school leaving certificate	16	18	3	12	...		**3A**
3B, Type 3	Senior secondary, Technical/vocational	Junior Secondary graduates	Secondary school leaving certificate	16	18 or 19	3 to 4	12 or 13	...		**3B**
5B (1st)	Diploma I programmes	Secondary school leaving certificate and an entrance examination	Diploma (DI)	19	19	1	...	1		**5B**
5B (1st)	Diploma II programmes	Secondary school leaving certificate and an entrance examination	Diploma (DII)	19	20	2	...	2		
5B (1st)	Diploma III programmes	Secondary school leaving certificate and an entrance examination	Diploma (DIII)	19	21	3	...	3	Entitles graduates to teach one subject at lower secondary level.	
5B (1st)	Diploma IV programmes	Secondary school leaving certificate and an entrance examination	Diploma (DIV)	19	22	4	...	4	Equivalent to Graduate Diploma (S1).	
5A (1st: Short and Long)	Degree stream	Secondary school leaving certificate and an entrance examination	Graduate Diploma (SI)	19	22 to 24	4 to 6	...	4 to 6	Most degrees are four years. Some like law and medicine take longer.	**5A**
5B (2nd)	Specialist I programmes	Diploma (DIV) or Graduate Diploma (SI)	Specialist I (SpI)	23	24 to 26	3 to 5	...	6 to 8	Certificate awarded in the non-degree stream equivalent to Master's. Usually requires original research or a special contribution to a field of study.	
5A (2nd)	Master's programmes	Graduate Diploma (SI)	Master's degree (SII)	23	24 to 26	2 to 5	...	6 to 8		
6	Specialist II programmes	Specialist I (SpI)	Specialist II (SpII)	25	27 upwards	3 to 5	...	9 to 11	Equivalent to a Doctorate. Usually requires original research or a special contribution to a field of study.	**6**
6	Doctorate programmes	Master's degree (SII)	Doctorate degree (SIII)	25	27 upwards	3 to 5	...	9 to 11	Includes professional degrees awarded in faculties of medicine, veterinary medicine and dentistry.	

JORDAN

ISCED97 Level for the WEI Data Collection	National title of programme	Entrance requirements	Qualifications awarded	Typical starting age	Typical completion age	Theoretical duration	Theoretical cumulative duration – primary/secondary levels	Theoretical cumulative duration – tertiary level	Notes	ISCED97 Flows
0	Preschool education			4	6	2	…	…	Run almost exclusively by private agencies.	0
1	Basic education-primary			6	12	6	6	…		1
2A	Basic education-preparatory			12	16	4	10	…		2A
3A	Comprehensive secondary education			16	18	2	12	…		3A
3C, Type 3 (counts as ISCED 3 completion)	Applied secondary education			16	18	2	12	…	Preparation of skilled workers in training centres and formal apprenticeship schemes. Apprenticeships are followed by one year of supervised employment.	3C
5B	Community college programmes	Passage of General (Academic) Secondary Education Certificate Examination	Diploma	…	…	2	…	2	All students meet the same general requirements and are awarded the same qualification. Community colleges provide a variety of programmes; one of them is teacher training.	5B
5B	Community college programmes	Passage of General (Academic) Secondary Education Certificate Examination	Diploma; entrance to ISCED 5A university programmes	…	…	2	…	2	Graduates with highest marks can enter labour force, or ISCED 5A university programmes if they wish.	
5B	Community college programmes	Passage of General (Academic) Secondary Education Certificate Examination	Diploma in technology	…	…	3	…	3		
5A (1st, Short and Long)	University programmes	Community college diploma and teaching experience	Bachelor's degree	…	…	3	…	3	Appointed teachers with community college diplomas can enter ISCED 5A university programmes through special government programme for upgrading teacher qualifications (they are exempt from 48 out of 132 hours required for bachelor's degree). In addition, about 5 percent of appointed teachers with community college diplomas can enter university through bridgement programmes.	5A
5A (1st, Short and Long)	University programmes	Passage of General (Academic or Vocational) Secondary Education Certificate Exam, or Community College Diploma with high marks	Bachelor's degree	…	…	4 to 6	…	4 to 6	5 year programmes in engineering, pharmacy and dentistry, 6 year programme in medicine.	
5A (2nd)	Education diploma programmes	Bachelor's degree	Diploma in education	…	…	1	…	5		
5A (2nd)	Master's programmes	Bachelor's degree	Master's degree	…	…	2 to 3	…	6 to 9		
6	Doctorate programmes	Master's degree	Doctorate	…	…	3 to 4	…	9 to 15		6

MALAYSIA

ISCED97 Level for the WEI Data Collection	National title of programme	Entrance requirements	Qualifications awarded	Typical starting age	Typical completion age	Theoretical duration	Theoretical cumulative duration – primary/secondary levels	Theoretical cumulative duration – tertiary level	Notes	ISCED97 Flows
0	Preschool	None	None	5	6	1	…	…		**0**
1	Primary (Years 1-6)	Schooling age	Primary school achievement test	6	12	6	…	…		**1**
2A	Remove class	6 years of primary education		12	13	1	…	…	Pupils from the national-type Chinese and Tamil primary school spend a year in the Remove class before the transition to secondary school to become proficient in Bahasa Melayu.	**2A**
2A	Lower-secondary (Forms 1-3)	6 years of primary education	Lower secondary assessment	12	15	3	9	…	Students who do not pass the Lower certificate of education examination enter the labour market.	
3C, Type 1 (does not count as ISCED 3 completion)	Upper-secondary (Forms 4-5) – academic stream	Lower secondary assessment	Malaysian Certificate of education	15	17	2	11	…	Based on performance in the Lower certificate of education examination, students are placed in the academic stream or technical and vocational schools.	**3C**
3C, Type 3 (does not count as ISCED 3 completion)	Upper-secondary (Forms 4-5) – technical and vocational schools	Lower secondary assessment	Malaysian Certificate of education	15	17	2	11	…		
3A	Pre-university (sixth form GCE A level)	Malaysian certificate of education	Higher School Certificate of examination/GCE	17	19	2	13	…	Two-year pre-university course that prepares students for the Higher School Certificate Examination.	**3A**
3A	Pre-university (matriculation)	Malaysian certificate of education		17	19	2	13	…		
4C	Teacher training (1 year programmes)	Malaysian certificate of education	Certificate	17	18	1	…	…	Training of preprimary and primary serving teachers.	**4C**
4C	Skill Training Programme	Malaysian certificate of education	Certificate	17	18	1 to 2				
5B	Higher education (teacher training – 2-3 year programmes)	Malaysian certificate of education	Diploma in teaching or Diploma in education	18	20 to 21	2 to 3	…	2 to 3	Training of preprimary and primary teachers.	**5B**
5B	Higher education (polytechnics)	Malaysian certificate of education	Certificate/ Diploma in various engineering, commerce and hospitality fields	18	20 to 22	2 to 4	…	2 to 4		
5A (1st, Short)	Higher education (3 year programmes)	Higher school certificate of examination/GCE	Bachelor's degree	20	23	3	…	3		**5A**
5A (1st, Long)	Higher education (5-6 year programmes)	Higher school certificate of examination/GCE	Bachelor's degree (medicine, dentistry, and veterinary science)	20	25 to 26	5 to 6	…	5 to 6		
5A (2nd)	Master's programmes	Bachelor's degree	Master's degree	23	24 to 25	1 to 2	…	5 to 6		
6	Doctorate programmes	Master's degree	Doctor of Philosophy (Ph.D.)	24 to 25	26 to 27	2	…	7 to 8	Requires submission of a thesis.	**6**
6 (2nd)	Higher doctorate programmes	Master's degree or Doctor of Philosophy (Ph.D.)	Higher doctor's degree (DLit, D.Sc., LL.D.)	24 upwards	29 upwards	5 to 7	…	10 to 15	Can be awarded in literature, law, and science.	

PARAGUAY

ISCED97 Level for the WEI Data Collection	National title of programme	Entrance requirements	Qualifications awarded	Typical starting age	Typical completion age	Theoretical duration	Theoretical cumulative duration – primary/secondary levels	Theoretical cumulative duration – tertiary level	Notes	ISCED97 Flows
0	Initial Education			3	6	3	...	...	Includes the stage of kindergarten of infants that assists children of 3 to 4 years and the preschool stage that assists children of 5 years.	0
1	Basic School Education, 1st and 2nd cycles			6	12	6	6	...	Obligatory.	1
2A	Basic School Education, 3rd cycle		Basic School Education, leaving certificate	12	15	3	9	...	Obligatory.	2A
2B	Basic School Education, technical cycle		Basic cycle technical, leaving certificate	12	15	3	9	...	Obligatory.	2B
3A	Humanistic, Scientist baccalaureate	Basic School Education – leaving certificate	Humanistic. Scientist baccalaureate title	15	18	3	12	...		3A
3C	Technical baccalaureate	Aptitude tests + entrance examination + Basic cycle technical-leaving certificate	Technical baccalaureate title	15	18	3	...	...		3C
5B	Non-university tertiary level; Post-secondary education	Aptitude tests + entrance examination + Humanistic, Scientist baccalaureate title or Technical baccalaureate title	Professor of Initial Education, Basic Scholar, education medium, or title of superior technician	18	21 to 22	3 to 4	...	3 to 4	Qualifications awarded are according to duration of the programme.	5B
5A	University	Secondary school leaving certificate and an entrance examination or probationary course	Licentiate or Degree title	18	22 to 24	4 to 6	...	4 to 6	Includes courses of medicine, dentistry, economics, etc.	5A
6	Post-graduate	Degree title	Doctorado or Master's degree	22 to 24	24 to 28	2 to 4	...	6 to 10	Requires submission of a thesis.	6

PERU

ISCED97 Level for the WEI Data Collection	National title of programme	Entrance requirements	Qualifications awarded	Typical starting age	Typical completion age	Theoretical duration	Theoretical cumulative duration – primary / secondary levels	Theoretical cumulative duration – tertiary level	Notes	ISCED97 Flows
0	Initial Education			3	6	3	…	…	Compulsory for all 5 years old.	
1	Primary			6	12	6	6	…		
2A	Secondary – 3 first grades	Completion of primary education		12	15	3	9	…		
3A	Secondary – 2 last grades Academic programmes	Completion of ISCED 2A		15	17	2	11	…		
3B	Secondary – 2 last grades Vocational programmes	Completion of ISCED 2A		15	17	2	11	…		
5B	Non-university Tertiary Programmes	Completion of secondary education	Technical and pedagogical certificates	17	20 or 22	3 or 5	…	3 or 5		
5A	Bachelor's programmes (most subjects)	Completion of secondary education	Bachelor's degree with or without 'licenciatura' certificates	17	22	5	…	5		
5A	Master's programmes	Bachelor's degree	Master's degree	22	24	2	…	7		
6	Doctorate programmes	Bachelor's degree	Doctorado	24	29	5	…	10		

PHILIPPINES

ISCED97 Level for the WEI Data Collection	National title of programme	Entrance requirements	Qualifications awarded	Typical starting age	Typical completion age	Theoretical duration	Theoretical cumulative duration – primary/secondary levels	Theoretical cumulative duration – tertiary level	Notes	ISCED97 Flows
0	Pre-primary	Birth Certificate		3	6	3	...	...		**0**
1	Elementary		Elementary-school-leaving certificate	6	12	6	6	...		**1**
2A	Secondary-General (First 3 years of secondary education)	Primary/Elementary-school-leaving certificate		12	15	3	9	...		**2A**
3A	Secondary-General (4th year of secondary education)		Secondary-school-leaving-certificate	15	16	1	10	...		**3A**
4A/B	Post-secondary technical vocational programmes	Secondary-school-leaving-certificate	Certificate of proficiency	16	18 or 19	2 to 3	12 to 13	...		**4A/B**
4C	Post-secondary technical vocational programmes	Secondary-school-leaving-certificate	Certificate of proficiency	16	17	...	< 2	11 to 12		**4C**
5A (1st, Short)	Tertiary programmes	Secondary-school-leaving-certificate	Associate of Arts	16	18	2	...	2	Agricultural technology, secretarial studies, business studies, fine arts, computer studies, midwifery, marine transportation, etc.	**5A**
5A (1st, Medium)	Tertiary programmes	Secondary-school-leaving-certificate	Bachelor's degree (most subjects)	16	20	4	...	4	Many tertiary institutions require students to pass an entrance examination. Graduates of teacher-training institutions are required to take the Licensure Examination for Teachers.	
5A (1st, Long)	Tertiary programmes	Secondary-school-leaving-certificate	Bachelor's degree (engineering, dentistry)	16	21	5	...	5	Graduates are required to pass a licensure examination to be able to practise their professions.	
5A (2nd course)	Tertiary programmes (2nd) stage – professional	Bachelor's degree	Professional qualification (law, medicine)	20	24	4	...	8	Graduates are required to pass a licensure examination to be able to practise their professions.	
5A (2nd course)	Tertiary programmes (2nd) stage	Bachelor's degree	Master's degree	20	22	2	...	6	Most fields require defence of a thesis.	
6	Doctorate programmes	Master's degree	Doctorate degree	22	24 or 25	2 or 3	...	8 to 9	Requires defence of a thesis/dissertation.	**6**

RUSSIAN FEDERATION

ISCED97 Level for the WEI Data Collection	National title of programme	Entrance requirements	Qualifications awarded	Typical starting age	Typical completion age	Theoretical duration	Theoretical cumulative duration – primary/secondary levels	Theoretical cumulative duration – tertiary level	Notes	ISCED97 Flows
0	Kindergarten			3	6	3	…	…		**0**
1	Primary			6 to 7	10	3 to 4	4	…		**1**
2A	Basic general education		Certificate 1	10	15	5	9	…	Lower secondary education is compulsory for all pupils (level 2A), awarded by certificate 1, duration 9 years (without preprimary education).	**2A**
3A	Secondary-general		Attestat	15	17	2	11	…	Upper level of secondary education is feasible in gymnasium, lyceum, secondary school, awarded by attestat or maturity (*zrelost*).	**3A**
3C	Secondary-vocational	Entrance examination	Certificate 2; Diploma 1	15	17 to 18	2 to 3	11 to12	…	Vocational lower secondary education is feasible in specialized school (*uchilische*), awarded by: (a) 2 years duration – certificate 2 with qualification of worker; (b) 3 years duration – diploma 1, confirm upper level education and worker's qualification.	**3C**
4C	Secondary-vocational	Entrance examination, Attestat	Certificate 2	17	18 to 19	1 to 2	12 to 13	…	Vocational education based on upper secondary education, duration 1 year; awarded by certificate 2 with worker's qualification (level 4C ISCED).	**4C**
3A + 5B	Secondary-special programme (technicum)	Entrance examination, Certificate 1	Specialist's diploma 1	15	19	4	13	2	Secondary special education is combination levels 2A and 5B, duration 4 years, awarded specialist's diploma 1, confirmed upper secondary level and first stage higher education, technician training, teacher training, and so on.	**3A+5B**
5B	Post-secondary special programme	Entrance examination, Attestat	Specialist's diploma 1	17	20	3	…	3	Postsecondary special programme based on upper secondary level (11 years), duration 3 years, feasible in colleges and technicums, awarded by specialist's diploma 1.	**5B**
5A (short)	Incomplete higher education	Attestat; Specialist's diploma 1; Exams	Certificate of incomplete higher education	17	19	2	…	2	Incomplete higher education – first stage of higher education, duration 2 years, awarded by diploma to students who discontinue their studies.	**5A**
5A	Basic higher education	Attestat; Entrance examination	Bachelor's degree	17	21	4	…	4	Basic higher education, duration 4 years in university or institution, awarded by bachelor's diploma.	
5A	Professional higher education	Attestat; Entrance examination	Specialist's diploma 2	17	22 to 24	5 to 7		5 to 7	Professional higher education, duration from 5 (in economics, humanities) to 7 years (in medicine), 5-6 years in engineering, awarded by specialist's diploma 2.	
5A	Professional higher education	Specialist's diploma	Specialist extended-education qualification	23 to 24	24 to 25	1	…	6 to 8	Further (upgraded) education – for specialists who wish to receive second specialty or improve their knowledge, duration 1 year, feasible in special department of university or institution.	
5A	Magistratura	Bachelor's degree	Master's degree	21	23	2		6	Educational programme with research elements in certain fields of science, graduates may work as a scientist, teacher in secondary school and at tertiary level.	
5A	Internatura	Bachelor's degree in Medicine	Internatura	24	25	1		8		
6	Aspiratura	Master's degree, Specialist's diploma 2	Kandidat nauk	22 to 24	25 to 27	3	…	8 to 9	Requires public defence of an independently elaborated thesis and by final examinations.	**6**
6	Doktorantura	Kandidat nauk	Doktor nauk	25 to 27	27 to 30	2 to 3	…	10 to 12	Requires defence of thesis offering new solutions to a major scientific/academic problem which is of substantial importance to the field or discipline.	

SRI LANKA

ISCED97 Level for the WEI Data Collection	National title of programme	Entrance requirements	Qualifications awarded	Typical starting age	Typical completion age	Theoretical duration	Theoretical cumulative duration – primary/secondary levels	Theoretical cumulative duration – tertiary level	Notes	ISCED97 Flows
0	Preschool			4	5	1	…	…	Not provided by national government, but by some local governments and private organizations on fee-paying basis. About 50 per cent of Sri Lankan children attend for some period of time.	0
1	Primary			5	10	5	5	…		1
2A	Junior secondary	Completion of primary	Completion of junior secondary	10	14	4	9	…		2A
3A	Senior secondary (Ordinary level)	Completion of junior secondary	General certificate of education (Ordinary level)	14	16	2	11	…		3A
3A	Senior secondary (Advanced level)	General certificate of education (Ordinary level)	General certificate of education (Advanced level)	16	18	2	13	…		
3B	Technical/ vocational		Certificates	14	16	2	…	…		3B
5B	Collegiate	General certificate of education (Ordinary level)	Diplomas and certificates	17	18 to 21	1 to 4	…	1 to 4	There are 24 technical colleges and 5 affiliated units operated by Ministry of Education offering wide variety of professional, academic, and craft courses.	5B
5A (short)	Collegiate	General certificate of education (Ordinary level)	Diplomas and certificates; entrance to university	18	20	2	…	2	There are 24 technical colleges and 5 affiliated units operated by Ministry of Education offering wide variety of professional, academic, and craft courses. Primary school teachers are trained at this level.	5A
5A (short and long)	University (first stage)	General certificate of education (Advanced level)	Bachelor's degree	19	22 to 25	3 to 6	…	5 to 8	There are 9 universities and 4 other institutions of higher education. Secondary school teachers are trained at this level.	
5A	University (second stage)	Bachelor's degree	Master's degree	22 to 25	23 to 27	1 to 2	…	6 to 10	There are 5 postgraduate institutes of higher education, all attached to universities.	
6	University (third stage)	Master's degree	Doctor's degree	23 to 27	25 upwards	2+	…	8 and above	There are 5 postgraduate institutes of higher education, all attached to universities.	6

THAILAND

ISCED97 Level for the WEI Data Collection	National title of programme	Entrance requirements	Qualifications awarded	Typical starting age	Typical completion age	Theoretical duration	Theoretical cumulative duration – primary/secondary levels	Theoretical cumulative duration – tertiary level	Notes	ISCED97 Flows
0	Pre-primary			3	6	3	...	...		
1	Primary			6	12	6	...	...		
2A	Lower secondary	Graduation from primary school (Grade 6)	Lower Secondary Education Certificate	12	15	3	9	...		
3A	Upper secondary-General	Graduation from lower secondary school (Grade 9)	Upper Secondary Education Certificate	15	18	3	12	...		
3B	Upper secondary-Vocational	Graduation from lower secondary school (Grade 9)	Vocational Education Certificate	15	18	3	12	...		
4C	Post secondary not tertiary	Graduation from upper secondary school	Post-secondary Certificate	18	19	1	...	...		
5B	Diploma programmes	Vocational Education Certificate	Diploma in Vocational Education	18	20	2	...	2		
5B	Technical degree programmes	Upper Secondary Education Certificate	Bachelor's degree	18	22	4	...	4		
5A (1st, Short)	University-level education	Upper Secondary Education Certificate	Bachelor's degree	18	22	4	...	4		
5A (1st, Long)	University-level education	Upper Secondary Education Certificate	Bachelor's degree	18	23 to 24	5 to 6	...	5 to 6	Most professional qualifications are earned here, including architecture, painting, sculpture, graphic arts and pharmacy (5 years) medicine, dentistry and veterinary science (6 years).	
5A (2nd)	Master's programmes	Bachelor's degree	Master's degree	23	25 to 26	2 to 3	...	6 to 7	Candidates are usually required to submit a research project and a thesis.	
6	Doctorate programmes	Master's degree	Doctor's degree (Ph.D.)	25 to 26	28 to 30	3 to 4	...	9 to 11		

ISCED97 Flows:

0 → 1 → 2A → 3A, 3B → 4C → 5B, 5A, 6

TUNISIA

ISCED97 Level for the WEI Data Collection	National title of programme	Entrance requirements	Qualifications awarded	Typical starting age	Typical completion age	Theoretical duration	Theoretical cumulative duration – primary/secondary levels	Theoretical cumulative duration – tertiary level	Notes	ISCED97 Flows
0	Pre-primary ('Pré-scolaire')			3	6	3	…	…		**0**
1	Primary (1st cycle of Basic Education)			6	12	6	6	…		**1**
2A	Lower Secondary (2nd cycle of Basic Education)			12	15	3	9	…		**2A**
3A	Upper Secondary-General	Completion of Basic Education	Baccalaureate title	15	19	4	13	…		**3A**
3B	Upper Secondary-Vocational (Formation professionnelle Level 1)	Completion of Basic Education	Certificat d'Aptitude Professionnelle	15	16 or 17	1 or 2	10 or 11	…		**3B**
3B	Upper Secondary-Vocational (Formation professionnelle Level 2)	Certificat d'Aptitude Professionnelle or 2 years of Secondary-General	Brevet de Technicien Professionnel	16 or 17	18 or 19	1 or 2	12 or 13	…		**5B**
5B	Vocational Programmes (Formation professionnelle Level 3)	Baccalaureate or Brevet de Technicien Professionnel	Brevet de Technicien Supérieur	19	21	2	…	2		
5A (1st, Short)	University-level education	Baccalaureate title	Bachelor's degree	19	21 or 22	2 or 3	…	2 or 3	Qualifications awarded are according to duration of the programme.	**5A**
5A (1st, Long)	University-level education	Upper Secondary Education Certificate	Master's degree	19	23 to 25	4 to 6	…	4 to 6		
5A (2nd)	Master's programmes	Bachelor's degree	Master's degree	22	23 or 24	1 or 2	…	4 or 5		**6**
6	Doctorate programmes	Master's degree	Doctor's degree (Ph.D.)	22 to 24	25 to 27	3	…	7 or 8		

URUGUAY

ISCED97 Level for the WEI Data Collection	National title of programme	Entrance requirements	Qualifications awarded	Typical starting age	Typical completion age	Theoretical duration	Theoretical cumulative duration – primary/secondary levels	Theoretical cumulative duration – tertiary level	Notes	ISCED97 Flows
0	Initial Education			3	6	3	…	…		
1	Primary			6	12	6	6	…		
2A	Basic cycle (básico)	Primary completion		12	15	3	9	…		
3A	Bachillerato Diversificado (Upper secondary general)		Bachillerato	15	18	3	12	…	The Bachillerato gives the right to enrol in the Faculty which corresponds to the option chosen in the second year of diversified education (humanities, science or biology).	
3B	Bachillerato Técnico (Upper secondary technical)		Bachillerato	15	18	3	12	…	The Bachillerato gives the right to enrol in the Faculty which corresponds to the option chosen (agriculture, architecture, engineering, administration or business & commerce).	
5B	Professional qualification	Bachillerato	Professional qualification	18	20 to 22	2 to 4	…	2 to 4	Programmes to train librarians, midwives, public administrators and business administrators.	
5B	Teacher training (primary schools)	Bachillerato	Maestro de educación primaria	18	21	3	…	3	Qualification which entitles the holder to teach in a primary school.	
5B	Teacher training (secondary schools)	Bachillerato	Profesor; Maestro Técnico	18	22	4	…	4	Qualification which entitles the holder to teach in a secondary or technical school.	
5A (1st short and long)	Licenciatura programmes	Bachillerato	Licenciatura	18	22 to 23	4 to 5		4 to 5	4 year programmes to 5A short, 5 year programmes to 5A long.	
5A (1st short and long)	Other professional degree programmes	Bachillerato	Ingeniero/ arquitecto/ químico farmacéutico	18	22 to 24	4 to 6	…	4 to6	4 year programmes to 5A short, 5 and 6 year programmes to 5A long.	
5A (long)	Medicine and dentistry programmes	Bachillerato	Doctor	18	23 to 25	5 to 7	…	5 to 7	Dentistry (5 years), Law (6 years), Medicine (7 years).	
6	Doctorate programmes	Licenciatura/ Ingeniero	Doctorado	22 to 24	24 to 26	1 to 2	…	6 to 8	Requires submission of a thesis.	

ZIMBABWE

ISCED97 Level for the WEI Data Collection	National title of programme	Entrance requirements	Qualifications awarded	Typical starting age	Typical completion age	Theoretical duration	Theoretical cumulative duration – primary / secondary levels	Theoretical cumulative duration – tertiary level	Notes	ISCED97 Flows
0	Preschool	None	None	3	6	2	...	...		0
1	Primary school		Primary school achievement test (Grade 7 certificate)	6	13	7	7	...		1
2A	Lower Secondary Form 2	7 years of primary education	Zimbabwe Junior Certificate	13	15	2	9	...		2A
3C	Senior Secondary «O» Level	Form 2	«O» level certificate	15	17	2	11	...		3C
3A	Upper Secondary	«O» level	«A» level certificate	17 to 18	19	2	13	...	Minimum entry requirement is five ordinary level subjects.	3A
4C	Vocational Training	Grade 7, Form 2 and «O» level	Certificate	17 to 18	19	2	...	2	Skill training courses.	4C
5B	Teaching courses	5 «O» level credits or 2 «A» level credits	Primary and Secondary Teaching Certificate	17 to 18	20	3	...	3	Courses of teaching either at primary or secondary.	5B
5B	Technical courses	«O» level	Technical diploma	17 to 18	20	3	...	3	College based training.	
5B	Apprenticeship programmes	«O» level	Technical diploma	17 to 18	21	4	...	4	Industrial based training.	
5A (1st degree)	Academic degree programmes	«A» level	Bachelor's degree	19	22	3 to 4	...	3 to 4	1st degrees.	5A
5A (2nd degree)	Masters courses	Bachelor's degree	Master's degree	22	25	3	...	6 to 7	Requires submission of a thesis.	
6 (2nd degree)	Doctorate medical courses	«A» level	Doctor of medicine	19	25	6	...	6	Medical degrees.	
6 (2nd degree)	Doctorate courses	Master's degree	Doctorate degree	25	28	3 to 4	...	9 to 11	Awarded in philosophy, litterature, law, science etc.	6

Acknowledgements

This publication results from a collective effort by countries participating in the
UNESCO/OECD World Education Indicators programme and the OECD and UNESCO.
The UNESCO Institute for Statistics team (responsible for the drafting of Chapter 1)
consists of Douglas Lynd, Albert Motivans, and Mathieu Brossard.
The team from the Statistics and Indicators Division of the OECD Directorate for
Education, Employment, Labour and Social Affairs (responsible for the drafting of Chapters 2 and 3)
consists of Andreas Schleicher, Michael Bruneforth, Maria Teresa Siniscalco and Karine Tremblay.

Other staff of the UNESCO Institute for Statistics and the OECD were involved in the data collection,
publication preparation and other activities in support of this report.

The following lists the names of the country representatives – policy-advisors, researchers and experts – who have taken part in the
preparatory work leading to this publication:

Mr. Felix Abdala (Argentina),
Mr. Ramon C. Bacani (Philippines),
Mr. Balakrishnan (India),
Mr. Ade Cahyana (Indonesia),
Mr. Ivan Castro de Almeida (Brazil),
Mr. Farai Choga (Zimbabwe),
Ms. Paula Darville (Chile),
Ms. Jehad Jamil Abu El-Shaar (Jordan),
Ms. Irene Beatriz Oiberman (Argentina),
Mr. João Batista Gomes Neto (Brazil),
Ms. Hilda Gonzalez Garcete (Paraguay),
Ms. Maria Helena Guimaraes de Castro (Brazil),
Ms. Vivian Heyl (Chile),
Mr. Mohsen Ktari (Tunisia),
Ms. Lin Zhi Hua (China),
Mr. Meng Hong Wei (China),
Ms. Khalijah Mohammad (Malaysia),
Ms. Silvia Montoya (Argentina),
Ms. Mara Perez Torrano (Uruguay),
Mr. Sumret Prasertsook (Thailand),
Mr. Mohamed Abdul Salam Ragheb (Egypt),
Mr. José Rodriguez (Peru),
Ms. Lilia Roces (Philippines),
Mr. Alexander Savelyev (Russian Federation),
Mr. Abhimanyu Singh (India),
Ms. Sirivarn Svasti (Thailand),
Mr. Senanayake Upasena (Sri Lanka),
Mr. Azmi Zakaria (Malaysia),
Ms. Gloria María Zambrano Rozas (Peru),
Ms. Dalila Noemi Zarza Paredes (Paraguay)

The WEI programme, including the preparation of this publication, was facilitated by a grant from the World Bank and
by financial and material support from several OECD countries and UNESCO member states.

■

OECD PUBLICATIONS, 2, rue André-Pascal, 75775 PARIS CEDEX 16
OECD Code: 96 2001 07 1 P 1 ISBN 92-64-18699-9 – No. 51885 2001
PRINTED IN FRANCE

UNESCO PUBLISHING, 7 Place de Fontenoy, 75352 Paris 07SP, France
ISBN: 92-9189-000-6